SINGLE CELL PROTEIN

SINGLE CELL PROTEIN

*Proceedings of the International Symposium
held in Rome, Italy, on November 7–9, 1973*

Sponsored by
Stanford Research Institute
Menlo Park, California, U.S.A.
and
Liquichimica S.p.A., Milan, Italy

Edited by
P. DAVIS
Department of Food and Plant Sciences
Stanford Research Institute

1974

Academic Press · London · New York · San Francisco
A Subsidiary of Harcourt Brace Jovanovich, Publishers

ACADEMIC PRESS INC. (LONDON) LTD.
24/28 Oval Road,
London NW1

United States Edition published by
ACADEMIC PRESS INC.
111 Fifth Avenue
New York, New York 10003

*TP
453
P1
555*

Library of Congress Catalog Card Number: 74–24956
ISBN: 0–12–206550–6

Printed in Great Britain by Page Bros (Norwich) Ltd, Norwich.

LIST OF SPEAKERS

J. Abbott, *Marketing and Credit Service, FAO, Rome, Italy.*

K. Aibara, *National Institute of Preventative Medicine, Tokyo, Japan.*

D. Calloway, *Department of Nutritional Sciences, University of California, Berkeley, California, USA.*

P. Davis, *Stanford Research Institute, Menlo Park, California, USA.*

S. Danielsen, *Dansk Gaering Industries, Copenhagen, Denmark.*

A.P. de Groot, *Central Institute for Nutrition and Food Research, TNO, Zeist, The Netherlands.*

R. Fahenstich, *Degussa, Frankfurt, West Germany.*

R. Ferrando, *École Nationale Vétérinaire, Alfort, France.*

R. Flannery, *Amoco Food Company, Chicago, Illinois, USA.*

M.J. Forman, *Agency for International Development, Washington, USA.*

E. Gaden, Jr., *Department of Chemical Enginering and Applied Chemistry, Columbia University, New York, USA.*

M. Ganzin, *Food Policy and Nutrition Division, FAO, Rome, Italy.*

G.L. Gatti, *Istituto Superiore di Sanità, Rome, Italy.*

F. Giacobbe, *Compagnia Tecnica Industrie Petroli, Rome, Italy.*

G. Giolitti, *Istituto di Ispezione degli Alimenti, Università di Milano, Italy.*

G.I. Griesmer, *Union Carbide, Geneva, Switzerland.*

H. Henderson, *Princeton, New Jersey, USA.*

S. Hibino, *General Institute for Feed and Livestock Research, Zen-Nho, Tukuba-machi, Tukuba-gun, Ibaragi, Japan.*

J.C. Hoogerheide, *International Union of Pure and Applied Chemistry, The Hague, The Netherlands.*

G. Kapsiotis, *Protein Food Development, Food Policy and Nutrition Division, FAO, Rome, Italy.*

K. Katoh, *National Food Research Institute, Tokyo, Japan.*

J. Littlehailes, *Imperial Chemical Industries, Teesside, United Kingdom.*

C.F. Lu, *Chief, Food Additives, World Health Organization, Geneva, Switzerland.*

M. Milner, *Protein Advisory Group of the United Nations System, New York, USA.*

B. Nicol, *Consultant for FAO, Rome, Italy.*

B.L. Oser, *Food and Drug Research Laboratories, Maspeth, New York, USA.*

P. Peri, *Liquichimia, S.p.A., Milan, Italy.*

P. Resmini, *Istituto di Industrie Agrarie, Università di Milano, Italy.*

J. Senez, *Centre National de la Recherche Scientifique, Marseille, France.*

C. Shacklady, *B.P. Proteins Limited, London, United Kingdom.*

K.W.G. Shillam, *Huntingdon Research Centre, Huntingdon, United Kingdom.*

E. Smit, *Philips/Duphar, Amsterdam, The Netherlands.*

G. Solomons, *Lord Rank Research Centre, High Wycombe, Bucks, United Kingdom.*

A. Spicer, *Lord Rank Research Centre, High Wycombe, Bucks, United Kingdom.*

H. Stone, *Department of Food and Plant Sciences, Stanford Research Institute, Menlo Park, California, USA.*

J. Taylor, *Bureau of Veterinary Medicine, Food and Drug Administration, Rockville, Maryland, USA.*

R. Ursini, *President of Liquichimica S.p.A., Milan, Italy.*

I.R.P. van der Wal, *ILOB, Wageningen, The Netherlands.*

M.C. Verghese, *United Nations Industrial Development Organization, Vienna, Austria.*

V. Young, *Massachusetts Institute of Technology, Cambridge, Massachusetts, USA.*

LIST OF PARTICIPANTS

AUSTRIA

K.G. Gilnreiner, *Biosaxon, Laudong 56/9, 1081 Vienna VIII°.*
M.C. Verghese, *UNIDO, P.O. Box 837, 1011 Vienna.*

BELGIUM

B.P. Burba, *FMC Corp., 177/179 Chaussée de la Hulpe, 1170 Brussels.*
E.A. Christopher, *Purina Protein Europe, 391 Av. Louise,*
    1050 Brussels.
Y. Hibino, *Kaneka Belgium N.V., 34 Rue de la Loi, 1040 Brussels.*
Ph. Mechelynck, *CEE, 207 Rue de la Loi, 1040 Brussels.*
J. Radisson, *Ralston Purina Europe, 391 Av. Louise, 1050 Brussels.*
A.M. Tachis, *CEE, 200 Rue de la Loi, 1040 Brussels.*
J. Tanghe, *CEE, 200 Rue de la Loi, 1040 Brussels.*

BRAZIL

M.S. Hartveld, *Petroquimica Uniao & Unipar, Rio de Janeiro.*
R. Kohlmann, *Bunge & Borne Ltda. S.A., 162 Rua Boa Vista, Sao*
    Paolo.
C. Molteni, *Petroquimica Uniao & Unipar, Rio de Janeiro.*
V. Moritz, *Direttore Ist. Ingegneria Biochimica, Università di*
    Rio de Janeiro.
A. Pinto Ribeiro Candal, *Ministero Industria e Commercio, Rio de*
    Janeiro.

CZECHOSLOVAKIA

R. Jilek, *Inst. of Veterinary Med. Research, Medlanky Hudcova 70,*
    Brno.

DENMARK

S. Danielsen, *Dansk Gaering Industries, Copenhagen.*
O.G. Kjaergaard, *Niro Atomizer, 305 Gladsaxevej, 2840 Soeborg.*

ENGLAND

H. Akazawa, *Mitsui & Co., Ltd., Royex House, Aldermansbury Sq.,*
    London ECEV 7LX.
E.F. Annison, *Unilever Research Laboratory, Colworth House,*
    Sharnbrook, Bedford.
D.W.J. Beatty, *ICI, Agricultural Division, Billingham, Durham.*
J.H. Byrne, *Pfizer, Sandwich, Kent.*
L.R. Dowsett, *Kingsley & Keith Chemical Group Ltd., George Street,*
    Croydon CR9 3QL.
J. Edelman, *RHN Research Ltd., Lincoln Road, High Wycombe, Bucks.*
A. Gabriel, *Shell Int. Chemical Co., Shell Centre, London SE1 7PG.*
J.F. Hearne, *Ministry of Agriculture, Fisheries & Food, Horseferry*
    Road, London SW1.

L. Hepner, *Bernard Wolnak & Associates Ltd.*, *Tavistock Square, London WC1.*

A.W. Holmes, *Food RA, Randalls Road, Leatherhead, Surrey.*

F.K.E.I. Imrie, *Tate & Lyle Ltd.*, *P.O. Box 68, Reading, Berks. RG6 2BX.*

P.G. Jones, *Pfizer, Central Research Division, Sandwich, Kent.*

C.C. Keith, *Kingsley & Keith Chemical Group Ltd.*, *George Street, Croydon CR9 3QL.*

J. Littlehailes, *ICI, Billingham, Durham.*

W.M. McKernan, *Kingsley & Keith Ltd.*, *George Street, Croydon CR9 3QL.*

P. Manning, *European Chemical News, 33/40 Bowling Green Lane, London EC1.*

C.K. Milner, *Shell Research Ltd.*, *Tunstall Lab.*, *Broad Oak Road, Sittingbourne, Kent.*

M. Moo Young, *Imperial College of Science and Technology, Dept. of Chemical Engineering, Prince Consort Road, London SW7.*

G.H. Pace, *ICI, Agricultural Division, Billingham, Durham.*

H.C. Palmer, *Pedigree Petfoods Ltd.*, *Mill Street, Melton Mowbray, Leics.*

Phillips, *Tate & Lyle Ltd.*, *P.O. Box 68, Reading, Berks. RG6 2BX.*

S.R. Ruff, *John & E. Sturge Ltd.*, *Denison Road, Selby, Yorks.*

C. Shacklady, *BP Proteins Ltd.*, *Moor Lane, London EC2Y 9BU.*

K.W.G. Shillam, *Huntingdon Research Centre, Huntingdon PE18.*

E.J.F. Spicer, *Dept. of Health & Social Security, Alexander Fleming House, Elephant and Castle, London SE1.*

G. Solomon, *Lord Rank Research Centre, High Wycombe, Bucks.*

D.A. Stringer, *ICI Ltd.*, *Research Station, Jealotts Hill, Bracknell, Berks.*

A. Tolan, *Ministry of Agriculture, Fisheries & Food, Horseferry Road, London SW1.*

D.B. Walton, *BP Proteins Ltd.*, *Moor Lane, London EC2Y 9BU.*

H. Watts, *BP Proteins Ltd.*, *Moor Lane, London EC2Y 9BU.*

A.B. Wilson, *ICI Ltd.*, *Alderley Park, Macclesfield, Cheshire.*

FINLAND

K. Forss, *Finnish Pulp & Paper Resin Ins.*, *Helsinki.*

H.G. Gyllenberg, *University of Helsinki, Department of Microbiology, 00710 Helsinki.*

J. Rinta, *Rintekno Oy, Kotkapolku 2, 02620 Karakallio.*

H. Romantschuk, *Oy Tampella A.B.*, *33100 Tampere 10.*

FRANCE

J.P. Bianchi, *Cie Francaise de Rafinage, 22 Rue Boileau, 75781 Paris.*

Delisle, *GFP, 2 Av. de Bois-Preau, Rueil-Malamaison.*

R. Ferrando, *École Nationale Vétérinaire, 94701 Alfort.*

E. Gatumel, *BP, 10 Quai P. Doumet, 92401 Courbevoie.*

G. Goma, *INSA, Av. de Rangueil, 31077 Toulouse.*

Kosse, *Rhone Progil, 79 Rue de Miromesmil, Paris 18.*
M. Jouannet, *S.A. Lorientaise Produits de Peche, 15 Rue Fl. Laporte, 56100 Lorient.*
J.P. Jourdan, *Rhone Progil, 79 Rue de Miromesmil, Paris 18.*
R. Molinero, *S.Te Dev. des Proteins BP, 10 Quai P. Doumet, 92 Courbevoie.*
J. Nougaro, *S.Te Dev. des Proteins BP, 10 Quai P. Doumet, 92 Courbevoie.*
J.C. Senez, *Centre National de la Recherche Scientifique, 31 Chemin J. Aiguier, 13274 Marseille.*

GERMANY

R. Fahnenstich, *Degussa GmbH, Frankfurt/Main.*
W. Feldheim, *Inst. für Ernahrungswissenschaft I, 20 Wilhelmstr., 6300 Giessen.*
H. Kawase, *Kuraray Co. Ltd., 18 Marienstr., 4000 Dusseldorf.*
M. Kinoshita, *Kyowa Hakko Europe GmbH, Dusseldorf.*
R.P. Krohn, *Farbwerke Hoechst A.G., 10 Lyoner Str., 6000 Frankfurt.*
H. Lenk, *Bundesgesund Heitsamt, Postfach, 1000 Berlin 33.*
H.D. Payer, *Kohlenstoffbiologie, Bunsen Kirchhoff Str. 13, 46 Dortmund.*
A. Pretzer, *Deutsche Raiffeisen Warenzentrale, Reuterweg 51/53, Frankfurt/Main 6.*
A. Toi, *Kyowa Hakko Europe GmbH, Dusseldorf.*
V. Wagner, *Verkauflantuertschaft, Futtermittelzusatze, Frankfurt.*

HOLLAND

A.J. Balfoort, *Cargill B.V., P.O. Box 8074, Amsterdam.*
Boeve, *Provimi, Veerlaan 17-23, Rotterdam.*
A.P. de Groot, *TNO, Zeist.*
M.J.L. Dols, *Bloencamplaan 10, Wassenaar.*
A. Franck, *Unilever Research, P.O. Box 114, Vlaardingen.*
J.C. Hoogerheide, *IUPAC, Loan Clingendael 129, Den Haag.*
O.R. Offringa, *Philips Duphar, Apollolaan 151, Amsterdam.*
P.T. Smit, *Philips Duphar, Apollolaan 151, Amsterdam.*
van den Bruel, *DSM, Geleen.*
T. van der Wal, *IOB, Wageningen.*
van der Wind, *Trouw & Co. Int., Nijverheidsweg 2, Putten.*
N. Zwiep, *Philips Duphar, Apollolaan 151, Amsterdam.*

ISRAEL

R.I. Mateles, *Hadassah Medical School, Hebrew Un., P.O. Box 1172, Jerusalem.*

ITALY

J. Abbott, *FAO, Via Terme de Caracella, 00100 Rome.*
P. Antonioli, *Cipzoo, Via Parenzo, 25100 Brescia.*
M. Amorosi, *CTIP, P. Douhet 31, 00144 Rome.*

P. Arlotti, *ANIC, S. Donato M.*
T. Baglioni, *Ist. Patologia Veterinaria, Via Celoria 10,*
   20100 Milan.
V. Balloni, *Ist. Microbiologia Agraria, P. Cascine 27, 50100*
   Florence.
A. Baldini, *Via Fortifiocca 50, 00100 Rome.*
F. Barbieri, *Hoechst Italia SpA, Via Traiano 18, 20100 Milan.*
W.H. Barreveld, *FAO, Hq Div. Agricoltura, Via Terme di Caracalla,*
   00100 Rome.
E. Barone, *Min. Agricoltura, Div. Alimentare, 00100 Rome.*
S. Bauso, *Lab. Chimica-Dogana Centrale, Via della Luce 35, 00100*
   Rome.
L. Bellani, *Ministero Sanità, Direzione Generale dei Servizi*
   Veterinari, 00100 Rome.
L. Benincampi, *CTIP, P. Douhet 2, 00144 Rome.*
E. Bergonzini, *Ist. Sperimentale Zootecnia, Via S. Geminiano 11,*
   41100 Modena.
G.C. Bianchi, *Istituto Clinica Medica, Via Gramsci 14, 43100 Parma.*
A.R. Borgati, *Istituto Biochimica Veterinaria, Via Napoli 5,*
   40100 Bologna.
H.J. Borngraber, *Ambasciata Repubbl. Democratica Tedesca, Via*
   Castro Pretorio 116, 00100 Rome.
A. Borghese, *Istituto Sperimentale Zootecnica, Via Onofrio*
   Panvinio 11, 00100 Rome.
L. Broggi, *ANIC, S. Donato M.*
P. Bruno, *Laboratorio Chimico Provinciale, Via Ridola, 75100*
   Matera.
G. Cagliari, *Eurotecnica, C. Como 13/9, 20100 Milan.*
V. Caglioti, *Presidente Onorario, CNR, 00100 Rome.*
B. Calcagno, *SIR, Via Grazioli 33, 20100 Milan.*
C. Cantarelli, *Istituto di Tecnologie Alimentari, Via Celoria 2,*
   20133 Milan.
F. Cantini, *SILO S.r.l., Via Borgo Albizi 10, 50100 Florence.*
V. Cariati, *Protec, Via Larga 23, 20122 Milan.*
A. Carzaniga, *SIR, Via Grazioli 33, 20100 Milan.*
R. Craveri, *Istituto Microbiologia Industriale, Via Celoria 2,*
   20100 Milan.
G. Chiriotti, *Rivista "Industria Alimentare", Via Caprilli 10,*
   10064 Pinerolo.
P. Cipolla, *UTIF, 96100 Siracusa.*
G. Criscuoli, *Eurand S.p.A., Via Priv. Pasteur 1, 20092 Cinisello.*
A. Corrias, *Ist. Zooprofilattico Piemonte e Liguria, Via Bologna*
   148, 10154 Turin.
C. Delfini, *Istituto Superiore Sanità, Via Regina Elena 299,*
   00100 Rome.
F. Delfino, *CIAPI, 89100 Reggio C.*
K. Derk, *FAO (AGAP), Via Terme di Caracalla, 00100 Rome.*
M. de Vita, *Pozzi Ferrandina S.p.A., 75013 Ferrandina.*
L. di Fiore, *SIR, Via Grazioli 33, 20100 Milan.*

E. di Giulio, *Montedison, Largo Donegani 1-2, 20100 Milan.*
V. Faenza, *Università di Trieste, Via Pienza (Villino 7), 00100 Rome.*
Fasella, *Istituto Chimica Biologica, 00100 Rome.*
M. Fenici, *Distillerie Cavarzere, Via Plana 46, 27058 Voghera.*
L. Ferro, *Istituto Nazionale Nutrizione, 00100 Rome.*
F.L. Fidanza, *Istituto Scienza Alimentazione, Via Canapina 3, 06100 Perugia.*
G. Florenzano, *Istituto Microbiologia Agraria, 50100 Florence.*
A. Fognano, *Italproteine S.p.A., Via Fara 41, 20100 Milan.*
R. Forquet, *ENI, P. E. Mattei 1, 00100 Rome.*
A. Frugoni, *Via Parioli 41, 00100 Rome.*
Galeota, *Ministero della Sanità, 00100 Rome.*
M. Ganzin, *FAO, Via Terme di Caracalla, 00100 Rome.*
M. Garattini, *Direttore Istituto Ricerche M. Negri, Via Eritrea 62, 20100 Milan.*
G.L. Gatti, *Istituto Superiore di Sanità, Via Regina Elena 299, 00161 Rome.*
S. Ghielmi, *Montedison, Largo Donegani 1-2, 20100 Milan.*
F. Giacobbe, *CTIP, P. Douhet 31, 00100 Rome.*
E. Giulianelli, *Montedison, Largo Donegani 1-2, 20100 Milan.*
M. Gobbi, *Italproteine S.p.A., Via G. Fara 41, 20100 Milan.*
R. Graziani, *U.S. Feed Grains Council, 00100 Rome.*
A. Grein, *Farmitalia - Istituto Ricerche, Via dei Gracchi 35, 20100 Milan.*
R. Guillet, *CTIP, P. Douhet 2, 00100 Rome.*
O.A. Iacazzi, *Camera Deputati, 00100 Rome.*
Igarashi, *Mitsui Italia S.p.A., P. Liberty 2, 20121 Milan.*
E. Kainov, *Rappres. Comm. le URSS in Italia, Via Gaeta 5, 00100 Rome.*
G.D. Kapsiotis, *FAO, Via Terme di Caracalla, 00100 Rome.*
J. Kobajashi, *Mitsui Italia S.p.A., P. Liberty 2, 20100 Milan.*
V. Kolcianov, *Ambasciata URSS, Via Gaeta 5, 00100 Rome.*
A. Liguori, *Ordinario Chimica e Fisica, Università di Roma, 00100 Rome.*
G. Longobardi, *CTIP, P. Douhet 31, 00100 Rome.*
A. Macri, *Ist. Superiore di Sanità/Lab. Veter., Via Regina Elena 299, 00100 Rome.*
F. Maestroni, *Sipa Pollo Arena, 37066 Sommacampagna.*
G. Malacart, *ANIC, 20100 S. Donato M.*
F. Malossini, *Ist. Sperimentale Zootecnia, 00015 Monterotondo.*
D. Mancini, *Via Val Padana 117, 00100 Rome.*
R. Marchese, *CIAPI, 89100 Reggio C.*
W. Marconi, *SNAM Progetti, Via Ramarini, 00015 Monterotondo.*
A. Marelli, *Ufficio Tecnico Federconsorzi, Via Curtatone 3, 00100 Rome.*
A. Mariani, *Istituto Nazionale Nutrizione, Città Universitaria, 00100 Rome.*
G. Martini, *Rivista "Industrie Alimentari", Cso Torino 139, 10064 Pinerolo.*

G. Marullo, *IRFIS, Via Principe di Paternò 74B, 90100 Palmermo.*
G. Mascheroni, *Ministero del Mezzogiorno, 00100 Rome.*
G. Mascherpa, *Farmitalia S.p.A., V. le Bezzi 24, 20100 Milan.*
G.C. Masini, *Presidente Unione Ital. Giornalisti Scientifici,*
   00100 Rome.
G. Matarrese, *Presidente della Silos & Mag. Tirreno, 00100 Rome.*
R. Materassi, *Istituto Microbiologia Agraria, 50100 Florence.*
Mayer, *FAO "AGA", Via Terme di Caracalla, 00100 Rome.*
C. Mazzanti, *Lab. Ricerche Tecnologiche, Via N. Bixio 19,*
   95030 Nicolosi.
V. Mazzaracchio, *00100 Rome.*
P. Mazziotti di Celso, *Ist. Sperimentale Zootecnica, Via O. Panvinio*
   11, 00100 Rome.
L. Mazzoni, *ICIPU, Via Q. Sella 2, 00100 Rome.*
M. Mioli, *Doxal, S.p.A., Via Crimea 33, 20100 Milan.*
G. Menigazzo, *Tecnipetrol, 00100 Rome.*
A.O. Mohamed, *Ist. Superiore Sanità - Veterinaria, Via Regina*
   Elena 299, 00161 Rome.
P.L. Manachini, *Istituto Microbiologia Industriale, 20100 Milan.*
G. Montuori, *00100 Rome.*
F. Mordenti, *Università di Bologna - Ist. di Zootecnia, 40100*
   Bologna.
A. Morelli, *Federconsorzi, Via Curtatone 3, 00185 Rome.*
D. Mura, *Ist. Zooprofilattico Sperimentale della Sardegna,*
   07100 Sassari.
A. Mussini, *Ist. di Ricerca "Mario Negri", Via Eritrea 62,*
   20100 Milan.
J. Neumann, *Hoechst Italia, Via Traiano 18, 20100 Milan.*
B. Nicol, *FAO/Nutritional Division, Via Terme di Caracalla,*
   00100 Rome.
M. Nora, *Consorzio Agrario, Via Monteverdi 17, 26100 Cremona.*
D.S.W. Pace, *Istituto Superiore Sanità, Via Regina Elena 299,*
   00100 Rome.
G. Pacetti, *Ufficio Tecnico Federconsorzi, Via Curtatone 3,*
   00100 Rome.
Pagano, *CTIP, P. Douhet 31, 00100 Rome.*
E. Palliola, *Istituto Superiore Sanità, Via Regina Elena 299,*
   00100 Rome.
U. Pallotta, *Via S. Giacomo 7, 40100 Bologna.*
Pandolfi, C. *Tecnipetrol, 00100 Rome.*
A. Panizzi, *Citterio S.p.A., Corso Europa 206, 20017 Rho.*
C. Paoletti, *Istituto Microbiologia Agraria, Università, 50100*
   Florence.
C. Pascucci, *B.P., Pza Spagna 15, 00100 Rome.*
E. Passaro, *Montedison, Largo Donegani 1-2, 20100 Milan.*
D. Pedrina, *F.R.A.G.D., Pza Erculea 9, 20100 Milan.*
G. Petralli, *SILO S.p.A., Via R. Fucini 5, 50053 Empoli.*
Petrini, *Lab. Ricerche Tecnologiche, 96100 Siracusa.*
P.P. Puglisi, *Istituto di Genetica, Università di Parma, 43100*
   Parma.

B. Pushaparay, *Istituto Microbiologica Agararia, 50100 Florence.*
H. Pihl, *Alfa Laval S.p.A., Via Pusiano 2, 20052 Monza.*
M. Ragaini, *ICIPU, Via Q. Sella 2, 00100 Rome.*
P. Rampolla, *CTIP, Pza Douhet 31, 00100 Rome.*
R. Ravenna, *Montedison, Largo Donegani 1-2, 20100 Milan.*
A. Reggio, *Montedison, Largo Donegani 1-2, 20100 Milan.*
A. Reiter, *Via Salaria 414, 00100 Rome.*
P. Robertucci, *Laboratorio Dogana, Via della Luce 35, 00100 Rome.*
E. Rognoni, *Università di Milano, Via Celoria 10, 20100 Milan.*
Ruter, *FAO "AGS", Via Terme di Caracalla, 00100 Rome.*
R. Scandurra, *Università di Roma, 00100 Rome.*
O. Schettini, *Chimica Bromatologia, Università di Napoli, 80100 Naples.*
V. Silano, *Istituto Superiore Sanità, Via Regina Elena 299, 00100 Rome.*
V. Sillani, *Montedison, Largo Donegani 1-2, 00100 Rome.*
E. Squillace, *Montedison, Largo Donegani 1-2, 00100 Rome.*
A. Stagni, *Silos e Magazzini del Tirreno, 00100 Rome.*
G. Succi, *Istituto Zootecnia, Via Celoria 2, 20100 Milan.*
L. Tuttobello, *Istituto Superiore Sanità, Via Regina Elena 299, 00100 Rome.*
Y. Uchida, *Mistui Italia S.p.A., Pza Liberty 2, 20100 Milan.*
Unger, *CTIP, Pza Douhet 31, 00100 Rome.*
V. Vaccari, *CTIP, Pza Douhet 31, 00100 Rome.*
F. Valfrè, *Istituto Superiore Sanità, Via Regina Elena 299, 00100 Rome.*
E.W. van Ness, *CTIP, Pza Douhet 31, 00100 Rome.*
Veronese, *Università Milano, 20100 Milan.*
von Wietersheim, *Alimont de Rica, 29010 S. Polo Pod.*
J. Wells, *CTIP, Pza Douhet 31, 00100 Rome.*
D.S.O. Zavattari, *Istituto Superiore Sanità, Via Regina Elena 299, 00100 Rome.*
Zeni, *CTIP, Pza Douhet 31, 00100 Rome.*

R. Ursini, *Presidente Liquichimica S.p.A., Via Roncaglia 12, 20146 Milan.*
L. Chierici, *Liquichimica S.p.A., Via Roncaglia 12, 20146 Milan.*
A. Ganni, *Liquichimica S.p.A., Via Roncaglia 12, 20146 Milan.*
E. Geuna, *Liquichimica S.p.A., Via Roncaglia 12, 20146 Milan.*
G. Pedetti, *Liquichimica S.p.A., Via Roncaglia 12, 20146 Milan.*
P. Peri, *Liquichimica S.p.A., Via Roncaglia 12, 20146 Milan.*
B. Rosi, *Liquichimia S.p.A., Via Roncaglia 12, 20146 Milan.*

JAPAN

K. Aibara, *National Institute of Health, 2-10-35 Kamiosaki, Shinagawa-Ku, Tokyo.*
S. Araky, *Mitsui Co. Ltd., 2-9 Nishi Shimbashi Itchome, Minato-ku, Tokyo.*
S. Hibino, *ZEN-NOH, Takuba-machi, Ibaragi-ken.*

M. Kanazawa, *Kanegafuchi, 3-3 Chome, Nakanoshima, Kita-ku, Osaka.*
K. Katoh, *National Food Research Inst., Tokyo.*
A. Kitai, *Sanraku Ocean Co. Ltd., 7-1 Chone Chuoko, Tokyo 104.*
N. Makiguchi, *Mitsui Toatsu Ch. Inc., Yokohama.*
T. Onihara, *ZEN-NOH, Takuba-machi, Ibaragi-ken.*
N. Tanahashi, *Kanegafuchi, 3-3 Chome, Nakanoshima, Kita-ku, Osaka.*

LIBYA

Bushwereb, *Min. Agriculture Research Centre, P.O. Box 2480, Tripoli.*
W.F. Kohl, *Ind. Research Centre, P.O. Box 358, Tripoli.*
A.A. Mohamed, *Ind. Research Centre, P.O. Box 3633, Tripoli.*

SPAIN

A. Akerman, *McKee CTIP, Av. da Generalissimo 71-A, Madrid 16.*
A. Briones, *Barcelona.*
G.J. Centeno, *S.A. Cros, Paseo de Gracia 56, Barcelona.*
de Mellinedo y Martinez, *Ind. Abastecimientos S.A., Nunez de Balboa 118-5, Madrid.*
A.R. Foguet, *S.A. Cros, Paseo de Gracia 56, Barcelona.*
A.J.L. Ladero, *Ministero Agricoltura, Po Infanta Isabel 1, Madrid.*
J. Lajara, *Cia Ind. Abastecimientos S.A., Nunez de Balboa 118-5, Madrid.*
L.O. Mingarro, *Explosivos Riotinto, Madrid.*
Quededo, *McKee CTIP, Av. da Generalissimo 71-A, Madrid 16.*
P.J. Rubio, *Ministero Agricoltura, Po Infanta Isabel 1, Madred.*
E. Waldburger, *Cia, Ind. Abastecimientos S.A., Nunez de Balboa 118-5, Madrid.*

SWEDEN

H. Faulkner, *Alfa-Laval A.B., Postfack, 14700 Tumba.*
Th. Johansson, *Alfa-Laval A.B., Postfack, 14700 Tumba.*
A. Lindberg, *The Swedish Ass. of Future Studies, Box 5073, 10242 Stockholm 50.*
L. Rutguist, *National Veterinary Inst., 10405 Stockholm 50.*

SWITZERLAND

W.F. Avery, *Union Carbide, 5 Rua Pedro Meylan, 1211 Geneva 17.*
B. Berti, *Union Carbide, 5 Rua Pedro Meylan, 1211 Geneva 17.*
G.J. Griesmer, *Union Carbide, 5 Rua Pedro Meylan, 1211 Geneva 17.*
E. Kaloussis, *Ste Ass. Technique Produits Nestle, 1814 La Tour D.P.*
A.W. Krieger, *Wander A.G., 3001 Bern.*
F.C. Lu, *WHO, Av. Appia, Geneva.*

USA

D.H. Calloway, *Dept. Nutrit. Sciences, Univ. California, Berkeley 94708.*

H. Clymer, *Smithkline Corp., Philadelphia.*
P. Davis, *Stanford Research Institute, Menlo Park, California.*
R.J. Flannery, *Standard Oil (Ind.), P.O. Box 400, Naperville.*
M.J. Forman, *Agency for Inv., Washington.*
E. Gaden, *Dept. Chem. Eng. & Applied Chemistry, Columbia*
   University, New York.
H. Henderson, *Writer, New York.*
J.F. Irwin, *Arthur McKee & Co., Cleveland.*
R.J. Jones, *Arthur McKee & Co., Cleveland.*
D. Kellor, *Cargill Inc., Minneapolis.*
D.D. Maclaren, *Exxon Enterprises Inc., 1251 Av. of the Americas,*
   New York.
M. Milner, *PAG, New York.*
B.L.Oser, *Food & Drug Research Lab., Maspeth, New York.*
H.J. Prebluda, *Editor, Chemurgic Digest, 3 Belmont Circle,*
   Trenton.
I. Reilly, *E.I. Du Pont de Nemours & Co., Wilmington.*
H. Stone, *Stanford Research Inst., Menlo Park, California.*
J. Stradford, *Berkeley.*
J. Taylor, *Bureau of Veterinary & Medicine Food & Drug Adm.,*
   Rockville.

SYMPOSIUM HONORARY COMMITTEE

President

On. le Mariano Rumor   Prime Minister

Members

On. le Mario Ferrari Aggradi	Minister of Agriculture
On. le Ciriaco de Mita	Minister of Industry
On. le Piero Bucalossi	Minister of Scientific Research
Prof. Adriano Buzzati Traverso	
Prof. Silvio Garattini	Director of Istituto "Mario Negri"
Prof. Giancarlo Masini	President of Italian Association of Scientific Journalists
Dr. Max Milner	General Secretary of PAG, New York
Prof. Alessandro Faedo	President of CNR
Prof. Vincenzo Caglioti	Honorary President of CNR
Prof. Giancarlo Bianchi	President of Istituto Studi sulla Nutrizione e sulle Tecnologie Alimentari

PREFACE

This volume contains the papers presented at the International Symposium on Single Cell Protein - Standardization, Evaluation, and Safety held in Rome, Italy, November 7 through 9, 1973. The symposium was presented by Liquichimica S.p.A., Milan, Italy, and Stanford Research Institute, Menlo Park, California.

Aspects of standardization, evaluation, and safety of single cell protein (SCP) were emphasized in the program because this was the first major conference on SCP held in Europe, and many individuals involved in the production and regulations of SCP had requested specific, detailed information on these topics.

The symposium was divided into the following four sessions: (1) Considerations of SCP as a Protein Source; (2) Nutritional Evaluation of SCP; (3) Current Position on SCP - Production, Standardization, and Use; and (4) Roundtable Discussions, Topic 1 - Control of SCP Processes, Topic 2 - Processing of SCP for Human Food, Topic 3 - Nutritional Value and Safety of SCP as Human Food, Topic 4 - Utilization and Safety of SCP as Animal Feed, and Topic 5 - Political and Social Aspects of SCP Utilization. These roundtable discussions provided the conferees an opportunity to participate in the symposium and explore all the aspects and ramifications of producing, testing, processing, selling, and using SCP.

I thank Liquichimica for so graciously sponsoring this symposium, and especially wish to thank Drs. Raffaele Ursini, Bruno Rosi, and Antonio Ganni for their great contributions to the success of the symposium. I also extend thanks to the speakers and participants who made this a most worthwhile conference. Special gratitude is due to the authors and all those who have contributed to the publication of this book.

Peyton Davis

Menlo Park, California
April 1974

FOREWORD

The Proceedings of the International Symposium on SCP which was held in Rome on November 7 to 9 are becoming available at a particularly important moment in the history of the so-called "non-conventional protein sources".

From the middle of 1974 to the end of 1975, in hardly more than one year, we shall in fact be able to observe the realization of some interesting activities in the field of industrial production of proteins by fermentation. Without distracting from the merits of the engineers who projected the plants and directed their construction, if single cell proteins are on the market in a few months' time, it will be largely due to those scientists, who with so much enthusiasm, not disjoined from an acute sense of criticism, have for many years debated about the production of SCPs on commercial scale and on the use of these new proteic meals.

In my opinion, at least one fundamental conclusion may be drawn from all the papers which were presented in Rome and that is that the doubts which still exist about SCPs' safety and nutritional properties, the optimal size of the plants, and the type of substrates to be preferred are not such as to totally condition the production of single cell proteins. They will disappear with the starting up of the plants, when control of production at each single stage and mass testing, with all the required accuracy, is possible. As soon as the results are available they will satisfy even the most sceptical potential user. It is at this stage that I would consider it most opportune that all those who have been so far concerned with SCPs express their enlightened criticisms. To this effect periodical meetings on specific subjects should be held. This is a logical consequence of the large meetings which were held in these last five years in various countries and which dealt with more general topics. We are accustomed to hearing that corn, soya and yeast for breadmaking are safe products, because both men and animals have been fed with them for centuries. I am convinced that what we must achieve is that one day people will say the same about SCP

Raffaele Ursini

Milan, Italy
April 1974

CONTENTS

OPENING REMARKS

Raffaele Ursini

President, Liquichimica SpA
Via Roncaglia 12, Milan, Italy

Liquichimica, together with Stanford Research Institute, has sponsored this symposium on the standardization, evaluation and safety of SCP. It is my honor to thank the Prime Minister, the Rt. Hon. Mariano Rumor, and all the other distinguished gentlemen who are members of the Honorary Committee. I also wish to give a warm welcome to all those persons who have accepted our invitation to contribute to this symposium which is now about to begin.

The number of highly qualified scientists who have come to Rome from all parts of the world is a valid index of man's impelling need to solve a basic problem which threatens our very existence, mainly chronic malnutrition. The lack of synchronization between population increase on the one hand, and adequate increase of protein in human diets on the other, is now universally accepted. It is also true that so far all national and international measures taken to reverse this imbalance have met with only partial success.

The current scarcity of protein for animal feedstuffs subsequently affects the production of protein for human consumption. However, the use of unconventional raw materials for the production of proteins is an effective solution to this problem. For example, 2,000,000,000 tons of crude oil per annum are extracted from the earth and used for an almost infinite variety

1

of purposes.   If only ten percent of this crude oil could be
used for the production of SCP substrate, one could obtain between 20 to 30 million tons of protein and this would help in
eliminating protein malnutrition.   Up till now the production
of unconventional proteins has been considered a scientific
curiosity;   however, it is now established that petroleum and
other uncommon materials can serve as substrates for the production of these needed proteins.

Important features of unconventional proteins are that they
are produced under controlled factory conditions which requires
very limited space;   they are not dependent upon atmospheric
conditions;   they spare marine fauna and other natural resources.
The microorganisms involved reproduce themselves in large fermentation vessels continuously.   At the moment, in connection
with the production of SCP by fermentation, there are many projects under way all around the world;   some are still at the
laboratory level, some are at pilot plant stage and a few are
in commercial production.   However, the best possible use for
their end products has yet to be defined.

While foreseeable production of SCP will not, in my opinion,
completely solve man's problem of protein deficiency, I am convinced that together with new high yielding cereals, proteins
obtained from oil seeds and animal proteins, they will greatly
contribute to alleviating malnutrition.

It is on the basis of these concepts just outlined that I
declare this symposium opened.   Its fundamental objective is to
collect and collate information obtained both in laboratory research and in industrial production, in order to set up standard
criteria for the acceptance, approval, distribution and use of
SCP.   Lastly, we should try to set up guide-lines for the use of
SCP in feed and food.

I hope that the fruits of this symposium will be to the benefit of us all.

SESSION 1

CONSIDERATIONS OF SCP AS A PROTEIN SOURCE

INTRODUCTION

Marcel Ganzin

Director, FAO Food Policy and Nutrition Division
Rome, Italy

The potential of SCP cannot be seen in isolation from the present world situation. This meeting opens at a time of near crisis on the world protein market. As you all know an acute shortage of two important commodities in the compound feed industry, soy bean and fish meal, has led to steep price rises, and has brought man and animal into competition for cereals which are the staple foods in many developing countries. Growing demand for meat has caused some meat-exporting countries to rely more heavily on grain staples produced internally as a component of their animal feeds.

The supply-demand situation became so finely balanced that the Director-General of FAO recently convened a meeting of major wheat exporting countries to discuss food security plans for the protection of poorer nations against commodity price fluctuations.

The recovery of the fish meal industry which is at the mercy of the supply of anchovetta, will remain slow in 1974 and will return to normal only in 1975 according to forecasts. Future prices are likely to remain high, and supplies uncertain for a number of years.

Long-term demand for soy bean, and recent crop failures will maintain high prices and shortages. The US produce at present 75% of the soy world market and one in seven acres of US crop land is now under soy bean, and this is reaching its limit. With the increasing demand for soy bean for the manufacture of tex-

tured vegetable proteins, aimed at the expanding market in the
USA and Europe, there is now a shift towards soy bean as a meat
replacer for human consumption.   It has been estimated that by
1980, 20% of the American meat market will have been replaced
by meat analogues.

In the face of uncertain crops and the ever-increasing world
demand for meat products, the compound feed industry is obviously
attracted by a product of constant composition with good biological value, which can be produced under highly-controlled conditions, and is independent of soil and climate.   It must be
remembered that the compound feed industry is itself growing at
the rate of over 10% per year.   Because of the progress made in
recent years, and because of the enormous production potential
for SCP there are good prospects that this industry can be supplied with good quality proteins that will not only fill the deficit created by expansion, but will also reverse the flow of
soy beans and cereals into animal feeds.

There has recently been a re-appraisal of the approach to
food and nutrition policies.   Recent revision of protein requirements indicate that in many cases there is no longer a protein
deficit at national level.   Nevertheless, clinical surveys show
that undernourishment is not decreasing.   Basic data on food
consumption and food requirements is lacking in many developing
countries and the aggregated figures available conceal inequal-
ities of distribution, both at a national level and very often,
at a family level.

Increasing supplies of SCP for animal feeds would therefore
improve human nutrition rather quickly by taking vegetable sources
of protein out of the human/animal competition and making them
available once more for human consumption in developing countries.

SCP which is the chief subject of this symposium is distinguished from the protein of other microorganisms because it can
be produced on hydrocarbon or hydrocarbon-derived materials, as

opposed to the conventional and traditional carbohydrate fermentation.

Hydrocarbon and microorganisms are an unfamiliar combination and like all new products which will find their way even indirectly into the human diet, they must first be carefully controlled. In the case of SCP those products now on the market are the results of several years of nutritional and toxicological testing on a variety of domestic animals, in most cases along the lines recommended by the P.A.G. This has led to some categories of SCP being cleared for animal consumption, but not for human consumption. Some years of testing lie ahead before there can be a decision on the direct use of SCP in foods. You will hear later Dr. Hoogerheide, of the International Union of Pure and Applied Chemistry (IUPAC), underline the importance of carefully defining substrates and final SCP products. IUPAC are cooperating with the PAG on the development of a guideline on SCP for animal feeding.

Progress in SCP production from hydrocarbons has had its counterpart in recent developments in the use of cellulose and other carbohydrate waste materials, as substrates for the growth of microbial proteins. The successful outcome of using these wastes which are constantly being renewed by photosynthesis will have the double advantage of upgrading waste materials and ameliorating the pollution hazard they present.

Substrates for SCP production will be the subject of Dr. Elmer Gaden, of the Department of Chemical Engineering and Applied Chemistry of Columbia University.

To give you a picture of the background against which these novel sources of protein are coming on to the market, we will first hear Dr. Bruce Nicol speak on recent developments in the status of international food and nutrition.

The economic aspects of SCP and its place in world protein supplies will be the subject of Dr. J. Abbott who heads the

Marketing Credit and Cooperative Services in FAO.

I have so far cited the case for the use of SCP in animal feeding and the possible advantages.   But a note of warning is also necessary.   We have recently seen in Japan that in spite of government's clearance of home-produced SCP from normal paraffins as animal feed, popular opinion has been so strongly against the product that several companies have been forced to postpone or cancel their production plans.

We should therefore recognize that public opinion should be - if not formed - at least informed of the potentialities of SCP.   The use of such emotive and inaccurate words as "synthetic" should be avoided when speaking of Single Cell Protein from hydrocarbons.

We then might well see SCP contribute significantly over the next few years to the stabilization of the world protein market and to the nutrition, directly and indirectly, of the world's population.

RECENT DEVELOPMENTS IN THE STATUS OF INTERNATIONAL FOOD AND NUTRITION

Bruce Nicol*

Consultant for FAO, Rome, Italy

INTRODUCTION

It has been my privilege during the last few years to have introduced the subject of world food supplies and their nutritional adequacy or inadequacy at a number of symposia convened by national or international bodies. The subjects of the symposia have varied from, for instance, "Easing the Pressure of Population", "Problems of World Medicine", "The Establishment of Co-operative Agricultural Research Programmes between Countries with Similar Ecological Conditions" to the "Causes and Prevention of Famine". All such audiences had an interest in world food supplies specific to their own concerns and I suspect that this symposium on "Considerations of Single Cell Protein as a Protein Source" has an interest much more specific than most of the others I have had the honour to address. However, the subject I have been asked to discuss, "The Status of International Food and Nutrition", is not concerned directly with single cell protein (SCP) and I will ask only a few tentative questions about its possible use at the end of my presentation.

---

* Although much of the data upon which this paper is based were provided to the author by FAO and WHO the way in which the material has been presented and the conclusions drawn are the author's responsibility and do not necessarily represent the views of the Organizations.

Dr. Abbott will consider in some detail the state of world protein supplies. Therefore I intend to deal rather briefly with the overall food situation and then turn to a consideration of the relationship between the state of nutrition at national and international level, as it can be identified by different indicators, and the state of national and regional food supplies and requirements for energy and protein.

THE WORLD FOOD SITUATION

In a paper presented recently at the United Nations Symposium on Population and Development (1) the Food and Agriculture Organisation of the United Nations (FAO) concluded that food production at world and regional levels has increased faster than population growth during the last two decades, although the margin between the two has narrowed. Production in a number of countries has lagged behind population growth and in others behind the effective economic demand for food. Past rates of food production in the developing countries need to be stepped up considerably to meet United Nations Second Development Decade targets. Even if those targets are met, the magnitude of nutritional problems, found mainly in underdeveloped regions, would remain at approximately present levels in spite of projected food and cereal surpluses at world level.

Short-term fluctuations in food production due to seasonal and climatic conditions will continue and concerted national and international food stock policies must be developed to protect the world, developed and developing, against the worst consequences of food scarcity due to crop failures.

The possibility of bringing about considerable increases in agricultural production exists, but is dependent upon the availability of modern inputs and related institutional and structural measures beyond the capacity of many developing countries. Hence there is an urgent need for international measures in the fields of trade and aid.

Boyd Orr drew attention to the importance of socio-economic
conditions as a major factor in the epidemiology of malnutrition
in the British context in his book "Food, Health and Income" in
1936 (2).   The same theme was expanded by Cépède in 1953 in his
treatise on "Economie Alimentaire du Globe" (3).   It is now
realised that undernutrition and malnutrition in lesser-developed
countries are to a large extent a function of poverty and that
their solution requires measures for the creation of income,
which in most of those countries must be derived mainly from
agriculture.   Increasing population and pressure on the land
are inhibiting factors in this creation of income.   A population
policy, therefore, becomes a major component of food and agricultural policies and an important element of plans designed to reduce undernutrition and malnutrition at national and regional
levels.

DISTRIBUTION OF FOOD SUPPLIES

The inequality of available food supplies between the developed and developing regions is a major and increasing cause
of concern.   Means to achieve a more equitable distribution
through agricultural adjustment, trade and aid must receive top
priority.

In the highly developed countries malnutrition, exemplified
for instance by obesity or possibly coronary heart disease, is
the result of affluence and ample food supplies processed, distributed and being put to use through efficient food industries
and marketing systems.   Lester Brown's presentation to the
Protein Advisory Group of the United Nations in June this year
was interesting in that he attributed the present shortage and
resulting high prices of wheat, maize and soya beans not only to
short-term crop failures in various parts of the world, but also
to the long-term affluence which exists in North America and

B

Europe.   This affluence has led to a large increase in the consumption of animal products in those regions, with a resulting
rise in demand for animal feeds, pressure on the land in developed
countries and a reduction in world-wide supplies of these protein
foods for direct human consumption.   He said that in the United
States, between 1940 and 1972, beef consumption increased from
around 25 kg to 53 kg per person per year;   that is to say from
about 70 g to 145 g of beef *per caput* per day.   Such quantities,
and an increase of such magnitude, are surely unjustifiable from
any nutritional point of view in the developed world.   Some
clinicians and pathologists are now saying that this high beef
consumption may add yet another dimension to what may be termed
"affluent malnutrition" in the form of cancer of the lower colon.

On the other hand, in developing countries undernutrition
and malnutrition result either from lack of total food supplies,
from shortage of foodstuffs of high nutritional quality such as
animal products, or from an inability to obtain such high quality
protein foods to supplement the staples.   In the latter case
this may result from poor social status, such as subsistence
farming or fishing, low purchasing power or both.   It is important to realise that in developing countries a considerable socio-
economic gradient exists, even in comparatively small village
communities, which affects food consumption and the satisfaction
of energy and nutrient requirements to a considerable degree.
Table 1 shows these social and economic differences and their
effects on food consumption and nutrient intakes quite clearly.
Table 2 indicates two other factors which are relevant in this
context, (a) ecology and (b) distribution of food within families.
In the Savannah areas of West Africa the staple foods are sorghum
and various millets, which contribute about 80% to both energy
and protein intakes.   Such diets provide adults and young children with ample amounts of protein to meet their nutritional
needs but the quantities consumed by young children do not cover

Table 1   Nutrient intakes of different socio-economic groups in Nigeria.

NUTRIENT (intake per day)	NIGER DELTA (freshwater and mangrove swamp)		BIDA AREA (Guinea savannah)	
	TRADERS	FISHERMEN	N.A. OFFICIALS	FARMERS
CALORIES	3000	2200	3200	2600
PROTEIN (g) animal	50	68	45	5
total	84	80	90	75
FAT (g)	86	39	50	44
VITAMIN A (i.u.) [a]	9000	5700	8000	5000
THIAMINE (mg)	1.02	0.30	3.60	3.20
RIBOFLAVINE (mg)	1.37	0.68	1.20	0.76
ASCORBIC ACID (mg)	71	40	100	98
CALCIUM (g)	1.3	2.9	1.3	0.5
IRON (mg)	21	24	56	40

(a) 1 i.u. preformed Vitamin A taken as equivalent of 3 i.u. of Vitamin A as carotene.

B. *Nicol*

Table 2 Ratio of energy and protein intakes (1) to requirements of children 4 to 6 years compared with those of adults in same families.

NIGERIAN PEASANT FAMILIES

VEGETATION ZONE	CALORIES per day 1/R × 100		PROTEIN g per day			
			1/SPA × 100		1/MR × 100	
	4-6 yrs.	Adults	4-6 yrs.	Adults	4-6 yrs.	Adults
SAHEL SAVANNAH	87	128	220	240	330	360
SUDAN SAVANNAH	95	110	190	200	280	300
GUINEA SAVANNAH	70	115	200	250	300	370
MONTANE	75	100	170	200	250	300
RAIN FOREST	77	95	70	85	105	130
DERIVED SAVANNAH	70	87	70	76	105	110

SPA, safe practical allowance as defined by FAO/WHO Expert Committee on Protein Requirements, 1957.

MR, minimum requirement as defined by same Committee.

their energy requirements.   In the Rain Forest and Derived Savannah areas yams (*Dioscorea* spp.) and cassava *(Manihot util-
issima)* are the staple foods and they also contribute about 80%
of dietary energy and protein.   Adults' diets provide about
their safe level of intake but energy needs are not adequately
met if judged at a level of moderate activity.   In such ecological zones the food consumed by children provides only about 70%
of their needs for energy and protein as proposed by FAO/WHO
Expert Committees.

I have explained elsewhere (4) that I believe the failure
of the Savannah Zone diets to meet energy requirements of young
children is due to their bulky nature and the fact that they are
fed only twice or three times a day.   In the Rain Forest areas,
however, a complete change in crop production and dietary patterns is needed if the prevalence of malnutrition in young children is to be reduced and the economic effectiveness of their
parents is to improve.   This example from West Africa can be
translated to other countries of the world with similar ecological variations.   The local environment also affects to a marked
degree the vitamin and mineral pattern of diets.

FOOD AVAILABILITY, CLINICAL, ANTHROPOMETRIC AND DEMOGRAPHIC CRITERIA

I would like to turn now from food supplies and their distribution to look at the relationship between the prevalence of
undernutrition and malnutrition and the food supplies available
for human consumption at national levels.   It is important for
governments interested in improving health and efficiency of
their peoples to know what this relationship is, and, if possible,
to know its nature.

I must say quite frankly that I am not in favour of the
mathematical/statistical attempts which have been made in the
past to estimate the number of undernourished and malnourished

people in the world, using food balance sheet (FBS) data on the
one hand and the requirements for energy and protein, as proposed by such groups as FAO/WHO Expert Committees on the other
hand, unless such attempts are related in some way to the clinical facts of life.   Food balance sheet data have their limitations of accuracy and do not give any idea of food distribution
within a population.   Our estimates of energy requirements are
dependent upon so many factors, particularly levels of activity,
about which we have so little good information, that many assumptions have to be made by the statistician in determining the numbers not receiving adequate food supplies.

Obviously the best way to compare food supplies with nutritional status at national level is to carry out surveys for
food consumption simultaneously with clinical, anthropometric and
other studies on the same samples of the population.   The samples should be representative of the whole in terms of the different socio-economic and age and sex groups, and of special
groups such as expectant and nursing women, the very young and
the elderly.   They should be carried out at those times of the
year which allow estimates of seasonal variations in food supplies
and consumption to be made.   Preferably they should use inter-
nationally standardised techniques, as simple in design as possible,
to allow comparison from one country to another.   I am told that
FAO and WHO are now in process of defining such techniques.

In spite of the cost of national surveys of this nature in
terms of time and money, a few have been carried out in developing
countries but the results are either not yet available or have
not been released for publication.   Food consumption surveys of
limited coverage on *selected* groups of people have been conducted
in some developing countries and clinical data has been obtained
at the same time, often on the same samples.   A number of clinical and anthropometric studies on *representative* samples of
national populations have been published but unfortunately they

have seldom been related to food consumption.   Therefore, in making this comparison of national food supplies and nutritional status, I have had to rely, reluctantly, upon FBS data which are available for most countries, upon various indicators of the state of nutrition of populations which can be obtained from statistical records published by the United Nations and the World Health Organization (WHO) (5,6,7) and from the clinical and anthropometric studies I have just mentioned.   Reference to many of these clinical and anthropometric surveys are given in the literature cited at the end of this paper.   Such an approach to the present state of international food and nutrition, while having the possible merit of being novel, is not entirely satis-factory.   I would anticipate criticism by saying that it appears to me to be the best one possible at the moment in view of lack of more detailed and correlated information.

Nutrition Indicators

The indicators chosen, which many agree are influenced to some extent by the nutritional background of a population, are first the age-specific death-rates, infant mortality rate (IMR), second year mortality and the mortality in the age group 1 to 4 years.   It seems reasonable to relate such statistics to food supplies available at national level.   The effects of malnourish-ment start to exert an effect on mortality in the second six months of life but may occur sooner if weaning takes place at an earlier age.   They continue through the second year of life and may be most pronounced at that time, when infectious diseases aggravate the results of inadequate feeding.   They decline with increasing age up to the fifth year (8).   Birth weight at full term, height at age 8 years and the point prevalence of protein-calorie malnutrition (PCM) have also been included because infor-mation upon them is available from a good number of countries, both developed and developing.   I am indebted to Dr. Bengoa of the Nutrition Unit of WHO for help in obtaining much of this in-

formation and to his own publications (9,10).   A close relationship has been shown to exist between birth weights, economic status
and maternal nutrition (11,12,13,14).   Height at some defined
point during the growth of young children is a measure of their
past nutritional experience (15,16).

Problems of sample size, age groupings and methodologies employed have made it necessary to select, from the data available,
those surveys which were as nearly as possible comparable and
representative of national situations.

Age-specific Death Rates and National Food Supplies

In Table 3 the age-specific death rates have been compared
with the availability, at *per caput* level, of energy and protein
supplies in relation to the requirements and safe levels of intake proposed by the FAO/WHO Expert Committee of 1971 on Energy
and Protein Requirements (17).   The developing and developed
countries are ranked according to the supply of energy as a percentage of requirement at the level of moderate activity.
Using International Labour Organization categories of employment
and numbers so employed in the different countries and the energy
requirements estimated by Durnin and Passmore for such types of
work (18) almost all countries, both developed and developing,
appear to fall in the moderate category of energy expenditure.
Much more information is needed on this question of activity and
energy requirements.

The mean safe levels of intake for protein *per caput* have
been determined as described in the FAO/WHO Expert Committee report.   As energy supplies increase to reach or surpass 100% of
requirements, the excess of protein over and above safe levels
of intake rises at an even faster rate and is surely associated
with an improvement in its quality.   This excess of protein
over safe level of intake is found for all but two or three
countries in the world where starchy roots and tubers are almost
exclusively the staple foods.

Table 3   National *per caput* energy and protein supplies (S) and requirements (R) compared with age-specific death rates.

CLASSIFICATION BY COUNTRY		S/R cals %	S/R prot %	Infant mortality 1000 live births	Second year mortality 1000 popul.	1 - 4 year mortality 1000 popul.
(Number of countries)		(95)	(95)	(86)	(37)	(52)
DEVELOPING						
S/R cals less than 90%	(13)	85	127	99.9 (8)	40.4 (2)	15.2 (4)
S/R cals 90-109%	(39)	97	156	67.5 (36)	24.7 (11)	9.2 (15)
S/R cals 110% and over	(7)	112	183	72.4 (7)	69.0 (2)	8.1 (3)
DEVELOPED						
S/R cals 90-109%	(6)	106	215	26.8 (6)	1.3 (2)	1.6 (3)
S/R cals 110-119%	(13)	116	213	29.6 (12)	3.4 (8)	1.2 (11)
S/R cals 120% and over	(17)	122	236	25.4 (17)	2.9 (12)	1.0 (16)

CORRELATIONS (all countries)	S/R cals %	S/R prot %	Prot/cals %
Infant mortality	r-0.59 P <0.005	r-0.60 P <0.005	r-0.42 P <0.005
Second year mortality	r-0.43 P <0.01	r-0.42 P <0.01	r-0.31 P <0.05
1 - 4 year mortality	r-0.67 P <0.005	r-0.62 P <0.005	r-0.40 P <0.01

Table 4 National *per caput* energy and protein supplies (S) and requirements (R) compared with certain anthropometric and clinical data.

CLASSIFICATION BY COUNTRY	S/R cals %	S/R prot %	Birth Weight full term kg	Height aged 8 years cm	Prevalence PCM 0-5 yrs %
(Number of countries)	(95)	(95)	(35)	(27)	(48)
DEVELOPING					
S/R cals less than 90% (13)	85	127	2.94 (5)	120.4 (2)	24.9 (10)
S/R cals 90-109% (39)	97	156	3.01 (15)	118.6 (11)	21.9 (36)
S/R cals 110% and over (7)	112	183	3.06 (2)	120.5 (4)	15.0 (2)
DEVELOPED					
S/R cals 90-109% (6)	106	215	3.03 (1)	124.8 (2)	Ø*
S/R cals 110-119% (13)	116	213	3.24 (4)	124.7 (3)	Ø*
S/R cals 120% and over (17)	122	236	3.36 (8)	126.4 (4)	Ø*

CORRELATIONS (all countries)

	S/R cals %	S/R prot %	Prot/cals %
Birth weight	r 0.84 P <0.005	r 0.82 P <0.005	r 0.61 P <0.005
Height 8 years	r 0.63 P <0.005	r 0.67 P <0.005	r 0.46 P <0.01
Prevalence PCM	r-0.37 P <0.01	r-0.33 P <0.05	r-0.22 P Ø

* PCM is recorded in some developing countries, particularly those with high infant mortality rates, but probably never reaches 5%.

IMR falls from a very high level in those countries with
the lowest energy availability until energy supply approximately
equals requirement. This fall in IMR is significant ($P < 0.02$).
As *per caput* energy and protein supplies increase in the developing countries to exceed requirement IMR still remains at a
high level. A downward trend is seen for 1 to 4 year mor-
talities, not statistically significant, as energy and protein
supplies in relation to requirement increase.

When all countries are considered together there are significant correlations between these age-specific death rates and
the supply of energy and protein relative to requirements or
safe levels of intake and also to the percentage of calories
supplied by protein.

An important point to be noted from Table 3 is the abrupt
fall in all three indicators between the highest ranked developing countries and the lowest ranked developing countries.
This sharp decline occurs in spite of the fact that energy and
protein supplies relative to requirement, *per caput,* are in the
same order of magnitude for both those groups of countries.
Death rates do not diminish significantly in the developed
countries as food supplies increase in quantity and quality over
and above estimated requirements.

Clinical and Anthropometric Data and Food Supplies

The three other indicators are considered in Table 4. Birth
weights at full term increase slightly with energy and protein
supplies in developing countries. They are significantly lower
($P < 0.05$) than those in developed countries. There is a very
significant correlation between birth weights and energy and
protein supplies when all countries are considered together. The
same holds true for the heights of boys and girls aged 8 years.

In developing countries the point prevalence of PCM in the
age group 0 to 5 years decreases as food supplies increase. PCM
is seldom observed in developed countries and only in those where

the IMR still remains at a rather high level.   The correlation
between the prevalence of PCM and calorie and protein supplies
in developing countries is much lower than that found for the
other five indicators here considered.   And this is not surprising in view of its epidemiology which is so closely related
to inequitable distribution of food supplies between socio-
economic groups, the synergistic relationship of malnutrition
and infections, and to other non-nutritional factors.   It is
surprising that there is any correlation at all between PCM and
energy and protein supplies at national *per caput* level.

Two other indicators not shown in the tables have been
examined from 18 countries, equally distributed between the developed and developing world.   They are mean heights and weights
of adults aged 20 to 40 years and the percentage of full-term
birth weights less than 2.5 kg.   Both are correlated to national
energy and protein supplies at the 1% probability level.
Nutritional and Food Supplies at Regional and Sub-Regional Level

Three of the indicators, IMR, birth weight and the prevalence of PCM, are compared in Table 5 with energy requirements
and safe levels of protein intake at sub-regional and regional
levels.   The poor food and nutritional state of affairs in
Africa, particularly in West and Central Africa, and in East and
South Asia is very evident.   Conditions in Latin America, the
Near East and Eastern Africa are somewhat better but bear no
comparison to the standards prevailing in the developed regions.

CONCLUSIONS

The comparison which has been made indicates a definite association, at a given time, between food supplies available at
national level and the clinical, anthropometric and other indicators which have been considered.   Birth weights at full term,
1 to 4 year mortality rate, and height aged 8 years appear to be
the best indicators of the worst state of national food supplies

Table 5 National *per caput* energy and protein supplies (S) and requirements (R) compared with some nutritional indicators by regions and sub-regions.

REGION AND SUB-REGION		S/R cal %	Prot cal %	Infant mor- tality 1000 live births	Birth Weight full term kg	Prevalence PCM 0-5 yrs %
(Number of countries)		(95)	(95)	(86)	(35)	(48)
CARIBBEAN	(18)	97	9.5	74 (4)	3.04 (2)	22.3 (3)
LATIN AMERICA	(18)	100	10.2	67 (18)	3.09 (6)	19.1 (15)
Central	(7)	99	10.1	60 (7)	3.07 (3)	19.1 (7)
South	(11)	100	10.3	70 (11)	3.11 (3)	19.1 (8)
NEAR EAST AND N.W. AFRICA	(13)	95	11.4	56 (12)	3.09 (4)	18.3 (9)
AFRICA	(18)	96	10.3	86 (12)	2.92 (6)	28.2 (14)
West and Central	(10)	95	9.8	115 (6)	2.89 (4)	29.4 (8)
Eastern	(8)	97	11.0	56 (6)	2.97 (3)	26.7 (6)
ASIA, E. AND S.	(8)	95	9.1	62 (6)	2.94 (6)	25.3 (7)
EUROPE	(27)	119	11.6	30 (27)	3.34 (10)	Ø*
West and Scand.	(19)	119	11.7	24 (19)	3.33 (7)	Ø*
Eastern	(8)	119	11.5	37 (8)	3.37 (3)	Ø*
NORTH AMERICA AND OCEANIA	(4)	124	12.0	19 (4)	3.33 (1)	Ø*

* PCM is recorded in some developed countries, particularly those with high infant mortality rates, but probably never reaches 5%.

as measured in terms of energy and protein related to requirements and safe levels of intake.   But this association must be
considered in its proper and much wider context.

There is the observed sharp change in degree of all the indicators considered which is found between countries classified
by the United Nations as either developing or developed.   This
change occurs at a point where, at national level, energy and
protein supplies in relation to needs are approximately the same.
It is particularly pronounced in the case of the prevalence of
PCM.   Therefore, and as expected, the association cannot be
attributed only to food supplies.

The infrastructure for putting available food supplies to
the best use is still lacking in most developing countries.
Food processing and distributing industries and marketing systems are too often still rudimentary.   Storage and preparation
of food in the home is not as good as it should be.   Knowledge
of how best to feed infants and young children is imperfect.
Environmental sanitation is primitive.   Even the roads, rail-
ways and bridges needed for bulk transport of crops to centres
where food industries could be set up are often lacking.

It is evident that the process of development eventually
leads to an improvement in the state of nutrition.   But "development" is a long-term process.   If undernutrition and malnutrition are to be reduced at a rate which will help to hasten
development by improving the health and productivity of populations, short-cuts to this end must be sought by the provision
of external aid of one sort or another.   This aid should be
designed not to have an inhibitory effect on national aspirations
in the approach taken towards development.   If such aids are to
be successful, much more locally-specific information on the
ecology, epidemiology and aetiology of malnutrition must be obtained in order to permit countries to develop food and nutrition
policies and intervention programmes which will be orientated in

the right direction for the country, and for people living in particular parts of that country where specific problems exist. Developing countries should be given every help to train national staff to obtain this lacking information and to formulate policies and programmes which are in line with national development plans and aspirations.

There is just as undoubted a lack of good quality protein in the diets of developing countries as there is an undoubted excess of it in more fortunate areas. Possibly it is in this field that SCP will find its best chance to assist in improving the state of nutrition of developing countries through helping to stimulate livestock industries. I know that some of the producers of SCP have had this in mind in the past but local circumstances militated against following it up.

Should SCP be produced in developing countries and combined there with the other necessary ingredients of animal feed? This would act as a stimulus to local agriculture, raise incomes and improve nutrition. Should feed which includes SCP be compounded elsewhere and provided to the developing countries through trade or aid? This might have inhibitory effects on local development. Alternatively, is it yet justifiable to include SCP as a component of high protein foods for children in developing countries in the way the proteins of dried skimmed milk, soya bean, groundnut and cotton seed have been used? These are questions I gladly leave to debate between economists, animal husbandrymen, nutritionists, toxicologists and the members of this symposium.

REFERENCES

1. United Nations Symposium on Population and Development, Cairo. "Population, Food Supply and Agricultural Development," E/CONF.60/BP/5, FAO, Rome (1973).

2. Orr, Sir J. Boyd "Food, Health and Income," 2nd ed, Macmillan & Co. Ltd., London (1937).

3. Cépède, M. "Economie Alimentaire du Globe," Librairie de Medicis, Paris (1953).

4. Nicol, B.M. "Protein and Calorie Concentration," *Nutrition Reviews*, 29, 83 (1971).

5. United Nations Demographic Yearbook, UN, New York (1972).

6. World Health Statistics Annual, WHO, Geneva (1973).

7. Fourth Report on the World Health Situation, WHO, Geneva (1971).

8. Gordon, J.E., Wyon, J.B. and Ascoli, W. "The Second Year Death Rate in Less Developed Countries," *Am. J. Med. Sci.* 254, 357 (1967).

9. Bengoa, J.M. "Nutritional Significance of Mortality Statistics," *Proceedings of Western Hemisphere Nutrition Congress III*, Futura Publishing Co. Inc., New York (1972).

10. Bengoa, J.M. "The State of World Nutrition," NUTR/73.1, WHO, Geneva (1973).

11. Ross, F.W. and Turshen, T. "Fetal Nutrition," *Bull. Wld Hlth Org.* 43, 785 (1970).

12. Meredith, H.W. "Nutrition and Birth Weights," *Hum. Biol.* 42, 217 (1970).

13. Saigal, S. and Srivastava, J.R. "Economic Aspects of Malnutrition," *Indian Pediatr.* 6, 773 (1969).

14. Puffer, Ruth and Serrano, C.V. "Patterns of Mortality in Childhood," PAHO/WHO Scientific Publication No. 262, WHO, Washington, DC (1973).

15. Patwardhan, V.N. and Darby, W.J. "The State of Nutrition in the Arab Middle East," Vanderbilt University Press, Nashville, USA (1972).

16. Beaton, G.H. and Bengoa, J.M. "The Practical Population Indicators of Health and Nutrition (in publication, personal communication) (1973).

17. "Energy and Protein Requirements." Report of a Joint FAO/WHO *ad hoc* Expert Committee: FAO Nutrition Meetings Report Series No.52, FAO, Rome; WHO Technical Report Series No. 522, WHO, Geneva.

18. Durnin, J.V.G.A. and Passmore, R. "Energy, Work and Leisure," Heinemann, London (1967).

ECONOMICS OF SINGLE CELL PROTEIN IN RELATION
TO WORLD PROTEIN SUPPLIES

J.C. Abbott

Chief, Marketing and Credit Service, FAO, Rome, Italy

I understand my task is to look at the economics of single
cell protein against a background of protein supplies from other
sources. What I propose to do first is compare the cost of protein from various sources on the basis of 1972 prices. This
leaves aside the very high prices of this year as reflecting a
special set of circumstances unlikely to recur in the same combination.

Then I shall set out the pattern of protein consumption in
the world and consider where it will go over the next 10 years
or so. A summary review of what seems likely to happen with the
main sources of protein will follow - with the focus on the market they leave open for SCP.

COMPARISON OF PROTEIN COSTS

The costs of some current and potential protein foods are
compared in Table 1. You may think I am ranging rather widely
in my protein coverage for a conference concerned with single
cell proteins. However, I want to deal with sources of protein
that are quite unrelated to SCP and, therefore, full competitors,
as well as with those whose production provides a major market
for SCP. Finally we should consider the scope for SCP as an
ingredient in made-up foods for direct human consumption.

The figures in this table are based on 1972 prices for average quality wholesale purchases at a major source of low cost

25

J.C. Abbott

Table 1   Relative cost of protein in major foods.

	Price of product Cents per kg	Protein content Percent	Price of protein Cents per kg
Chick peas[a]	14.1	20	9
Beans[b]	18.3	22	29
Wheat flour[c]	17.2	11	31
Fish, dried[d]	63.4	37	134
Skim milk powder[e]	65.8	36	156
Chicken[f]	61.4	19	257
Cheese[g]	117.5	25	425
Pork[h]	58.5	10	447
Beef[i]	82.3	15	702
Eggs[j]	65.1	11	466
Lamb[k]	97.7	12	702
***	***	***	***
Soy flour[l]	33.0	50	51
Single cell protein[m]	39.6	66	51

a)   Banda, Uttar Pradesh, India 1972
b)   Dry, Mexico City 1972
c)   Toronto, Canada export price 1971
d)   Dried and salted cod exports, Norway 1971
e)   New Zealand commercial exports 1971/72
f)   US ready-to-cook broilers, Chicago 1972
g)   New Zealand white, London Provision Exchange 1972
h)   Average all weights, Chicago 1972
i)   Australia average first and second export quality 1972
j)   Netherlands export price 1972
k)   New Zealand frozen carcasses, Smithfield, London 1972
l)   US price for use as a meat extender
m)   Estimated price Western Europe of $400 per ton

supplies of each product. To allow, at least very roughly, for the value of the calories in each food these have been priced at 15 cents per kilogramme, and deducted (1). It is understood, of course, that costs calculated in this way reflect other attributes of these foods as well as protein content; beefsteak is not eaten for protein alone. Furthermore, import duties and restrictions, transport costs, distribution margins, etc. can change radically inter product cost relationships in a particular country. Account should also be taken of the biological value of the protein which is generally higher in foods of animal origin.

Subject to such reservations it is striking how much lower in cost is the protein in legumes and cereals, particularly wheat, than in what are commonly regarded as high protein foods. Of these, the lowest priced in terms of protein is dried salt cod, the Italian baccala - also sold widely in West Africa. That its price has not gone up much over the last year or so may reflect, however, a limited popularity. The other animal product which has not increased much in price, and thus with inflation became relatively cheaper is, of course, chicken. American high productivity strains and production techniques have been adopted successfully in Europe and the Near East, and in Asian countries like Sri Lanka. Battery production of chicken is one of the obvious markets for SCP as an ingredient in compound feed mixes.

Dried skim milk is a low cost source of animal protein. It is used in India and elsewhere for reconstitution with local ingredients, but must compete in this use with its alternative outlet as a livestock feed. Its price has gone up by 50 percent recently, as meat prices have risen and fluid milk surpluses have disappeared. Milk production in the United States peaked out in the early 1960s. Since then dairy cow numbers have fallen steadily, compensated in part by increasing average output per cow. This trend will surely be followed in Europe eventually, but in the meantime the Common Market countries are expected to

have 400,000 tons of dried milk in surplus every year; this
figure might go up to 1 million tons by 1975.

The last two prices in Table 1 are for protein ingredients
rather than foods acceptable as such to the consumer. Though
above the cost of protein in cereals and legumes, they are only
one third of the cheapest animal protein. The SCP price applied was $400 per ton. Perhaps you will consider this too
high for use in realistic comparison; however, the 66% protein
percentage may also be high. That the price per kilogramme of
protein comes out the same as for soy flour can hardly be coin-
cidence.

PROTEIN FOOD CONSUMPTION PATTERNS

There are wide variations as between the different parts of
the world in the balance of foods from which people obtain their
proteins. Recent estimates of average *per caput* consumption of
protein by food groups are shown in Table 2. Some of you will
be surprised how much protein people obtain from the bread, pasta,
chapatties, tortillas and corn meal mixes which make up a large
part of the average diet in many countries. Cereals, the staple
food in most countries, are also the main source of protein fur-
nishing almost half the total supply.

Another surprise may be the high average protein intake of
the population in Eastern Europe and the USSR. They eat, in
fact, more protein than the average person in Western Europe.
Nearly half of this protein, however, comes from cereals; consumption of the more highly valued protein foods such as meats,
eggs, fish and milk is only 70 percent of the West European
level. Since the working man's family in Eastern Europe and
Russia has relatively more of its earnings available to spend on
food than in the West, this is some indication of the potential
demand for animal protein foods in the East if they could be made
available.

Table 2 Protein consumption *per caput* by major food groups.

	Cereals	Starchy roots	Pulses and nuts	Vegetables and fruits	Meat, eggs fish and milk	Total
			Grammes per day			
North America	15.9	2.4	4.1	4.9	70.7	98.2
Australia and New Zealand	22.6	2.4	2.2	3.5	63.4	94.4
Western Europe	27.0	4.3	2.9	5.2	48.5	88.2
Eastern Europe	42.3	5.9	3.2	3.4	35.8	90.9
USSR	43.6	6.4	3.5	2.9	35.6	92.2
Argentina, Paraguay Uruguay	26.5	4.2	2.4	3.4	57.4	94.0
Japan	25.8	0.7	12.7	5.9	31.8	76.9
Central America	31.6	0.5	11.9	2.0	22.8	58.0
Caribbean	21.4	3.3	8.3	2.2	22.8	58.0
Africa	33.3	5.2	8.5	1.9	12.1	61.0
Near East	45.1	0.6	4.7	3.3	12.2	65.9
South Asia	32.3	0.5	8.6	0.6	6.3	48.8
China	31.8	2.9	10.8	2.2	8.8	56.6

Source. FAO Food Balance Sheets, for 1970 or extrapolations from the most recent year available. External trade, changes in stocks and non-food utilization are taken into account.

The trend of consumption as consumer incomes rise is demonstrated by the figures for North America, where consumers eat 70
grammes of meat protein per day and take only 16 grammes from
cereals.   Moving rapidly now along this course is Japan.   Animal
protein consumption has risen sharply there in reflection of expanding consumer income, and demand for the traditional soy products is static.   Traditionally fish has been the main source
of animal protein for most Japanese consumers.   However, beef
imports into Japan have doubled this year and we can expect to
see the growth of Japanese multinational cattle ranching ventures
in Australia and South America.

Consumption of animal protein is around 12 grammes per person daily in Africa and the Near East.   It is about half this
in Southern Asia;   here pulses play a more important role in protein food intake and the average proportion from plant sources
reaches 80 percent.   Three rupees a day, less than 50 US cents,
is the usual wage for the large mass of agricultural and un-
skilled urban workers in this part of the world.   With this income the average daily expenditure on food per family member
cannot be more than 10 cents.   Given the size of the populations
involved - in Asia particularly - it will be a long time before
incomes rise in these areas to the point that much larger proportions of animal protein can be consumed.

Projections to 1980

What changes in overall protein supply demand relationship
can be expected from the continuance of present trends over the
next decade?   The FAO Commodity Projections 1970-80 provide
some indications (2).   They show that, assuming prices remain
constant, *per caput* food demand in developing countries would
grow by 8 percent in terms of value over the 1970s with an annual
rate of a little under 1 percent.   The food available for the
populations of Africa and South East Asia will still, however,
not be enough to meet recommended energy requirements.   Overall

protein consumption is expected to be higher than now on a *per caput* basis, but with the gap between the better off and the lower income parts of the world even wider.

Dr. Nicol has just shown that many people in the world do not get enough protein, although supplies are fully adequate on an average basis.

While this audience may not be directly concerned with measures by which protein calorie malnutrition within population groups may be overcome, you may be interested in their possible implications for protein marketing. Production of a convenient low-cost ingredient for inclusion in food aid programmes has been a consideration in the establishment of some protein food enterprises in North America and Europe. Relevant measures are:

Subsidized Feeding Programmes for Vulnerable Groups

These are efficient because they can be directed specifically to meet a need. Feeding of children at school, of nursing mothers at clinics, and sale of amino-acid or otherwise fortified basic foods through special outlets in low-income quarters can achieve this purpose. How far they can be implemented on the scale required depends on the means a government has to pay for them. In the poorest countries these means are necessarily restricted, so the ingredient must be cheap. Where there is international support it tends to take the form of providing supplies of products in surplus in the donor country.

Special Formulae Commercial Foods

At one time there were great hopes for combination foods, augmented with a bland protein ingredient and distributed through commercial channels. SCP could fit into these. Unfortunately, while such ventures continue it is difficult to point to many that have a major impact on the consumers most needing better food, or incidentally, that provide a significant market for protein ingredients.

PROTEIN SOURCES

Up till now we have been talking about the demand for protein in various forms and how both growing market demands and the
nutritional need for increased consumption by substantial segments of the world population could be met.

Let us now look at alternative protein sources.

Cereals and Legumes

Wheat, barley and corn contain 10 to 12 percent protein.
Together with beans and chickpeas - around 20 percent protein -
they are major sources of food protein for the world.   Breeding
in more protein of better amino-acid composition will enhance
this.   Their role as direct protein providers tends to decline
as incomes rise because of the bulk that must be consumed with
the protein.

Meat

Meat is the preferred source of protein in most countries.
Demand has increased rapidly as consumer incomes have risen in
North America, in Europe (particularly Italy where, formerly, it
was very low), in the Near East, and in Japan.   Production is
slow in expanding to meet this demand, and the lag in response
has sent prices up sharply, especially for beef.   Some consumers
- in Britain, for example, where real incomes have not risen so
fast as in some other countries - have had to shift to the cheaper
meat of chicken and turkey.   While this movement may be matched
by a corresponding shift away from pork and towards beef in West
Germany for example, the ease with which pig and poultry production
can be expanded to meet demand means that it will assure a buoyant
market for protein in compound feeds.

Expansion of beef production is constrained by our inability
to devise a satisfactory commercial technique for obtaining more
than one calf per year per breeding cow.   For every animal that
enters the meat production process, one adult animal must be fed

and maintained for a year. Efforts to find a way round this
are bringing up some rather startling projects - for example,
that to set up ranches in Africa linked to calf fattening centres
in southern Italy. A puzzler to me is how such a movement of
young animals will get past traditionally strict disease trans-
mission controls; some Mediterranean island must be designated
as a quarantine station. A stage further along this road would
be for the Japanese to pick up the male calves from the 230
million cattle and buffaloes in India; this is a quarter of the
world's cattle population. At present most of the male calves
are allowed to die once they have stimulated a lactation. Latin
America is seen as a more immediate source. The World Bank is
being asked to finance a large-scale calf raising project in
Brazil for subsequent fattening in Europe. Meanwhile Polla
Arena at Verona is hiring jumbo jets to fly in calves from Canada.

While the fastest response to the rising demand for beef
will undoubtedly come from factory type feedlots in the consuming
countries, provided they can get the calves, established exporting countries such as Australia using more extensive methods are
expected to provide continuing competition. The increased
demand for livestock feed, both in exporting and consuming
countries, that will result from these developments is evident,
even though more animals will also be raised on grain and roughage.

Fish

Fish must be seen both as a direct source of protein food
and a source of protein meal for livestock feeding. World fish
production in 1972 failed to expand for the second year running,
bearing out forecasts made a few years ago that the steeply up-
ward trend of the 1960s would not be resumed until large un-
utilized resources were brought into use. Most of the major
fishing countries caught less or only slightly more fish than the
year before, and global production was estimated to be 7 percent
below 1971.

Contributing greatly to the recent high cost of protein
feed and, in consequence, to the sharpening of investment interest
in SCP, has been the failure of the anchovy catch in Peru. The
specialists' view is that 9 to 11 million tons of fish equivalent
to 2 million tons of meal can be produced annually under average
conditions. This would mean a return to the average yield of a
few years ago when fishmeal was a preferred source of protein
feed, and the reappearance of a strong competitor to SCP. However, this cannot be counted upon. Nor can potential catches
of "nonconventional" marine species such as krill which are not
marketed commercially now. Sometimes these constitute food for
the species consumed at present.

More responsive probably to commercial incentives will be
fish farming. This involves a considerable input of supplementary
feed and so constitutes a potential market for SCP. Illustrative
is catfish production in the Southern USA - estimated at 12
million pounds of processed fish in 1972. Some people say that
catfish are at the stage where broilers were 30 years ago. Only
one and a half pounds of 32% protein floating food is needed to
produce a pound of catfish. Similar developments with shrimps
are under way. I understand that carp, eels and trout have all
responded well to diets including high percentages of SCP.

Oilseed

At present, oilseeds are the mainstay of most intensive livestock production. They can also be processed into foods for
immediate human consumption. A great agricultural boom of the
sixties was grain and oilseed feed for livestock and poultry.
Demand is expected to grow at a slower pace over the next decade.
Nevertheless, FAO projects a consumption in 1980 of 70 to 75
million tons as against the present 60 and it could go higher.
This demand is derived from that for compound livestock feeds;
they are cheaper than traditional fodder, mainly because they
contain less high-priced cereals. Moreover, the compound feeds

are better suited to increasingly consolidated and modernized farm operations. The critical issue for us is which protein ingredient will benefit from the coming increase in European and Japanese feed demand.

Until now the soybean with its high protein quality and quick response in supply has been the front runner. Lester Brown of the Agricultural Development Council has caught the public ear recently with a rather pessimistic outlook for soy production in the USA. However, the official view is that output could expand much more if there is a continuing incentive. Production will also expand rapidly in other countries, particularly Brazil with its Japanese-linked 'export corridors', and Argentina. We must recognize, therefore, that the price of soybean will go down from present levels. How far, is a critical question for SCP economics.

World production of oilseed and fishmeal protein is shown in Table 3. Hot news in Europe at the moment is rapeseed. It fits conveniently into cereal rotations in the more northerly countries, and enables them to compete in a market hitherto largely dominated by warm climate agriculture. In Britain and in Sweden production is expanding rapidly with new processing plants under construction. There is the disadvantage, however, that rapeseed does not, as yet, provide a very attractive feed product. It is likely to be priced accordingly.

Tropical oilseed growers are also expanding production. However, the quantities for export cannot have much impact on the overall oilseed market. It is difficult to see any oilseed challenger to soybean in the feed market. If there is to be a challenge it will have to come from single cell protein.

Oilseed Protein for Direct Human Consumption

After a protracted gestation the meat substitute industry has now reached take-off point. Products are now available that can compete with a wide range of natural meats.

J.C. Abbott

Table 3   Production of oilseeds and fishmeal protein.

	1966-70	1971	1972
	(.... million tons ....)		
Soybean	11.5	13.2	14.1
Cottonseed	3.1	3.0	3.4
Groundnut	2.1	2.2	2.2
Sunflowerseed	1.4	1.4	1.5
Rapeseed	0.9	1.4	1.4
Linseed	0.6	0.8	0.5
Copra	0.2	0.3	0.3
Sesameseed	0.3	0.3	0.3
Palm kernel	0.1	0.1	0.1
Fish meal	3.1	3.5	2.7

Source.   FAO "Commodity Review and Outlook 1972-73."

As meat extenders, soy protein extracts, isolates or concentrates, can improve the taste, chewability and water absorption of the final product.   They reduce shrinkage and retain fat and natural juices.   Protein content can be increased.   Meat extenders do not need a special texture or taste, since in a blend with meat they should remain unnoticed; so they can be produced at relatively low cost.   Some 25,000 thousand tons will be sold in the United States this year.

Oilseed protein can also be processed to resemble specific meats in texture, colour and flavour.   The protein content is higher and fat can be lower than in natural meats.   This suits consumers in developed countries where low calorie and low fat foods with high protein content are preferred.

Meat analogues are not likely to replace meat in cuts with particular muscle texture and flavour, e.g. steaks, roast beef and chops; but a lot of meat is consumed in less specific forms and here substitutes can compete through price and promotion.

The weight behind these developments can be measured by the degree of commercial commitment.   A few years ago there were only three firms in the US producing human commercial grade oil-seed products and one or two in Northern Europe.   Now there are 15 to 20 in the United States, 10 or 11 in Europe, 6 or 7 in Japan and one in Israel (3).

At 33 cents per kilogramme soy protein substituted for 25% of the lean ground beef brings down the price of a hamburger by 48 cents per kilogramme.   Better quality products result from the use of spun protein costing about $1.50 per kilogramme dry weight.   Savings of 1 to 25 cents per serving from using it in place of meat are claimed.

Government regulation of production, labelling and marketing of foods have always been geared to protect agricultural producers against unfair competition as well as consumers and manufacturers. The quantitative restrictions on the use of oilseed protein as meat extenders and in meat product blends has induced the industry to find its outlets through institutional channels such as res-taurants, hospitals, schools, canteens, etc. and by producing pro-ducts without any meat, but which imitate meat in all its charac-teristics.

Changing living customs are favouring ready-to-cook and easy-to-prepare foods.   It is in this sector of the market that the manufacturers of meat-like products could most easily penetrate, taking full advantage of the changes in demand because of their ability to tailor their products to specific consumer requirements.

The FAO forecasts of the extent meat substitutes will cut into the total meat market by 1980 range from 1 to 6 percent depending on the liberality of government restriction policies, promotional success in overcoming consumer resistance, and the margin in price below meat.

I have dwelt at some length on developments in using oilseed

protein as a meat substitute because of its direct implications
for SCP.   As a meat extender capable of raising protein levels
and reducing fat proportions SCP has an important potential market.   Food technologists tell me it cannot as yet be texturized;
to this extent it will be at a disadvantage as against soyprotein
in this market.

Pet Foods

This is one of the current growth industries founded on convenience in handling and ample pet-owner incomes.   A fairly recent estimate of pet food turnover was $2,300 million with an in-
take of around 500,000 tons of meat and offal.   Conservationist
pressure against the use of whale meat and game has forced the
industry back on to conventional sources of protein.   It is correspondingly receptive to offers of suitable meat substitutes.
While some of my pet-lover friends insist that their animals will
back off in disgust, the industry says it could shift 15% of its
protein input to non-animal sources.   Given our present command
of textures and flavours, I would bet on a percentage very much
higher if the price is right.

Petroleum Based Protein

Pilot plants for the production of petroleum based protein
suitable for livestock and eventually human feeding have been in
operation for some time.   We have now reached the stage of large-
scale investment in plants for commercial production.   The following table provides some indication of current plans.   It is
intended mainly for verification of our information.   However,
the location of the larger plants also provides some indication
of the territorial markets which their sponsors expect to serve.

Production in Japan has been suspended temporarily in face
of a consumer movement's publicity campaign against "petropro-
teins".   Japanese manufacturers are now looking for other locations where they can earn a profit on their technology, as in
Eastern Europe and Libya.

Table 4   Petroleum based protein production plans, 1973

Country	Tons per year	Enterprise and location
Britain	4,000	BP, Grangemouth
	100,000	ICI, Billingham
France	20,000	BP, Lavera
Italy	100,000	Liquigas, Reggio Calabria
	100,000	BP, Sardinia
Japan	(300,000)*	Dainippon (60,000) Magoya Kanegafuchi (60,000) Takasago Mitsubishi Asahi Kyowa Hakko Kogyo Mitsui Toatsui
Rumania	60,000	Ministry of Chemical Industry/ Dainippon Jassy
Russia	16,000	Biomass Plant by Rosedown UK
	100,000	Planned for 1974

* Suspended temporarily.

In the United States, work on developing single cell protein for livestock feed has not gone beyond the pilot stage - apparently because it is economically preferable to use conventional fodder such as soybeans and, some would say, because the soybean political lobby is too strong.   Reluctance to be dependent on imports of American soybean is, of course, an immediate motive for the official sanction of the present petroleum protein developments in Europe.   The French Government is going so far as to subsidize British Petroleum.   The location of the larger West European plants in southern Italy also reflects access to subsidized regional development finance.

Acceptability.   The protagnonists of petroleum protein feed

for livestock are quite confident on this score. Research that
began in 1965 in Western Europe suggests that livestock continu-
ally raised on chemically-nurtured proteins are no different from
those that obtain their protein from natural fishmeal - except
that they do not taste of fish. From Russia Professor Pocrovsky
reports that eggs and meat from livestock fed petroleum protein
have been eaten by 100 consumers over a considerable time with
no ill effect.

The UN Protein Advisory Group has concluded that "development has reached a point where large-scale commercial production
of SCP from carbohydrate, hydrocarbon, or petrochemical substrates
is economically and technically feasible. At the present time,
this is established for animal feeding in industrialized countries
that have a rising demand for animal protein and an increasing dependence on imported feed. There are reasonable prospects, however, that there will also be a demand for SCP for human consumption within a few years." The UN Protein Advisory Group is concerned, however, over the fact that each batch of petroleum-based
protein may not be the same. This puts in doubt the continuing
validity of assurances based on a particular set of tests.   In
the meantime, it seems to be accepted that up to 7 percent SCP
protein can be fed to calves below six weeks old as a milk replacement, and from then on 10 percent, and to pigs and poultry 20
percent.

Even as a partial replacement for other feed protein the
scope of the market is still immense. Current consumption of
soymeal is running at the rate of 44 million tons per year, counting US production alone. The EEC countries import 4 million tons
of protein annually. Japan spent $357 million on soybean in
1972. Supplies of meat and other livestock products lag far behind consumer demand in Eastern Europe. Much more feed is needed
if they are ever to catch up. The potential market is such that
even if the petroleum protein producers got a one million ton share

of it, the goal towards which present plans are directed, there
would still be ample room left for vegetable protein feed suppliers.

There will be obstacles to overcome.　According to the local
press the firm building the plant in Calabria already faces pay-
off demands from the Mafia.　Some European newspapers will certainly run protest campaigns against food from animals fed
"unnatural" nutrients.　Developing a favourable public image is
essential.　For this a way must be found round the use of terms
such as "petroleum", "single cell" or "microbial" protein in promotion and labelling.　Here "bioproteina" is the favoured word.

Prices

Remaining for consideration in the economic assessment of
the competitive position of SCP is, of course, the price at which
it will be sold.　The current sales line is that it replaces
fishmeal now in short supply and is priced accordingly at around
US$425 per ton of 66 percent protein.　However, the production
cost is said to be in the area of $280 per ton.　With several
firms involved, the sales price can be expected to work down to
this level as commercial production gets under way.

Following his visit to the USSR Professor Humphrey has
spoken of a feasible price range of $130 to $250 per ton (5).
The lower end of this range is rejected by West European industry
spokesmen on the grounds of the inescapable cost of the paraffin
oil;　but methanol is expected to be cheaper.　Stability of
supply independent of climatic factors and the consequent ability
to make long-term supply contracts has been claimed as a competitive advantage of SCP over products of agricultural origin.
However, recent events suggest that the SCP producer had best
also control his own supplies of raw material.

This leads to the question whether the possible inadequacy
of the world's petroleum supplies in relation to its rapidly expanding energy requirements will bear upon the supply of petroleum

c

raw materials for protein food manufacture.   While some price
transfer can be expected, supplies are not likely to be affected
significantly.   Conversion of petroleum into protein is a highly
efficient process with a one-to-one input/output ratio.   In competition with the consumption of petroleum for energy, petro-
protein production would surely claim priority once market outlets had been developed.   Moreover, the quantity needed is relatively small.   According to some sources the whole world's protein requirements could be met from only 1 percent of its present
annual consumption of gas and oil.

OTHER SOURCES OF PROTEIN

Over the longer run there is competition to consider, from
other sources of protein still more unconventional than growing
it on petrol.   In Mexico there is a firm selling biscuits incorporating protein from algae, a food reserve for the Aztecs many
centuries ago.   Much more important in my view is the recycling
of human and animal waste.   Already pigs are being fed experimentally in California on protein from algae grown on sewage.
In Milan recently a prominent official in the Australian Department of Primary Industry told me that with the establishment of
a new 10,000 sow piggery would go a plant to recycle the manure.
Environmentalists would demand it if the pig raiser did not.

Markets in Developing Countries

Some of you will be wondering what are the chances of petroleum protein finding good markets in the developing countries.
The establishment there of SCP plants has already been studied
(6).   No technical difficulty is envisaged, provided there is
access to an appropriate substratum on which to grow the protein.
In a number of countries such as Algeria, Indonesia and Nigeria
the raw material may be available locally;   in others foreign
exchange would be needed to import it.   Much more of a problem
may be to market the product.   Levinson (7) and Wells (8) have

considered the issues involved.   They are the same as those
which arise in regard to the marketing of oilseed protein products in developing countries.   If the SCP is to be sold for
livestock feed then there must be an established feed-mixing and
distributing system and a sufficient number of farmers buying
such mixes on a regular basis.   If it is to be sold directly
for human consumption then there must be some accepted processed
food into which it can be incorporated conveniently without
raising significantly its price.   However, we know that consumers buying processed foods are a small proportion of the total
in typical developing countries, and they are not those most needing more protein.   Those who do need more protein have often the
means to buy only basic ingredients such as wheat flour, rice,
pulses;   they make up their foods at home.

This is not to say that SCP will not find a market in developing countries, but that there are substantial obstacles to overcome there - lack of purchasing power, limited, scattered demand,
food preparation and distribution practices which are not well
adapted to incorporating new ingredients on a large scale.   Without much doubt it will be in the developed countries of Europe
and Japan where SCP is taken up first: prestige and familiarity
acquired there will eventually help it in overcoming the obstacles
to wide use in the countries that are less well off.

CONCLUSIONS

1)   The developed world will go on demanding more meat and other
animal protein foods.   There will be increased emphasis on factory type animal feeding calling for complete, easy-to-handle compound feeds.   This will be the main market for SCP.

2)   Some propaganda against the use of SCP in animal feeding may
have to be faced;   and some meat producers may use this to promote
products from animals fed only "natural" foods.   But this will be
a fringe reaction.   The size of the feed market will be deter-

mined in the end by price.

3)   While the total demand for feed protein will continue to
grow, increased supplies of fishmeal, soybean and other protein
sources will oblige SCP producers to lower their prices if they
are to be competitive.

4)   Alternative sources and forms of protein will be increasingly
accepted for direct human consumption through advances in texturizing, flavouring and presentation.   Promotion, coupled with
convenience in distribution and consumption will be powerful in
supporting this trend in the developed countries.   These products are still expensive for the developing countries and their
convenience advantage less likely to be appreciated there.

5)   Vegetable protein sources will supply in the medium term
the bulk of raw material for meat substitution.   Over the longer
run, protein derived from algae, yeasts, etc. will become increasingly important because of its high speed of multiplication, no
need for land, and range of substrata on which they can be grown.
Direct human consumption will follow after they have become
familiar in livestock feed uses.

6)   The dietary deficiencies of the vulnerable groups in developing countries can be overcome most economically by special feeding programmes.   Mainly they will use food of domestic origin,
with imports coming mainly from countries with surpluses.

7)   To be competitive SCP will have to be priced on a par with
fishmeal and soybean.   In spite of rising demand, competitive
pressure from such sources will keep prices on a relatively downward trend - SCP will have to accept this.

REFERENCES

1.   The wholesale price of sugar, a near pure calorie food in
      wide international demand was about 7 cents in 1972. This
      is also a fair estimate of the price of the calorie element
      in wheat.

2.   FAO, "Agricultural Commodity Projections, 1970-1980," Vols.

I and II, Rome (1971).

3. "Meat-like Products and their Possible Impact on the Demand for Meat," FAO Paper, Rome (April 1973).

4. Statement to the UN Protein Advisory Group.

5. New York Times (June 23, 1973).

6. Fussman, F. *et al.* "Effect of Site Factors on the Economics of Petro-Protein Manufacture," *Expert Group Meeting on the Manufacture of Proteins from Hydrocarbons*, Vienna, Austria (October 1973).

7. Levinson, F.J. and Austin, J.E. "Marketing SCP in Low Income Countries: a Double Perspective," *International Conference on Single Cell Protein*, Cambridge, Massachusetts (May 1973).

8. Wells, J. "The Marketing of Fermentation Proteins in Developing Countries," *Expert Group Meeting on the Manufacture of Proteins from Hydrocarbons*, Vienna, Austria (October 1973).

SUBSTRATES FOR SCP PRODUCTION

Elmer L. Gaden, Jr.

Department of Chemical Engineering and Applied Chemistry
Columbia University, New York

INTRODUCTION

The purpose of this contribution to the symposium is to compare the various substrates which have been used or proposed for the manufacture of microbial protein - or SCP. My primary aim is to evaluate the future roles of these materials in the light of the "price revolutions" which erupted last year and continue unabated. The plural "revolutions" is appropriate because we are faced with several economic upheavals whose origins are quite separate. Nevertheless, because of their simultaneous occurrence and the close-knit structure of the world economy, their secondary effects have become closely intertwined.

I will not offer, as part of this presentation, any new or revised cost estimates for microbial protein production. In absolute terms such calculations have a notoriously short half-life. Furthermore, they are better made by industrial people [1] who have access to realistic and current cost data and who can incorporate into their estimates the various constraints and advantages which apply to each specific situation. Instead, I will attempt to evaluate the various substrates for protein production against the following general criteria:

(1) *availability*.

(2) *technical suitability*, especially pretreatment requirements and biomass yields.

47

(3) *Competitive pressures.*

The last of these criteria is especially significant.   So
long as we enjoy - or suffer under, depending on the point of
view - an uncontrolled world economy, raw materials will flow
toward the point of highest profit.   Political considerations
may modify these flows somewhat - Middle Eastern oil is a current
example - but historical experience shows such modifications to
be short-lived.   This is certainly the case with respect to the
raw materials for microbial protein production.   All of them are
subject to alternative demands which establish their free-market
costs and hence their potential utility as substrates.

One final point should be noted in these introductory remarks.   There are at least two fundamentally different approaches
to the overall problem of microbial protein production.   On the
one hand we can envision the large-scale manufacture of protein
for world, or at least for substantial regional, markets.   Such
a material would be incorporated into animal feeds or human foods
as a basic ingredient, supplanting or supplementing more conventional protein sources.   Primary product criteria would be nutritional quality, physical characteristics, and cost, and the
choice between substrates would be made on economic grounds alone
so long as a product of satisfactory quality can be generated.
The only significant commercial manufacture of microbial protein
in the past, yeast production from molasses, is an example of
this type of operation, although the amounts involved have never
been very large.   Current world production of dried yeast (ex-
cluding baker's yeast) is probably less than 200,000 tons per
year.

An alternative approach to microbial protein production dif-
fers in "philosophy" rather than in technical detail.   Here the
substrate is determined *a priori*, usually because it is a by-
product or waste from some other operation and enjoys no competitive outlet.   The protein product is then sold for whatever it

will bring with the revenue being considered as a credit against disposal costs. Yeast production from sulfite waste liquor is a classic case.

The fundamental difference between these two approaches to microbial protein production must be recognized in any consideration of substrate availability and utility. Raw materials which arise as by-products or wastes from other manufacturing operations can be eliminated by technological development in the primary industry. Sulfite waste liquor is an excellent case in point; increasing use of the Kraft process is steadily reducing the amounts of sulfite liquor available and the major U.S. yeast plants using this substrate have been shut down. No one has sought an alternative raw material to keep them in operation because the product has not been competitive on its own merits in the American protein market.

THE PROCESS

Regardless of the substrate employed or the type of organism propagated on it, the production of microbial protein always involves certain basic steps:

(1) provision of an assimilable substrate carbon-source, usually through some combination of chemical and physical treatments applied to the raw materials.

(2) preparation of a suitable medium containing this substrate plus sources of nitrogen, phosphorus, and other essential nutrients. (In the case of algae utilizing carbon dioxide, the prepared medium will not include the substrate. Instead, CO_2 will be absorbed from the gas phase as it is used.)

(3) propagation of the desired microorganism in this medium to convert substrate carbon to cellular (biomass) carbon.

(4) separation of cell matter from the spent medium.

(5) post-treatment of the cell matter with or without specific purification operations.

Steps 2, 3 and 4 (medium preparation, conversion, and cell separation) are always necessary but the first and last steps may or may not be included, depending on (1) the nature of the raw material and (2) the form and intended use of the product.

In addition to these basic process steps a number of auxiliary operations are also required regardless of the substrate type and product form. These include cooling, aeration to provide oxygen during the propagation stage (carbon dioxide instead of oxygen will be used for algae), and the elimination of "spent" medium in the separation stage. In some circumstances this "spent" medium will still be very high in BOD and further treatment may be required before it can be discharged to the environment.

Traditional microbial processes, including those for protein biosynthesis, have been characterized by a high degree of flexibility in the use of raw materials. The basic process steps, and even specific equipment design features, have been little affected by changes in the raw material employed. Introduction of hydrocarbon substrates has altered this picture somewhat, at least with respect to fermenter design, because of the substantially higher oxygen demands and heat evolution rates encountered. Even with these substrates, however, the overall process sequence and auxiliary operations are essentially the same.

SUBSTRATES FOR SCP

With the exception of the algae, all the organisms which have been used or proposed for the manufacture of microbial protein require complex carbon sources. Until the introduction of hydrocarbons a decade ago virtually all commercial production was based on carbohydrates. Now, in addition to these glucose-yielding materials, substrates in use or under consideration include alkanes ranging from methane to middle-distillate materials, lower alcohols from methanol to isopropanol, and various organic acids. The more important features of these substrates, in terms of the criteria set forth earlier in this discussion, are summarized in Table 1. The calculations of Abbott and Clamen (1), cited earlier, in which substrate and conversion costs for microbial protein production from various substrates are compared, are also most valuable.

THE CARBOHYDRATES

Carbohydrate substrates fall into two major classes: saccharide and polysaccharide. The saccharides include the simpler five- and six-carbon sugars which are directly assimilable by many organisms. For the purposes of this discussion we may also include in this group disaccharides like sucrose, maltose and lactose. Most organisms of interest for microbial protein production can also utilize these substrates because they possess the enzymatic equipment necessary to first hydrolyze them to their monosaccharide components. Examples of raw materials containing saccharide substrates are molasses, whey, sulfite waste liquor, and potato waste water.

Polysaccharide substrates are of two types; starchy and cellulosic. Starchy materials, such as grains or cassava, must be chemically or enzymatically treated in order to convert the starch to dissimilable sugars. Cellulosic materials, although abundant, require hydrolysis of the cellulose to saccharides. Typical examples are wood wastes, bagasse, corn cobs, oat hulls and, of course, a significant part (40-60%) of common municipal solid waste.

The carbohydrate substrates normally used for microbial protein production are agricultural wastes or by-products. Advantages cited for the use of carbohydrates are their abundance, theoretical inexhaustibility, and low cost. Their use also often yields a credit by relieving disposal problems. On the other hand, these materials also suffer from fluctuations in

Table 1   Substrates for microbial protein production.

MATERIAL	AVAILABILITY[1]		TECHNICAL		COMPETITIVE USE
	PLACE	TIME	PRE-TREATMENT	YIELD[7]	
Saccharide					
Molasses - cane	Widespread	Seasonal	Simple	0.25-0.3	Animal feeding
- beet	Concentrated	Seasonal	Simple	0.27-0.33	Animal feeding
- corn	Limited	Seasonal	Simple		
- citrus	Limited	Seasonal	Simple	0.18	Animal feeding
Whey	Limited	Year-round	Simple	0.03	Fractionation
Sulfite waste liquor	Concentrated	Year-round	Simple	0.008	(2)
Potato waste	Limited	Seasonal	None		
Fruit/vegetable packing wastes	Limited	Seasonal	None or simple	0.03[3]	
Polysaccharide					
Starch - grains	Widespread	Seasonal	Hydrolysis	0.5-0.6	Food
- cassava	Concentrated		Hydrolysis		
Cellulose - wood	Concentrated	Year-round	Hydrolysis	0.03[4]	Fuel
- bagasse	Concentrated	Seasonal	Hydrolysis	0.1-0.3	Fuel/Animal feed
- corn cobs	Limited	Seasonal	Hydrolysis	0.13	
- hulls	Limited	Seasonal	Hydrolysis		
- municipal wastes	Concentrated	Year-round	Hydrolysis		

Hydrocarbons					
Methane	Concentrated	Year-round	None	$0.3-1.4^{(5)}$	Fuel/Chemical feedstock
n-paraffins	Widespread	Year-round	Separation	1.0	Fuel/Chemical feedstock
Alcohols					
Methanol	Widespread	Year-round	None	$0.25-0.5^{(6)}$	Fuel
Ethanol	Widespread	Year-round	None	0.6-0.7	Fuel
Propanol (n,i)	Limited	Year-round	None	0.4	
Other					
Acetate, maleate	Limited	Year-round	Dependent on source	0.35	

NOTES:

(1) Terms used under "Availability" are defined as follows:

"Widespread" - available throughout the world in potentially useful amounts.

"Limited" - relatively small amounts available at a number of locations within larger regions.

"Concentrated" - relatively large amounts available at a few locations.

(2) Sulfite waste liquor availability is decreasing (see text).

(3) Yield figure is for citrus press juice.

(4) Yields for cellulosic materials are based on weights of material as delivered, including normal moisture.

(5) Reported yields on methane vary widely; 1.0 is suggested as a reasonable norm.

(6) A yield of 0.4 is suggested as a norm for methanol.

(7) All yields are reported in terms of kg dry cells (biomass) kg substrate supplied.

availability due to seasonal harvests and climatic conditions.
In addition they may be scattered about over a large region and
the cost of collection adds considerably to the raw material
cost.   Prices also fluctuate for the same reasons as availability.

Saccharide Substrates

Molasses in its four major forms (beet, cane, citrus, and
corn) is the most abundant and readily available saccharide substrate for microbial protein production.   As we have seen, its
use for this purpose is widespread and well-developed.   Cane
molasses is mainly the by-product of the one-commodity, plantation-
type agriculture found in less-developed, tropical regions.   The
only exceptions to this generalization are the United States
(especially Hawaii) and Australia.

Both cane and beet molasses are seasonal products but the
use of selective planting and improved crop management has made
it possible to keep cane sugar mills in operation for 6 to 8
months each year.   Only Hawaii manages a year-round operation.
Beet production, on the other hand, is concentrated in developed,
temperate countries which have internal markets for the molasses.
Beet production is very seasonal and the mills produce sugar (and
molasses) only about two to three months per year.

Cane and beet molasses both require limited pretreatment
before they can be used for microbial protein production.   Simple
chemical treatments are used to reduce the mineral content and to
remove excess suspended organic matter.   Beet molasses must also
be heated and aerated to remove SO_2.   In normal practice one can
expect a dry cell yield of 25% based on the weight of molasses
used.   Since the cells are approximately half protein, about
7-8 kg of molasses are required per kg of protein produced.

The changing pattern of molasses utilization over the last
twenty-five years is a cardinal factor in determining its availability as a substrate for microbial protein manufacture.   In
1946 less than one-third of the molasses consumed in the United

States was used for livestock feeding; the rest went to other uses, primarily chemical manufacture (ethanol, citric acid, etc.). U.S. molasses consumption today is more than double that in 1946 and well over 80% is used for liquid animal feeds. Molasses alone is an energy source and as such serves mainly as a replacement for grains in animal rations. When supplemented with nitrogen, in the form of urea, and phosphorus, however, it can replace protein sources, especially soy beans.

In the last few years the burgeoning livestock industry of northern Europe has generated an additional demand for molasses. It is expected that the Common Market countries plus Scandinavia will import as much molasses next year as will the United States (2).

Whey from cheese-making is another potentially attractive raw material for microbial protein production; it contains from 4-5% lactose. Pilot studies with yeast (there has been no regular commercial production to date) indicate that a yield of about 20% (kg dry cells/kg sugar) can be realized as a relatively high-protein (nearly 60%) product. The steady increase in dairy product consumption plus growing restrictions on direct disposal of this high BOD material to the environment have made the case for whey as an SCP substrate appear better and better. Still, commercial cheese production is limited to the most highly developed economies where many protein sources compete. Furthermore, recent developments in separation techniques have made it possible to fractionate whey directly into a series of relative pure - and saleable - products.

As noted previously, sulfite waste liquor has been widely used for yeast production in both Europe and North America but recent changes in wood pulping technology have changed this picture. The replacement of sulfite pulping with the sulfate, or Kraft, process has already brought about the closing of U.S. production facilities.

Finally, the many other sugar-containing materials which result from agricultural and food processing operations, potato waste water for example, are typical of the second approach to microbial protein manufacture cited in the introduction. Their availability is "limited" (Table 1), that is relatively small amounts are generated at a number of sites, and they cannot be considered as potential substrates for large-scale protein production.

Polysaccharides

Grains, though perfectly reasonable raw materials for microbial protein production, are far too valuable as foods themselves to be used in this way. The situation with cassava is similar. In the tropical and semi-tropical areas where it is cultivated abundantly, it is a basic ingredient of the diet and a major supplier of calories.

Cellulosic raw materials, on the other hand, are abundant and cheap at the point of origin. They tend, however, to be widely dispersed in relatively small amounts - corn cobs on the farm, sawdust at the saw mill, etc.. The cost of collecting and moving these low-density materials to central processing sites therefore adds significantly to the real raw material cost. Municipal solid wastes are another matter, however. Here relatively large amounts of materials averaging about 50% cellulose in composition, are available in concentrated areas.

The greatest disadvantage of these materials lies in the requirement for hydrolysis of the cellulose to assimilable sugars. Available methods, involving high-temperature and high-pressure treatment in the presence of mineral acids, are expensive and the final substrate cost becomes much higher than equivalent amounts of molasses, for example. The successful utilization of cellulosic raw materials for microbial protein production requires the development of a simple and inexpensive hydrolysis technique. The current high level of research interest in production and utilization of cellulases is a response to this need.

HYDROCARBONS

The ability to utilize hydrocarbons as energy sources is widespread in the microbial world. A wide variety of yeast and bacteria - many still lacking complete identification and often in mixed culture - grow rapidly on hydrocarbons. Their general preference is for straight-chain types (alkanes) in the range C_{10} - C_{20}. Liquid hydrocarbons of smaller chain lengths appear to be toxic while larger ones are so insoluble as to be only slowly utilized.

Methane offers some very attractive advantages as a substrate, the absence of residual hydrocarbon in the product for example. As a result it quickly attracted attention when the study of hydrocarbon raw materials began about 10 years ago. A number of bacterial strains have now been isolated which grow reasonably well on methane but high growth rates and rapid conversions have been found only with mixed cultures. Furthermore, the high demand for natural gas as a fuel coupled with an apparently critical supply situation, at least in North America, have severely clouded the prospects for methane.

The potential advantages of hydrocarbon substrates are very great. They are ordinarily available in large quantities at one location and are independent of agricultural and climatic factors. They are not seasonal and prices have tended to be stable - although this advantage is questionable today. Furthermore, the amounts which might be required for microbial protein production will have little impact on the overall supply. Finally, cell yields and protein contents are both higher, in general, than those for carbohydrate processes.

On the other hand hydrocarbons are relatively expensive and processing costs are higher because propagation involves much greater oxygen requirements and the need to remove the higher heats of fermentation encountered.

ALCOHOLS

The lower alcohols, methanol and ethanol in particular, are especially attractive substrates for microbial protein production. They offer a compromise between the advantages of carbohydrates (water solubility, product free of substrate contamination) and the hydrocarbons (higher biomass yield).

Adoption of methanol as a substrate avoids the technical difficulties inherent in direct utilization of methane and the cost of producing it from natural gas has fallen substantially during the last decade. In fact, the same period which has witnessed the rapid growth of interest in microbial protein has also seen the development of radically new technology for methanol synthesis. This technological progress has been so effective that methanol is now being considered either as a potential fuel for direct use in power generation or as an economically attractive means for long-distance transporation of methane.

Ethanol may well be the most attractive of all substrates for protein production. Reported biomass yields are high (over 0.6 kg of cells/kg alcohol) and the little information publicly available indicates that the protein content of the cells is of high quality. No problem arises from substrate incorporation into the product and, until recently, competitive demands for ethanol were well established and stable.

Recently, however, the energy supply situation has rekindled interest in ethanol as a fuel. During the agricultural depression of the 1930's, the use of ethanol-gasoline mixtures (sometimes called "gasohol") in internal combustion engines was studied. Ethanol is a good motor fuel and its use offers environmental benefits as well as a saving in hydrocarbons. It must be remembered that any raw material which can provide glucose equivalents is a potential substrate for both protein and

ethanol production.   If the supply of gasoline continues to be
uncertain, ethanol can become a prime candidate for motor fuel
use.   A second-order effect could then follow with the diversion
of fermentable carbohydrates, including cellulose-derived glucose,
to the production of ethanol.

PROSPECTS

The rapid, worldwide escalation of protein prices, especially
soy bean, during the last year has certainly improved the climate
for microbial protein manufacture.   In his opening address to
the recent SCP Conference at M.I.T., Professor Humphrey ventured
the opinion that, had facilities been in existence, microbial
protein could have been produced profitably from a number of substrates during the last year (3).

At the same time, however, several potent factors inimical
to the prospects for microbial protein are operating.   Some of
these derive directly from the same pressure - the world protein
shortage - which has enhanced SCP prospects, for example:
(1)   The rapidly growing demand for molasses for incorporation
in liquid animal feeds draws off and increases the cost of a
proven and widely used substrate for microbial protein manufacture.
Only too recently molasses traders considered $24/ton to be a
"normal" price for cane molasses (79.5 Brix, FOB New Orleans);
now $63/ton is typical (2).   Not only does this reaction reduce
the availability of molasses for SCP but it relieves market pressures on soy bean meal for cattle feed use, thereby diminishing
somewhat the major force for increased use of microbial protein.
(2)   Cellulose, another obvious raw material candidate, may also
find other competitive markets.   One of these has, in fact,
resulted from the search for improved techniques for the degra-
dation of cellulose to glucose in order to make it available as
a substrate for protein biosynthesis.   It has been found that
an extremely simple chemical treatment, using dilute alkali,

greatly increases the nutritional availability of cellulose to ruminants. At the same time, studies of the microbial conversion of feed lot waste (manure) to a high-protein feed ingredient show considerable promise, especially in view of growing concern over the environmental effects of these wastes.

The other factors working against realization of the microbial protein dream have their roots in our current energy problems. The most obvious of these are:

(1) Intense market pressures on methane, and possibly methanol, as preferred fuels.

(2) The need for more octane improvers in motor fuels with the possible diversion of a greater fraction of the paraffin content of crudes to this end through increased use of reforming.

(3) The prospects for ethanol as a fuel ingredient in internal combustion engines, thereby diverting it from SCP production. Also, as noted earlier, successful use of ethanol in motor fuels could draw carbohydrate raw materials, including even municipal solid wastes into ethanol production.

REFERENCES

1. Abbott, B.J. and Clamen, A. *Biotechnol. Bioengr.* 15, 117 (1973).

2. Curtin, L. (National Molasses Corp.), Personal communication.

3. Humphrey, A.E., Personal communication.

PROPOSED GUIDELINES FOR TESTING OF SINGLE CELL PROTEIN, DESTINED AS MAJOR PROTEIN SOURCE FOR ANIMAL FEED: ITS STANDARDS OF IDENTITY

J.C. Hoogerheide

International Union of Pure and Applied Chemistry
The Hague, The Netherlands

INTRODUCTION

After thousands of years of slow growth the world population has increased rapidly during the past 100 years and has reached already the $3\frac{1}{2}$ billion mark.   United Nations' estimates are that in the next 25 years the world population will be doubled.   This means that agriculture and fishery, within a period of 25 years, must produce twice as much food as at present to feed this additional population, not taking into account any improvement of the large-scale undernourishment still existing in many underdeveloped countries.

Although extrapolation is always risky, past experience indicates that doubling of world food production within a period of 25 years will be setting an extremely high goal.

For this reason it becomes mandatory that very serious attention must be paid to the development of new and novel sources of food and feed, in particular products of high protein content, with the ultimate aim that such products become an equivalent supplement to conventional agricultural and fishery food products.

Research in this field should have a high priority; it should be encouraged and financially supported, especially if such projects could be combined with utilization of agricultural and industrial waste products which at present pollute our lakes and rivers and poison our drinking water.

Whether we appreciate it or not, at present we have arrived at the threshold of an era wherein, of dire necessity, we may have to get accustomed to the idea that in the future part of our food may not come any longer from the farm or the sea but will be produced industrially from highly unconventional raw materials, such as petroleum fractions, natural gas, methanol, wood, leaves, or even from such obnoxious products as cow dung.

Experience, particularly in Japan, has shown that large segments of the population still have difficulties in accepting this seemingly inevitable development, even as an ingredient for animal feed. This is highly regrettable and clearly shows that this problem cannot be attacked by a scientific approach alone, but in addition requires intelligent public relations efforts via press, radio and television in order to convince people that food produced industrially is just as acceptable as that from conventional sources. This however requires an open policy; secrecy or withholding essential facts will cause suspicion and feeds political opposition.

For this reason an abundance or even an excessive amount of evidence is required, to convince not only the scientists but also the layman of the safety and nutritional value of SCP.

With these objectives in mind the SCP Advisory Committee of the Fermentation Section of IUPAC has prepared a set of standards and specifications to be used as guidelines for future producers of SCP destined as animal feed ingredient. Close contact was maintained with the PAG *ad hoc* Committee on SCP, a United Nations organization with similar aims, albeit more specifically for its use as a human food ingredient.

These standards and specifications, severe as they may seem to be, are not meant to discourage industry to produce SCP. On the contrary, our Committee is fully convinced of the necessity of such a development and has assured itself that industry can easily meet these high standards using normal hygienic precautions and the usual modern microbiological process technique.

The question may be asked why there should be such strict specifications for an animal feed; there are no such specifications for present animal feed ingredients such as soya flour, and pigs may eat highly contaminated food waste products without apparent harm. This is partially true, although retardation due to the presence of toxic products, outbreak of infectious diseases, rejection of infected animals or their organs at the slaughterhouse stage may be the inevitable result of taking such risks.

Moreover, for economic reasons, modern methods of breeding for egg and meat production are directed on crowding as many animals as possible into very restricted areas. This, inevitably, will result in future higher demands on the hygienic quality of the feedstuffs supplied to these animals. Should the use of a new, unconventional feed ingredient such as SCP result in only a small calamity among animals, or in case such a small calamity could possibly be connected with the use of such an unconventional feed ingredient, industrial production of SCP might get a serious setback, perhaps for years to come.

With very little additional cost industry is able to produce a high-quality blameless product of proven, unquestionable safety and high nutritional value that can easily meet severe standards and specifications. Strict specifications for animal feed ingredients are also necessary since animals, fed with unsafe feed ingredients, are ultimately consumed by humans; the same is true for edible products derived from such animals, for example milk, butter, cheese and eggs.

Let us now come to the six recommended basic requirements to be met before a SCP product can be marketed!

1)   Although in principle all types of bacteria, fungi and algae

can be used for SCP production, adequate evidence must be given that the organism selected for SCP production is not pathogenic for man, animal or plant, and that it produces no toxic products that cannot be easily removed to a level that falls below an acceptable limit.

2) No novel source of protein should be admitted as animal feed ingredient unless it has been evaluated thoroughly with respect to safety and absence of toxicity.

3) Evaluation must be conducted on samples derived from a fully stabilized process, yielding products of fully reproducible quality. If, on the basis of the outcome of the evaluation of such samples, full-scale plant production is undertaken, sufficient proof should be submitted that the plant production samples are identical in every essential respect with the pilot plant samples, evaluated for safety and absence of toxicity. To this end, chemical analysis and short-term (e.g. acute) toxicity studies with laboratory animals should be carried out with such plant production samples.

4) The manufacturer of such a novel SCP product should be required to divulge (in confidence) to the authorities charged with quality control all essential data regarding the manufacture and processing of the product and, in particular, those data necessary to establish efficient safety and quality control measures. As examples may be mentioned the type of micro-organism used in the production; the raw materials used as major nutrients (e.g. gas oil, purified alkanes, methanol, methane, sulphite waste liquor etc.); whether unusual chemicals have been added (e.g. defoaming agents, substrates to break emulsions); whether a solvent extraction process has been used; the drying process used; sanitary precautions taken during production and processing, etc.

5) Any change in organism or process should be reported to the appropriate authorities with sufficient proof that such changes did not influence safety and nutritional value of the product.

6)   On the basis of the data submitted, an appointed Commission
of nutritionists and toxicologists (preferably a universally-
accepted International Commission) should decide whether the data
submitted by the manufacturer warrant the conclusion that the
product is sufficiently safe and nutritionally adequate as a
major source of protein for nutrition of farm animals.   Such a
decision should be based exclusively on scientific evidence;   no
discrimination should be applied because of its unconventional
origin.

What tests should be applied to prove safety and nutritional
quality?   For reasons discussed in the Introduction, we feel
that the major procedures suggested by the Protein Advisory Group
of the three United Nations Agencies, and presented in their
Guideline #6 entitled: "Guideline for Preclinical Testing of
Novel Sources of Protein", should also be used for the evaluation
of novel sources of protein destined for animal feed ingredient.
Investigations according to the above-mentioned Guideline include:
1)   Microbiological examination for viable and non-viable contaminants, including presence of pathogenic organisms or toxin
producers, as an indication of sanitary production and processing
conditions.
2)   Chemical analysis, including moisture content;   ash and its
composition;   heavy metals;   contaminants such as solvent residues;   presence of hydrocarbons, including polycyclic aromatic
hydrocarbons;   protein content and the amino acid composition of
the proteins;   non-protein nitrogen components, including nucleic
acid content;   lipid content and its components.
3)   Safety tests on animals in order to prove absence of toxicity
and of toxic products such as heavy metals (Pb, Hg, As);   toxic
lipid components;   teratogenic or mutagenic substances.   Animal
tests should include, in addition to continued gross inspection
of the animals, clinical laboratory tests and pathological observation of organs of such animals, fed for extended periods with

feed containing the test material in different concentrations. In addition, reproduction and lactation studies should be made. 4) Protein quality studies such as protein digestibility, PER and NPU tests as well as nitrogen balance procedures.

For further details reference must be made to PAG Guideline #6.

In addition to safety and nutritional tests, conducted primarily with rats according to PAG Guideline #6, it is essential that additional feeding tests are conducted with farm animals, such as chickens and pigs, for which the product is ultimately destined.

ADDITIONAL SEMI-CHRONIC TOXICITY TESTS ON CHICKENS AND PIGS

In addition to toxicity data, these tests also provide important data on the nutritional efficiency of the SCP under study. This is important, especially from the economic point of view. A relatively small decrease in growth rate, feed conversion and reproduction exceeding 5% may result in unacceptable economic repercussions. The mixed-feed manufacturer must be sure that substitution on the basis of digestible nutrient content leads to the expected results.

Preferably, three different concentrations of SCP should be used, a minimum of 5-7% and a maximum of 20-25% of the ration. Rations of the experimental groups and the control groups should be equalized relative to percentage of digestible nutrient components and energy availability.

Young animals of the same age, weight, sex and source must be evenly divided over control and test groups. Each group should consist of 125 chicks (25 males + 100 females) and of 15 piglets (5 males + 10 females, preferably housed separately). The groups should be housed under similar conditions.

Feeding tests with poultry should be continued for 10 months and with pigs for 18 months. Growth rate, feed conversion and

general health condition of the animals should be established
at regular times during the test period.   During the latter
period of the test, egg production as well as hatchability of
these eggs should be determined in comparison with those of the
control group.   With pigs, fertility, size of litter, weight
and health condition of the piglets should be recorded and compared with the control group.   At three-monthly intervals, blood
and urine analysis and haematological data should be obtained
from some of the animals in each group.

At the conclusion of the test a thorough post-mortem analysis
should be made.   Weight of liver, kidneys, spleen, heart, thymus,
adrenals, testes, ovaries and brain is determined;   a histological
study of these and other organs is made, in particular from organs
showing signs of abnormality.

Sufficient animals should be included in the test in order
to be able to detect statistically differences in growth rate
and feed conversion exceeding a 5% limit between the experimental
groups and the control group.   If this accuracy cannot be obtained, the test should be extended.

STANDARDS OF IDENTITY

Once the product is approved on the basis of data submitted
commercial production will start.   How can we be sure that commercial production batches at all times will be identical with
the samples subjected to the above-mentioned extensive tests?
Experience has shown that considerable variation in SCP quality
may occur as a result of variations in the technological production process or due to variations in the raw materials used
for production.   Undoubtedly, the manufacturer will strive, in
fact must strive for a closely controlled reproducible production process and careful quality control of the raw materials
used in its production.   Nevertheless, product variations could
considerably exceed the variations in conventional agricultural

feed ingredients. For this reason it is essential that standards of identity should be established which reasonably ensure that production batches are of reproducible quality and as far as possible are identical with the control batch used for safety tests.

It is fully realized that no set of standards of identity tests, be it chemical or biological, can fully guarantee such identity and uniformity of quality. Nevertheless, such quality control measures should be able to detect any *major* divergence from the standard test sample, differences which could result in toxicity or a reduction in nutritional quality.

Because of the variety of possible substrates and of microorganisms suitable for SCP production it is impossible to establish a single comprehensive set of standards to cover all SCP. Consequently, the standards of identity proposed will be divided into two categories:

- general standards applying to all sources of SCP
- specific additional standards relevant to a particular substrate and a particular micro-organism.

Table 1 lists the general standards of identity for SCP products destined as a major ingredient for animal feeds. They consist of a number of bacteriological specifications which guarantee that manufacture and production of SCP took place under satisfactory sanitary conditions, resulting in a product of unquestionable bacteriological safety. The following parameters are of particular importance: aerobic plate count, coliforms, coagulase-positive staphylococci, salmonella, perfringens and Group D streptococci. Alternative specifications given in PAG Guideline #11 for the sanitary production and use of dry protein foods may also be used as a guarantee of bacteriological safety and hygiene.

In addition, a limited moisture content is essential in order to guarantee that the product will keep and to prevent bacterial and fungal deterioration during storage.

Table 1   General standards of identity for SCP used for animal feed.

Microscopic Examination:

The product must consist primarily of the dead cells of the micro-organism used for its production.   No major infection with foreign organism, dead or alive, should be present.

	per gram
Viable bacteria count (total aerobic bacteria)	< 100,000
Viable yeasts and moulds	< 100
Enterobacteriaceae	< 10
Salmonella	< 1 per 50 gm
Staph. aureus	< 1
Clostridia total	< 1,000
Cl. perfringens	< 100
Lancefield Group D Streptococci	< 10,000
Moisture content	< 10%
Ash content	to be declared
Lead	< 5 ppm
Arsenic	< 2 ppm
Mercury	< 0.1 ppm
Total nitrogen	to be declared
Nucleic acid nitrogen	"
Ammonia and urea nitrogen	"
Total lysine	"
Available lysine as % of total	"
Sulphur amino acids	"
Crude lipids	"
Pepsin digestibility	"
Protein efficiency ratio (PER)	"
Net protein utilisation	"

Heavy metal content (Pb, Hg, As) should be below a permissible limit.

The Committee is of the opinion that there is no point in setting minimum requirements for protein content or for other natural cell components, nor for data related to nutritional quality, since these parameters may vary considerably from product to product derived from different sources or processes without affecting qualitatively the nutritional value.   However, the

manufacturer should declare these specifications for the product
he manufactures and guarantee that his product reproducibly ful-
fils these specifications.

Many SCP products have a very high nucleic acid content and
in addition may contain other nitrogen-containing compounds,
such as ammonium salts, of no or questionable nutritional value.
Total nitrogen determination and multiplication with the factor
6.25, as is customary with conventional feed products, could result in a highly exaggerated "crude protein" content.   It is
suggested, therefore, that apart from the total nitrogen, determined by the Kjeldahl method, free ammonia and nucleic acid
nitrogen should also be declared.

As pointed out the feed manufacturer is accustomed, by careful mixing of ingredients, often with quite different nutrient
content, to meet the exact nutritional needs of the animal.   In
order to accomplish this with new unconventional ingredients it
is essential that the content of digestible nutrients of such a
product is known.   Protein content, in combination with lysine
and sulphur amino acids determinations, gives some indication
of the potential nutritional value, whereas "available" lysine,
expressed as a percentage of the total amount of lysine, may give
an indication of the deleterious effect, possibly resulting from
an excessive heat treatment.   Finally, pepsin digestibility,
a high PER or NPU value are additional parameters of the nutritional quality of the protein components.   Lipid content of
SCP may also vary between relatively wide limits, frequently as
a result whether or not extraction procedures are used.   No
general maximal limits for lipid content are recommended, since
frequently such lipids contribute to the nutritional value of
the product.   However, the lipid content should be declared.

No specifications are recommended for the vitamen content
of SCP.   Due to a poorly reproducible vitamin scale of SCP
batches it seems safer that the feed manufacturer adds the re-

Table 2   Specific standards of identity for SCP from hydrocarbons.

Benzo(a)pyrene (as indicator of presence of polycyclic aromatic hydrocarbons)	< 5 parts per billion
Total residual hydrocarbons	< 0.5%
Total residual aromatic hydrocarbons	< 0.5%

quired amount of essential vitamins to his feed without taking
into account the vitamin content of the SCP component.

Table 2 lists the additional specific standards of identity
applicable for SCP production obtained using hydrocarbons as raw
material for its production.   It includes both SCP prepared from
gas oil and from the purified alkane fraction of gas oil.   Particular attention should be paid that no polycyclic aromatic hydrocarbons, present in small quantities in crude oil, are present
in detectable amounts since many of these compounds are suspected
to be carcinogenic.   In addition, residual hydrocarbons and in
particular aromatic hydrocarbons should remain below a permissible limit.   Such hydrocarbons may be left behind as undigested
or undigestible compounds in the cell during growth or could be
added and insufficiently removed when used as solvent during an
extraction step.

Obviously, such specific standards of identity must be extended to additional substances in case the manufacturer adds
unusual products and compounds either during the growth period
or as part of the recovery process.

In conclusion, it must be mentioned that the above specifications cannot and do not guarantee full identity with the safe
and nutritionally adequate samples investigated previously in
great detail.   However, if production samples comply with the
recommended standards it is felt that a possible abnormality in
quality is reduced to a bare minimum.

SESSION 2

NUTRITIONAL EVALUATION OF SCP

INTRODUCTION

P. Davis

Stanford Research Institute, Menlo Park
California, USA

This section is on the nutritional evaluation of SCP. It
includes papers on the tests necessary to evaluate SCP for feed
and food. We will also hear about the feeding trials in which
SCP was fed to a variety of animals, and how they metabolized
and used yeast proteins. In addition, the use of SCP by man
and attitudes of food manufacturers and potential consumers concerning the use of SCP will also be discussed.

There is much to learn about the feeding and nutritional
quality of SCP for animals and man. Some parameters that need
illuminating are the proper dietary levels, the degree of forti-
fication that is necessary or desirable, the toxicological aspects of substrates, any changes that might occur in the metabolism or histology of the species, the development of forms and
function properties, and the ultimate consumer acceptance of the
product.

Many fine papers have already been published or delivered on
various aspects of these subjects. However, the SCP industry is
relatively new, and there has not been time to assemble an adequate compendium of data on these topics. Thus, we have the
opportunity of contributing to that library of data during this
symposium.

73

D

MINIMAL TESTS NECESSARY TO EVALUATE THE NUTRITIONAL QUALITIES AND THE SAFETY OF SCP

A.P. de Groot

Central Institute for Nutrition and Food Research TNO, Zeist, The Netherlands

INTRODUCTION

The ever-increasing amount of literature on toxic substances occurring naturally in foods has contributed to the recognition of possible health risks in all types of foods and feeds. Even such reputable health foods like eggs, milk, beans, potatoes and wheat are known to contain detrimental components. The idea to investigate the merits and risks of new foods is, therefore, far from revolutionary.

Novel protein sources are often derived from a group of organisms which harbour toxin-producing species. Moreover, during their production, the materials are often submitted to treatments by heat, solvents, or alkali, each of which may impart undesirable, or even toxic properties to the resulting product. It would seem essential, therefore, to demonstrate the safety of all single cell protein products, not only in view of their public health aspects, but also in the interest of the producer and the image of this new source of foods.

After having touched the question "why" testing is necessary, the next question is "how" this should be done. Toxicologists and nutritionists generally dislike detailed instructions concerning the conduct of their studies. Nevertheless, several national authorities and supra-national bodies have drawn up elaborate

guidelines and protocols for the various types of information
required for the evaluation of the toxicity of food additives
and contaminants (1,2,5,6,7,8,10,16).

The purpose of the present paper is to make an attempt at
outlining the minimum amount of information that should be available before a SCP is considered for acceptance in foods and feeds,
and even before it is justified to initiate the phase of clinical
testing in humans.   These minimal requirements for a testing
programme will be based on the well-known PAG Guideline #6, for
pre-clinical testing of novel sources of protein (13), on a review of the subject by Oser (11) and on experience obtained in
our institute with testing many samples of SCP (9).

In spite of the excellent opportunity to shelter behind the
magic significance of the PAG #6 Guideline, I realize that by men-
tioning dogmatic minimums for the tests required, numbers of diet
groups and test animals, and types of observations, I am offering
an attractive target for attacks and criticism.   For tactical
reasons it seems sensible to introduce some protective terminology
and to place my subject under the heading "proposed guideline for
minimum requirements".

There is reason to suppose that the testing programme for
SCP intended as feed for farm animals could be less extensive than
that required for human foods.   However, toxic factors ingested
by farm animals could be accumulated in their edible products
(meat, fat, milk, eggs) and in this way constitute a risk to human
health.   As far as the extent of the safety evaluation programme
is concerned it does not seem desirable, therefore, to discriminate
between SCPs on the basis of their intended use.

CATEGORIES OF INFORMATION REQUIRED

From the various categories of information needed according
to the PAG Guideline #6, those on chemical composition, protein
quality, microbiological status, and biological safety testing,

are important for the scope of the present review.   The major
part will be devoted to the safety testing programme in laboratory
animals.   The evaluation of the merits of the product for feeding
farm animals will receive little attention, mainly because it is
beyond my competence.

ANALYTICAL DATA

The analytical information which should be available in the
initial phase of the testing programme partly concerns the nutritive quality and partly the safety.   Table 1 shows details of the
information needed.   The proximate composition, amino acid pattern,
and levels of calcium and phosphorus provide the data essential
for designing balanced diets to be used in the feeding studies.
Residue analyses of organic solvents, auxiliary substances used
in the production or purification of the product (e.g. emulsifiers,
anti-foaming agents) and of possible other contaminants (e.g.
lubricants, PCBs) may be helpful to prevent failures of the feeding studies.   The same applies to information on trace elements
which may prevent both deficiency and toxicity.

Table 1   Analytical data concerning nutritive value and safety.

Nutritive value		Safety	
Moisture		Solvent residues	
Nitrogen:	crude protein	Nucleic acids:	purines
	amino acids		pyrimidines
	available lysine	Contaminants:	auxiliary substances
Crude fat			
Total ash:	calcium	Trace elements:	Hg, Pb, F, As, Se
	phosphorus		

Table 2   Microbiological criteria.

Total aerobic count	$< 10^4/g$
Mould spores	$< 10 /g$
Enterobacteriaceae	absent in 0.1 g
Clostridia group	$< 10^2/g$
Lancefield group D streptococci	$< 10^2/g$

MICROBIOLOGICAL DATA

With respect to the microbiological status of novel protein sources, acceptable limits for different types of micro-organisms have been proposed in several documents of the PAG, for example for fish protein concentrates (14) and edible soy products (12).

Minimal requirements for SCP which seem to be acceptable to microbiologists are presented in Table 2.   The standards mentioned may be considered as tight, and products surpassing them by a factor of 10 could still be considered acceptable for use in most animal feeds.

PROTEIN QUALITY ASSAY

Determinations of protein quality are conducted with a variety of biological, chemical or microbiological methods.   The most relevant information is provided by each one of the three biological methods which are widely used by nutritionists.   These bio-assays are performed with young rats, by feeding the product to be examined as the sole source of protein in the diet at a level providing 10% crude protein.

The *protein efficiency ratio* (PER) is calculated from the gain in body weight and protein consumption of male rats over a test period of 4 weeks.   The resulting PER, calculated by means of a standard value of 2.5 for casein, is a measure of the combined effects of digestibility and utilization.   Therefore, a

Table 3   Rat-assays for protein quality.

PER	:	10 weanling males per group
		gain in body weight, protein intake
		test period: 28 days
		reference protein: casein
NPU + D	:	groups of 4-12 rats, 28-30 days old
		N in food, N in carcass and faeces
		test period; 10 days
N-balance	:	groups of 5-10 young rats
		N in food, N in faeces and urine
		collection period: 3-5 days

low PER may be the result of either inadequate amino acid composition, or poor digestibility, or both.

The *net protein utilization* (NPU) is defined as the percentage of the N consumed, which is retained in the body.   This value
is also the result of two different properties: amino acid composition and digestibility.   However, the method offers a simple
opportunity to differentiate between digestibility and amino acid
pattern, by conducting N analyses of faeces from the test rats and
from the controls on a protein-free diet.

The *N-balance method*, which differentiates between digestible
and utilizable N, is based on measurements of N-intake and N-
excretion in faeces and urine.   This bio-assay is the most laborious one, and for this reason less widely used than PER and NPU.

Although the PER is the most simple method, NPU is preferred,
because more information can be obtained if digestibility is determined in the same assay.   Details of each of the three bio-assays
are shown in Table 3.

SAFETY EVALUATION IN LABORATORY ANIMALS

The studies intended to establish the safety of SCP form the
major part of the testing programme.

The most suitable animal species for the feeding studies is
undoubtedly the rat, although at least part of the information
needed should be obtained in a second species of laboratory animal
(dog, monkey) or in a farm animal (pig or chicken).   It is clear,
however, that these species are not suitable for life-time or carcinogenicity studies, because an experimental period of at least
five years would be required.

With respect to the test diets, it is important to incorporate the SCP at two or more graded levels in nutritionally well-
balanced diets by omitting corresponding amounts of the high protein compounds from the basal diet.   Semi-purified diets are sometimes used for short-term studies, but practical-type diets are
to be preferred for long-term studies because of their proven
reliability.   Moreover, SCPs are more comparable in composition
with natural feed ingredients than with components of semi-
purified diets, which makes them more suitable for substitution.

Screening Test

The most practical way of starting any safety-evaluation programme is by means of a simple sub-acute feeding test with 10 male
and 10 female weanling rats, on a diet containing the SCP at the
highest level which will not disturb the nutritional balance of the
diet too much.   With SCP, varying in protein content from 50 to
70%, the dietary level will vary between 60 and 40% in order to
keep the protein content of the diet around 30%.

Attention should also be paid to the high P-level of SCP,
which may lead to renal damage as a result of too much available
dietary P or poorly balanced Ca:P-ratio.

The observations to be made in the screening test may be
limited to those mentioned in Table 4, which are known to be sensi-

Table 4   Screening test in rats.

Feeding level	30-60% SCP-product
Test group	10 male + 10 female weanlings
Feeding period	2-6 weeks
<u>Observations</u> :	growth, food intake
	haemoglobin content
	gross pathology
	weight of liver and kidneys
	microscopy of liver and kidneys

tive and often affected in toxicity studies.

This sub-acute test, even when continued for only 2 weeks, is very suitable for screening large numbers of samples to investigate the effect of various process conditions on the safety of the product, and to discover and correct a defective material at an early phase of product development.

Sub-chronic (90-day) Study

If the screening test does not reveal any deleterious effects, it is justified to continue the programme with the much more elaborate 90-day study. This study is conducted with groups of 10 male and 10 female weanling rats on diets containing the SCP at two or more graded levels. In addition to growth and food intake, haematological data and biochemical blood values are collected and examinations of urine sample are made in the final week of the testing period. Details of these examinations are shown in Table 5.

The study is terminated by careful gross examination of all rats at autopsy. A number of organs (usually 8-10) are weighed. Tissue samples of these organs and a number of other organs and tissues (usually 20-30) are collected from all rats and fixed in formalin for microscopical examination, as far as necessary. Table 6 mentions the organs which are usually weighed and those

A.P. de Groot

Table 5 Standard criteria of toxicity studies.

General	Haematology	Blood biochemistry	Urine	Kidney function
Mortality	haemoglobin	glucose	appearance	concentration test
Condition and behaviour	haematocrit	urea-N	pH	phenol-red excretion
Growth	erythrocytes	protein	glucose	UGOT
Food and water intake	leucocytes	alb/glob. ratio	protein	
Appearance of faeces		SGOT	occult blood	
		SGPT	ketones	
		SAP	sediment	

SGOT = serum glutamic oxalacetic transaminase

SGPT = serum glutamic pyruvic transaminase

SAP = serum alkaline phosphatase

Table 6   Pathological observations.

Organ weights	Microscopic examination
Liver, kidney, heart, spleen, brain, gonads, adrenals, thyroid, thymus	Organs weighed, as well as lung, prostate, urinary bladder, salivary glands, lymph nodes, gastro-intestinal tract (six levels), pancreas and all other organs showing gross abnormalities

sampled for microscopy.   Fortunately, not all of the many hun-
dreds of tissue samples need to be processed through paraffin,
sectioned and stained, because microscopical examination may be
restricted mainly to the highest dose group and the control
group.   Organs of the highest dose group showing no changes that
might possibly be caused by the test material are not examined
in the intermediate groups.   This is a quite acceptable and considerably decreases the impressive amount of histological work
involved in any extensive toxicity study.

Chronic (2-year) Feeding Study

In spite of the extremely valuable information provided by
a well-conducted 90-day study, no indications are obtained of
possible real long-term effects like shortening of the lifespan
or carcinogenicity.   For this purpose it is inevitable to conduct life-time studies, using the rat as the most suitable animal
species.

Groups of 30 males and 30 females are considered sufficient
for chronic studies, but groups of 50 males and 50 females are
strongly recommended if there is any suspicion of carcinogenicity.

Although the average lifespan of rats is longer, 2 years is
generally considered a sufficiently long experimental period.
At this age rats have already developed many ageing symptoms,
including tumours.

The two-year study is conducted in essentially the same way

Table 7 Design of sub-chronic and chronic studies in rats

	Sub-chronic	Chronic
Period	90 days	2 years
Rats per group	20	100
Observations		
Health	daily	daily
Body weight	weekly	monthly
Food intake	at intervals	at intervals
Haematology	week 12	6, 12, 24 months
Blood biochemistry	week 12	6, 12, 24 months
Urine composition	week 12	6, 12, 24 months
Autopsy	week 13	week 104
Organs weighed	8	–
Gross pathology	all rats	all rats
Histopathology:		
Groups	controls + top dose	controls + top dose
Rats	20	40
Organs	10-15	10-20
Tumours	–	all tumours

as the 90-day study, apart from the longer duration and the larger number of animals involved. The clinical observations, which are made only terminally in the 90-day study, are made at intervals of 3-12 months in the chronic experiment.

The gross pathology involves all rats in all groups. The histopathology may be restricted to 20 males and 20 females of the highest dose group and the controls, if the organs showing possible treatment-related changes are examined also in the intermediate dose groups. The grossly visible tumours, and the lesions suspected of being tumours, are examined microscopically in all rats of all groups, not only the survivors but also those which died during the experiment. Table 7 shows the design of the sub-chronic and chronic studies.

Multigeneration Study

In addition to possible chronic and carcinogenic properties, effects on fertility and lactation performance should also be examined. This is done in reproduction studies, which generally run parallel with the chronic study on the same diets, but with separate groups of rats.

The scheme of this study is shown in Fig. 1. The experiment is conducted with at least two dosage groups and one control group, each consisting of 10 male and 20 female rats. After three months the rats are mated within their diet group. The litters are weighed and counted shortly after birth, and at weaning. Then the young are discarded. The parents are mated again and the second litters are counted and weighed as the first litters. At weaning age 10 males and 20 females are selected from different litters in each group and continued on the same diet for the production of further generations. These F_1-generation rats are treated in the same way as the parent rats, which means that two successive litters are produced and observed for growth and mortality. This procedure is repeated with the F_2-generation rats up to weaning age of the second litter. At this stage the ex-

A.P. de Groot

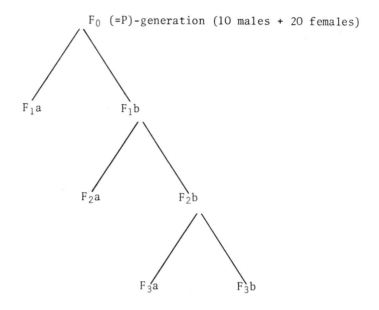

Observations: Mortality
               Body weights of parents and pups
               Number of young litter
               Implantation sites
               Extensive examinations of F_3b litters

Fig. 1   Design of multigeneration study.

periment is terminated by macroscopical and microscopical examination of 10 male and 10 female rats from each diet group.

Information on prenatal mortality is obtained by sacrificing
the mothers of each generation after weaning their second litters
and counting the uterine implantation sites.   From the ratio of
implantation sites and numbers of young born, the resorption
quotient is calculated.   An increase in resorption quotient indicates early embryonic mortality.

Teratogenicity Study

The multigeneration study as described before may provide indications of teratogenic and/or mutagenic properties, but is not
suitable to demonstrate the absence of these effects.   More

Table 8   Teratogenicity test

Pregnant rats per group	10
Test groups	2
Control groups	1
Treatment period	day 6-15 of pregnancy
Autopsy	day 20 of pregnancy
Observations:	resorption sites
	live and dead foetuses
	soft-tissue examinations
	skeletal examinations

specific and more sensitive methods have been developed for this purpose.

For detecting teratogenic properties, the following procedure is recommended as a necessary part of any safety-evaluation programme (Table 8).

Groups of 10-20 pregnant rats are treated with at least two high levels of the test material during the period of organogenesis of their embryos, which is from day 6-15 of pregnancy. One day before term the mothers are killed. Resorption sites, and live and dead foetuses are counted. The foetuses are weighed, sexed and examined grossly for malformations. Examinations of the soft tissues are made on two-thirds of the number of embryos, according to the Wilson technique, while the remaining one-third is examined for skeletal abnormalities after Alizarin staining. A comparison of the type and frequency of the birth defects in the different groups is the basis for deciding whether or not the test material exerted a teratogenic effect.

Mutagenicity Study

Genetic hazards from food contaminants can now be examined in mammals by several, relatively simple methods including *in vivo* cytogenesis, host-mediated assay and dominant-lethal assay. The

latter method seems to be promising for being integrated in routine toxicity testing in rats and mice.

This method is intended to discover mutations which indicate
major genetic damage, resulting in pre-implantation losses of
non-viable zygotes, early foetal deaths and sterility.   A practical and economic procedure has been described (3,4) and recommended for application to all food additives and contaminants
(Table 9).

Table 9   Mutagenicity test (dominant-lethal.

Males per group	5
Test groups	1
Control groups	1
Treatment period	5 days
Mating periods	4x one week
Autopsy of females	day 10-17 of pregnancy
Observations: total and living implants	
early and late foetal deaths	

Groups of at least five adult male rats or mice, are treated
orally with the test material at a maximally tolerated dose for
5 successive days.   A comparable group of five non-treated males
serves as a control group.   Thereafter, each male is caged
together with two non-treated virgin females at weekly intervals
for a total period of at least 4 weeks.   All females are autop-
sied at day 13 after mid-week of their presumptive mating, and
scored for pregnancy, total implants, living implants and early
and late foetal deaths.   The mutagenicity may be expressed as
1) the mutagenic index, which is the number of early foetal deaths
divided by the number of total implants × 100, or as 2) the number
of early foetal deaths per pregnant animal.

SAFETY EVALUATION IN FARM ANIMALS

A complete toxicity testing programme usually involves studies with two or more mammalian species, one of which should be a non-rodent.   For testing additives and contaminants in human foods, the rat is generally used as the first species and the dog as the second species.   Since SCPs are often developed for use in animal feeds, the practical application will be preceded by well-controlled feeding studies on the farm animals for which the product is intended (pigs and poultry).   This offers an excellent opportunity for including these species, as the second and third species for evaluating the safety of SCP, not only in sub-chronic studies but also sometimes in reproduction studies.

Before initiating any extensive studies on farm animals, it is safe first to collect some information in simple tentative feeding tests with small numbers of animals on diets with high levels of the product during only a few weeks.   If the product turns out to be satisfactory in tentative tests, more elaborate studies are started to obtain meaningful data both with respect to safety and to nutritive value.

For this purpose, the SCP is incorporated in the diet of pigs and chickens at one relatively low level, comparable to that used under practical conditions (e.g. 7.5%), and at one high level which provides all the protein needed on top of the amount already present in the energy-providing components of the rations. This level will be in the order of 15-25% depending on the protein content of the SCP.

The number of animals in each group is at least 20 for pigs and 60 for chickens.   If the experiment is continued for 6-12 months it covers roughly one-tenth of the normal lifespan of each species, which is comparable to the sub-chronic (90-day) feeding study in rats.

Table 10   Sub-chronic safety-evaluation studies in pigs and poultry.

Pigs per group	20
Chickens per group	60
Test groups	2
Control groups	1
Duration	6-12 months

Observations: condition and behaviour
weight gain and food intake
haematology, blood biochemistry
urine examination
autopsies: gross examination
weights of liver and kidneys
microscopy of the major organs (10-20)

The observations should include the groups of criteria mentioned in Table 10, which are generally considered obligatory in toxicity studies.

If the studies in farm animals have provided satisfactory results, and no indications of deleterious effects have been observed in the various studies in rats, little doubt is left concerning the safety of the product for animals and humans. However, more extensive information is certainly desirable with respect to the merits of the SCP as a major constituent of animal feeds.   Guidelines for such studies have recently been proposed (15) and are now under review.

REFERENCES

1.   Association of Food and Drug Officials of the United States. "Appraisal of the Safety of Chemicals in Foods, Drugs and Cosmetics," Texas State Department of Health (1959).

2.   Environmental Protection Agency.   "Pesticide Chemical Safety;   Proposed Toxicology Guidelines," Federal Register

37, No. 183, 19383 (1972, Sept. 20).

3. Epstein, S.S. and Bateman, A.J. "Dominant Lethal Mutations in Mammals." *In:* "Chemical Mutagens; Principles and Methods for their Detection." (Aex. Hollaender, ed), Vol.2, Chapter 21, Plenum Press, New York/London, pp. 541-568 (1971).

4. Epstein, S.S. and Röhrborn, G. "Recommended Procedures for Testing Genetic Hazards from Chemicals, Based on the Induction of Dominant Lethal Mutations in Mammals." *Nature* **230**, 459-460 (1971).

5. FAO/WHO. "Procedures for the Testing of Intentional Food Additives to Establish their Safety in Use." 2nd report of the Joint FAO/WHO Expert Committee on Food Additives. FAO Nutrition Meetings Report Series No. 17 (1958).

6. FDA Advisory Committee on Protocols for Safety Evaluation; Panel on Reproduction. "Report on Reproduction Studies in the Safety Evaluation of Food Additives and Pesticide Residues." *Toxicol. appl. Pharmacol.* **16**, 264-296 (1970).

7. FDA Advisory Committee on Protocols for Safety Evaluation; Panel on Carcinogenesis. "Report on Cancer Testing in the Safety Evaluation of Food Additives and Pesticides." *Toxicol. appl. Pharmacol.* **20**, 419-438 (1971).

8. Food Protection Committee, Food and Nutrition Board. "Principles and Procedures for Evaluating the Safety of Food Additives." Nat. Academy Sciences - Nat. Res. Council, Publ. no. 750 (1960).

9. Groot, A.P. de, Til, H.P. and Feron, V.J. "Safety Evaluation of Yeast Grown on Hydrocarbons. III. Two-year Feeding and Multigeneration Study in Rats with Yeast Grown on Gas-oil." *Fd Cosmet. Toxicol.* **9**, 787-800 (1971).

10. Ministry of Agriculture and Forestry. "Toxicity and Residue Tests Necessary for Registration of Agricultural Chemicals in Japan." Japan Pesticide Information No. 14 (1972).

11. Oser, B.L. "The Safety Evaluation of New Sources of Protein for Man." *In:* "Evaluation of Novel Protein Products." Proc. Symposium Stockholm, 1968, Pergamon Press, Oxford (1970).

12. Protein Advisory Group. "Guideline for Edible, Heat-processed Soy Grits and Flour." Guideline No. 5 (1969, Dec. 8).

13. Protein Advisory Group. "Guideline for Pre-clinical Testing of Novel Sources of Protein." Guideline No. 6 (1970, Jan. 30).

14. Protein Advisory Group. "Tentative Suggestion for Fish Protein Concentrates for Human Consumption." Document 2.8/ 26 (1970, Jan. 15).

15. Wal, P. van der. "Guidelines for Nutritional and Toxicological Evaluation of New Protein Sources for Use in Animal Feed." Portion of a paper presented at a Symposium on New Developments in the Provision of Amino Acids in Diets of Pigs and Poultry. (Sponsored by FAO and the Committee on Agricultural Problems, Economic Commission for Europe, December 1972).

16. WHO. "Procedures for Investigating Intentional and Unintentional Food Additives." Report of a WHO Scientific Group. WHO Techn. Report Series No. 348 (1967).

ENZYMATIC DIGESTION OF YEAST IN SOME ANIMALS

S. Hibino and H. Terashima

Central Institute for Feed and Livestock Research
ZEN-NOH, Tukuba-machi, Tukuba-gun, Ibaragi, Japan

Z. Minami and M. Kajita

Nagase & Co., Ltd., Division of Research and Development
Ohama, Amagasaki, Japan

INTRODUCTION

Many studies have been reported regarding the high nutritional availability of the yeast from n-paraffin for poultry, pigs and fish (1,2,3). The authors reported that, in chickens and pigs, the nutritional availability of the yeast was higher at a young age than for the very young (4,5). In order to clarify the mechanism of such a high utilization of the yeast, the following experiments were carried out.

Firstly, the enzyme levels were determined in the digestive organs of animals fed with yeast from n-paraffin. The activities of proteinase, chitinase, β-1,3-glucanase, ribonuclease and amylase were examined. These enzymes are supposed to contribute to the digestion of the yeast, as the yeast cell wall is mainly composed of glucan, mamman, protein and chitin (6).

Secondly, to check on the change of the yeast in each digestive tract, preparations of yeast were made in guts and were observed by an electron microscope.

Lastly, some intestinal bacteria which may contribute to the digestion of the yeast were studied.

S. Hibino et al.

Table 1   Digestibility and energy level of yeast.

| | Chicken | | Pig | |
	Broiler (4 weeks)	Layer (19 months)	Baby (10 kg)	Young (65 kg)
Digestibility				
Crude protein %	87.5	92.5	85.2	93.7
Organic matter %	52.8	72.4	88.8	94.0
Energy level*				
ME Cal/g	3.15	3.71		
DE Cal/g			4.16	4.51

* On dry basis.

Table 2   Chemical composition of yeasts (% on dry-air basis).

| | Yeast from n-paraffin | | Fodder yeast | Baker's yeast |
	A	B		
Crude protein	50.7	59.6	50.5	35-65
Crude fat	8.4	8.7	7.0	3-7
Hexosamine	2.0	1.4	0.1-0.5	0.13**
Glucan	6.6*			11**
Mannan	2.8*			12**

*   Harada *et al., Proc. IFS: Ferment. Technol. Today*, 479-485 (1972).
** Bacon *et al., Biochem. J.* **114**, 557 (1969).

DIGESTIBILITY AND ENERGY LEVELS OF YEAST

Table 1 shows digestibility and metabolizable energy (ME) or digestible energy (DE) of the yeast for chickens and pigs. In chickens and pigs, digestibility of crude protein (CP) and organic matter were higher at a young age than for the very young.

Table 3　Preparation and Assay of Enzymes.

Preparation:　Removal of each organ* → Homogenization →
　　　　　　　Centrifugation

Assay:　　　(Reaction temperature,** 40°C)

Enzyme	Substrate	pH	Time min.	Reference
Peptic-enzyme	casein	1.8	10	Hagihara (1956)
Tryptic-enzyme	casein	7.6	10	Hagihara (1956)
Chitinase	chitin, pptd.	4.5,7.0	60	Jeuniaux (1966)
Ribonuclease	yeast RNA	4.5,6.5,7.0	15	McDonald (1955)
β-1,3-glucanase	laminarin	5.0	60	Mandel (1959)
Amylase	starch	7.0	5	Bernferd (1955)

* Stomach, duodenum, small intestine, cecum, rectum, colon, pancreas.
** In fish, especially, proteinases were assayed at 30°C and chitinase, ribonuclease, β-1,3-glucanase and amylase were assayed at 35°C.

ENZYME ASSAY

Chemical Composition of Yeast

　　Table 2 shows the main chemical composition of the yeasts. Yeast from n-paraffin contains more hexosamine than fodder and baker's yeast.　The former may have much more chitin, polymer of N-acetylglucosamine, than the latter.

　　It is reported that glucanase, chitinase and proteinase are very effective for the digestion of yeast (7,8,9).　Therefore, we determined the activities of glucanase and chitinase, in addition to ordinary enzymes, in digestive organs.

Determination of Enzyme Activities

　　Table 3 shows the outline of enzyme preparation and the methods of enzyme assay.　After removal, each organ was homogenised with saline.　Centrifuged supernatants were used as stock solutions for enzyme assay.　Each enzyme assay was performed as shown in the table.

S. Hibino et al.

Table 4   Composition of diets for chickens.

A.   Control diet

	Broiler (3 weeks)	Layer (19 months)
Maize	75%	71.5%
Soybean meal	10	12
Fish meal	10	8
Alfalfa meal	2.3	-
Limestone	1.0	6
Dicalcium phosphate	1.0	2
Salt	0.2	0.2
Mineral mix	0.1	0.1
Furazolidone (10%)	0.1	-
Antibiotic (2%, BC)	0.1	-
Vitamin mix	0.2	0.2

B.   Test diet

   Broiler: 80% control diet + 20% yeast.
   Layer: Soybean meal and fish meal in control diet
              were replaced by yeast.

Table 5   The pH of the digesta of digestive tracts.

Organ	Broiler (3 weeks)				Layer (19 months)	
	Control		Test		Control	Test
	Pen*1	Pen 2	Pen 1	Pen 2		
Glandular stomach	5.08	5.66	6.27	6.15	5.12	6.17
Gizzard	3.64	3.53	3.74	4.02	4.60	4.45
Duodenum	6.32	6.52	6.46	6.50	6.35	6.37
Small intestine	6.75	6.67	6.43	6.21	6.52	6.30
Cecum	6.86	6.86	6.38	6.35	6.25	6.10

* Each pen consists of 5 birds.

Table 6   Enzyme activities of the organ (broiler, 3 weeks).

| Organ | Enzyme Activities* | | | | | |
| | Proteinase | | Chitinase | | Ribonuclease | |
	Control	Test	Control	Test	Control	Test
Glandular stomach	5,655	6,625	5,910	7,125	132	84
Gizzard	30	15	550	685	12	12
Pancreas	7,700	12,400	160	260	2,650	2,250
Duodenum	322	250	675	625	175	187
Small intestine	1,307	1,340	970	1,550	103	118
Cecum	351	1,190	680	1,240	57	54

* Units per g of wet organ.

STUDIES ON CHICKENS

Composition of Diets

Table 4 shows the composition of diets.   The test diet for broilers contained 20% yeast and 80% control diet.   In the case of layers, soybean meal and fish meal in the control diet were replaced by yeast.   After feeding each diet for 3 weeks, the birds were killed to assay the enzyme activities.

Enzyme Levels

In Table 5 the pH of the digesta are shown.   Tables 6 and 7 show the enzyme levels of broiler and layer, respectively. Enzyme activities were expressed as units per gram of wet organ. Proteinase activity was very high in the glandular stomach and pancreas.   Chintinase activity was also high in the glandular stomach, and was found in the small intestine.   Ribonuclease was detected mainly in the pancreas.

To compare the enzyme levels of a baby broiler that those of a layer, the values of proteinase and chitinase activities in the main organs of Tables 6 and 7 were abstracted into Table 8A. Table 8B shows converted enzyme levels per bird.   From Tables 8A and 8B, it may be said that the layer had rather higher enzyme levels than the baby broiler.   This fact may affect the

S. Hibino et al.

Table 7   Enzyme activities of the organ (layer, 19 months).

| Organ | Enzyme Activities* | | | |
| | Proteinase | | Chitinase | |
	Control	Test	Control	Test
Glandular stomach	6,989	8,300	7,800	8,100
Gizzard	431	527	385	368
Pancreas	15,185	12,979	-**	-
Duodenum	282	236	900	900
Small intestine	846	564	2,340	2,520
Cecum	41	5	-	-

*   Units per g of wet organ.
** Not determined.

Table 8   Comparison of enzyme activities of broiler (3 weeks)
with layer (19 months).

| | | | Proteinase | | | Chitinase | |
			glandular stomach	pancreas	small intestine	glandular stomach	small intestine
(A)*	Broiler	Control	5,655	7,700	1,307	5,910	980
		Test	6,625	12,400	1,340	7,125	1,550
	Layer	Control	6,889	15,185	846	7,800	2,340
		Test	8,300	12,979	564	8,100	2,520
(B)**	Broiler	Control	13,459	30,064		14,066	14,026
		Test	14,906	42,696		16,031	28,303
	Layer	Control	42,000	67,298		46,878	69,802
		Test	38,097	52,167		37,179	72,450

* Units per g of wet organ.
**Units per bird.

digestibility and ME value of young and baby chicks.

Electron Microscopic Observation

Figures 1 to 6 show changes of the yeast cell in each diges-

tive tract of a chicken, by the electron microscope. Layers of
10 months were fed with a diet containing 50% of the yeast.
After feeding for one week, birds were killed. Preparations
for microscopic observation were obtained from digesta of each
organ. Photographs were taken by the Model JEM 50.

Figure 1: Intact yeast.

Figure 2: Yeast, in the gizzard, almost unchanged.

Figure 3: Yeast in the duodenum. The yeasts are not
sharp in comparison with the intact cell. From
the duodenum, the yeast may begin to release its
contents.

Figure 4: Yeast in the anterior part of the small intestine. Yeast is surrounded with faint cell-wall-
like substance. Judging from the short shadow,
the content of the cell may be considerably released.

Figure 5: Yeast in the posterior part of the small intestine. Bud-scars of the cell wall can be seen,
which are the marks left on the surface of the
budding yeast.

Figure 6: Yeast in the cecum. The cell is almost empty.
Translucent cell-wall residue can be seen.

STUDIES ON PIGS

Composition of Diets

Table 9 shows the composition of diets. The test diet for
baby pigs contained 20% yeast and 80% control diet. In the case
of young pigs, soybean meal and fish meal were replaced by yeast.
After feeding each diet for 12 days, the pigs were killed to assay
the enzyme activities.

Enzyme Levels

In Table 10 the pH of the digesta are shown. Tables 11 and
12 show the enzyme levels of baby pigs and young pigs, respectively.

Fig. 1 Intact yeast.

Fig. 2 Yeast in gizzard.

Fig. 3 Yeast in duodenum.

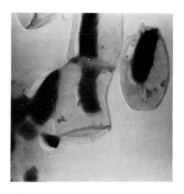

Fig. 4 Yeast in anterior part of small intestine.

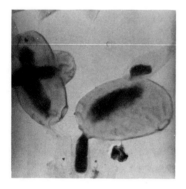

Fig. 5 Yeast in posterior part of small intestine.

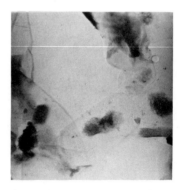

Fig. 6 Yeast in cecum.

Table 9   Composition of diets for pigs.

A. Control diet

	Pig, baby (46 days)	Pig, young (4 months)
Maize	58.1%	68.5%
Soybean meal	10	15
Fish meal	6	5
Alfalfa meal	15	-
Defatted rice bran	-	5
Wheat bran	3	-
Molasses	6	4
Limestone	0.55	1.05
Dicalcium phosphate	0.5	0.7
Salt	0.5	0.5
Premix	0.35	0.25

B. Test diet

Baby pig: 80% control diet + 20% yeast.
Young pig: Soybean meal and fish meal in control diet were replaced by yeast.

Table 10   The pH of the digesta of digestive tracts.

	Pig, baby (46 days)		Pig, young (4 months)	
	Control	Test	Control	Test
Stomach (cardiac gland region)	3.50	4.17	2.89	5.58
(pyloric gland region)			3.09	5.28
Duodenum	5.82	6.41	6.66	6.84
Jejunum	6.38	6.22	6.24	6.44
Ileum	7.03	6.85	-	-
Cecum	5.88	5.58	5.59	6.00
Rectum	5.96	5.74	5.72	5.86
Colon	6.09	6.29	5.78	5.87

Enzyme activities were expressed as units per gram of wet organ. Proteinase activity was found mainly in the stomach and the pancreas, and seemed to be a little higher in the test group than in

Table 11   Enzyme activities of the organ (pig, 46 days)

	Enzyme activities*							
	Proteinase		Chitinase		Ribonuclease		β-1,3-glucanase	
	Control	Test	Control	Test	Control	Test	Control	Test
Stomach	70	118	122	177	22	68	14	11
Pancreas	418	1,240	526	600	15,678	24,288	–	–
Duodenum	–	15	trace	trace	106	176	7	5
Jejunum	17	82	47	96	182	409	6	19
Ileum	135	170	trace	trace	122	97	26	24
Cecum	3	7	trace	trace	33	34	42	203
Rectum	4	5	trace	trace	29	48	54	205
Colon	4	21	trace	trace	39	60	37	164

* Units per g of wet organ.   – Not detectable

Table 12   Enzyme activities of the organ (pig, 4 months)

	Enzyme activities*							
	Proteinase		Chitinase		Ribonuclease		β-1,3-glucanase	
	Control	Test	Control	Test	Control	Test	Control	Test
Stomach	855	997	105	94	77	99	7	12
Pancreas	6,250	8,750	2,300	2,075	91,500	90,000	**	**
Duodenum	10	27	–	–	152	157	**	**
Jejunum	159	102	27	21	311	248	26	23
Ileum	–	–	–	–	–	–	15	3
Cecum	–	–	–	–	–	–	27	161
Rectum	–	–	–	–	–	–	22	56
Colon	–	–	–	–	–	–	18	136

* Units per g of wet organ.   ** Not detected.   – Not determined.

Table 13   Comparison of enzyme activities of pig (46 days) with pig (4 months).

		Proteinase		Chitinase		β-1,3-glucan-ase
		stomach	pancreas	stomach	pancreas	cecum
(A)*	Pig 46 days Control	70	418	122	525	42
	Pig 46 days Test	118	1,240	177	600	203
	Pig 4 months Control	855	6,250	105	2,300	27
	Pig 4 months Test	997	8,750	94	2,075	161
(B)**	Pig 46 days Control	30,070	11,555	56,002	14,603	6,156
	Pig 46 days Test	37,356	36,570	69,478	18,297	33,961
	Pig 4 months Control	700,355	440,750	85,055	164,065	16,092
	Pig 4 months Test	636,690	722,850	57,220	173,375	82,447

* Units per g of wet organ.
**Units per pig.

the control group.   Chitinase activity was found in the stomach, pancreas and jejunum.   Ribonuclease activity was very high in the pancreas.   β-1,3-glucanase activity was detected in the cecum, rectum and colon, and seemed to be much higher in the test group than in the control.

To compare the enzyme levels of baby pigs and those of young pigs, the values of proteinase, chitinase and β-1,3-glucanase activities in the main organs in Tables 11 and 12 were abstracted into Table 13A.   Table 13B shows converted enzyme levels per pig.   From Tables 13A and 13B, it may be said that young pigs had higher enzyme levels than baby pigs.

This fact may affect the digestibility and DE value of young and baby pigs.

Electron Microscopic Observation

Figures 7 to 12 show changes of yeast cell in each digestive tract of the pig, by the electron microscope.   Pigs of 4 months

S. Hibino et al.

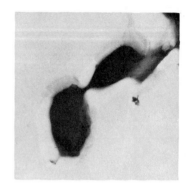

Fig. 7   Intact yeast.

Fig. 8   Yeast in stomach.

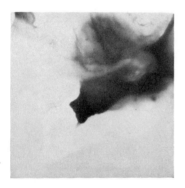

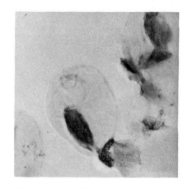

Fig. 9   Yeast in jejunum.

Fig. 10   Yeast in ileum.

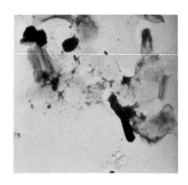

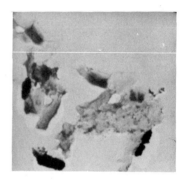

Fig. 11   Yeast residue in cecum.

Fig. 12   Yeast residue in rectum.

were fed with a diet containing 50% yeast.   After feeding for
one week, the pigs were killed to prepare specimens of the yeast
cell.

Figure 7 :   Intact yeast.

Figure 8 :   Yeast, in the stomach, almost unchanged.

Figure 9 :   Yeast in the jejunum.   The yeast is not sharp
in comparison with the intact cell.

Figure 10:   Yeast in the ileum.   Translucent cell-wall
residue can be seen.

Figure 11:   Yeast residue in the cecum.   Only digested particles can be seen.

Figure 12:   Yeast in the rectum.   The Figure is similar to
Fig. 11.

β-1,3-glucanase Producing Bacteria in the Cecum

β-1,3-glucanase, which was found at high levels in the cecum,
rectum and colon of the pig, was assumed to be secreted from bacteria in the digestive tracts.   The complexity of the microflora
in the cecum is well known.   Therefore, we especially investigated
β-1,3-glucanase producing bacteria in the cecum.

Table 14 shows microflora in the cecum of the pig.   Predomi-
nant bacteria were Streptococcus and Bacteroidaceae.

Table 15 shows cell numbers of bacteria producing β-1,3-
glucanase.   Cell numbers were expressed per gram of wet digesta
in the cecum: 10^7 to 10^8 bacteria producing glucanase per gram of
digesta were found.   The main bacteria were obligate anaerobic
rods.   Table 16 shows the main characteristics of the β-1,3-
glucanase producing bacteria;   from these characteristics, they
may belong to Bacteroidaceae.

Figures 13 and 14 show Gram stained β-1,3-glucanase producing
bacteria.

Figure 15 is a photograph of a plate-in-bottle.   The culture
plates, small pan with activated steel-wool and folded tissue
paper can be seen in the bottle.

E

S. Hibino et al.

Table 14   Microflora in the cecum (pig) (Cell numbers per gram of wet digesta).

	Control	Test
Yeast	3.4×10^3	$<10^5$
Mould	1.0×10^3	5.8×10^2
Enterobacteriaceae	2.4×10^7	2.9×10^8
Streptococcus	1.4×10^9	4.6×10^9
Staphylococcus	$< 10^5$	4.6×10^4
Corynebacterium	$< 10^7$	$< 10^8$
Bacillus	1.0×10^5	1.1×10^3
Lactobacillus	4.3×10^7	7.2×10^8
Bifidobacterium	$< 10^9$	$< 10^9$
Catenabacterium	1.4×10^8	5.8×10^5
Bacteroidaceae	2.8×10^9	1.4×10^9
Peotostreptococcus	$< 10^9$	1.4×10^8
Clostridium	$< 10^9$	2.9×10^8
Veillonella	$< 10^8$	$< 10^9$
Spirillaceae	$< 10^9$	1.4×10^6
Spirochaetaceae	$< 10^9$	$< 10^9$
Total	4.4×10^9	7.4×10^9
GNase$^+$	2.9×10^7	1.1×10^8

Table 15   Cell numbers producing β-1,3-glucanase.

Medium		Control	Test	Incubation method
M 10	Total*	2.0×10^9	3.7×10^9	Plate-in-bottle
M 1OL	Total	2.3×10^8	5.3×10^9	method. (Anaerobic) (Mitsuoka et al.,
	GNase^{+**}	1.3×10^7	1.1×10^8	1969)
EG	Total	1.0×10^8	7.2×10^9	Steel wool method
EGF	Total	1.2×10^8	2.7×10^9	(Parker, 1955), replaced air with
EGFL	Total	7.9×10^7	2.0×10^9	CO_2.
	GNase$^+$	2.9×10^7	$>1.4 \times 10^6$	(Anaerobic)
TS	Total	2.7×10^7	1.4×10^9	
TSF	Total	5.5×10^7	1.7×10^9	Aerobic
TSFL	Total	4.0×10^7	1.4×10^9	
	GNase$^+$	$>1.4 \times 10^3$	$>1.4 \times 10^4$	

* Total cell numbers per g of wet digesta in cecum.
** Cell numbers producing β-1,3-glucanase per g of wet digesta in cecum.

Table 16   Some characteristics of β-1,3-glucanase producing bacteria isolated from cecum.

Gram stain	-
Anaerobic growth	+
Aerobic growth	-
Spore	-
Cell form	Rod, Pleomorphism
Motility	-

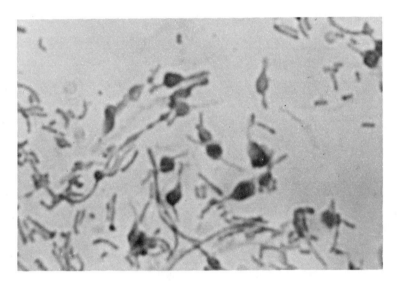

Fig. 13   Gram stain of a bacterium producing β-1,3-glucanase (strain L₅).

STUDIES ON FRESH-WATER FISH

Chemical Composition of Foods for Aquatic Animals

Table 17 shows the chemical analysis of the yeast from n-paraffin, fish meal and some natural foods for fish.   All, except fish meal, contain chitin.

Enzyme Levels

Figures 16 and 17 show the enzyme activities of each organ in *ayu*, carp, rainbow trout and eel.   These four kinds of fresh-water fish are most popular in Japan and they can be cultured by

S. Hibino et al.

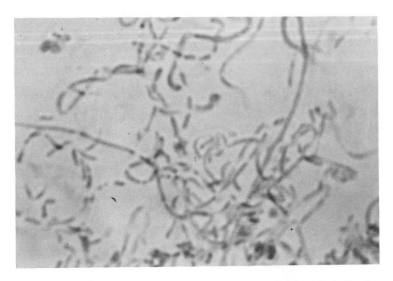

Fig. 14   Gram stain of a bacterium producing β-1,3-glucanase
(strain 1L-2).

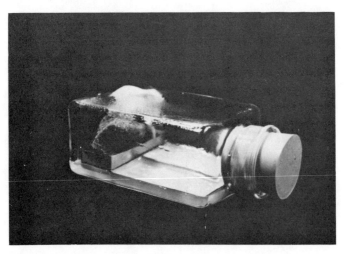

Fig. 15   Plate-in-bottle.

formula feeds.   *Ayu* is found only in Far East Asia;   it resembles
trout, but is smaller.

Peptic activity and tryptic activity were very high in the
eel and *ayu*, respectively.   Chitinase activity was found in these

Table 17 Chemical composition of yeasts, fish meal and some natural foods for aquatic animals. (% on dry-air basis)

	Yeast from n-paraffin		Daphnia		Rotifera	Artemia*	Diatom	Fish meal
	A	B	D**	I***				
Hexosamine	2.0	1.4	3.3	2.9	3.6	0.6	1.1	(0.4)[(a)]
Crude protein	50.7	59.6	56.1	48.2	51.7	49.9	30.1	67.7
Crude fat	8.4	8.7	13.2	9.3	12.8	28.4	7.1	5.7

*   Immediately after hatching.
** Domestic product.
*** Imported product.

(a) May not be derived from chitin.

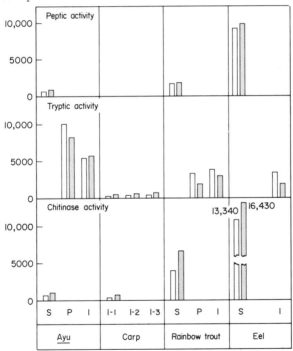

Fig. 16 Enzyme levels of fresh-water fish.   S: stomach, P: pyloric caeca, I: intestine. ▭: Control, ▬: Test. Enzyme activities are expressed as units per g of wet organ.

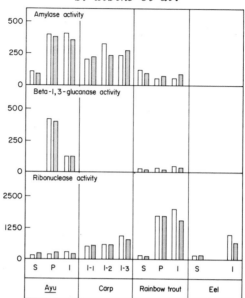

Fig. 17   Enzyme levels of fresh-water fish.   S: stomach,
P: pyloric caeca, I: intestine. ▭ : Control, ▬ :
Test.   Enzyme activities are expressed as units per g of wet
organ.

four fish and was very high, especially in the eel and in the

rainbow trout.   β-1,3-glucanase and ribonuclease activity were

very high in *ayu* and rainbow trout, respectively.

Chitinase-Producing Bacteria

Chitinase and chitinase-producing bacteria in marine fish

are already reported by Okutani (10).   Chitinase-producing bac-

teria were isolated from the digestive tracts of fresh-water

fish in relatively highly frequencies.

The common characteristics of the chitinase-producing bac-

teria are shown in Table 18.   From these characteristics, the

bacteria may be considered to belong to Aeromonas.

Table 18   Common morphological and biochemical characteristics of chitinase-producing bacteria isolated from fresh-water fish.

Form	Rod
Gram stain	-
Motility	+
Flagellation	Single, polar flagellate
Relation to oxygen	Facultatively anaerobic
Hugh and Leifson test	Fermentative
Reduction of nitrate	+
Production of indole	+
Liquefaction of gelatin	+
Hydrolysis of casein	+
Hydrolysis of starch	+
Susceptibility to 0/129	-
Cytochrome oxidase	+
Catalase	+ or (+)
Chitinase	+
Growth at 37°C	+

+ Positive reaction; - Negative reaction; ( ) Weak reaction

DISTRIBUTION AND LOCALIZATION OF SOME ENZYMES IN THE ANIMALS STUDIED

Table 19 shows a summary of the distribution and localization of proteinase, chitinase and β-1,3-glucanase.

Proteinase activity was higher in the pyloric caeca of *ayu* and in the stomach of the eel than in the other fresh-water fish. Proteinase activities of the pig and the chicken are also shown in Table 19.

Chitinase activity was higher in the stomach of rainbow trout and eel than in the other fish. Chitinase activity was very high in the glandular stomach of chickens and in the stomach and pancreas of pigs.

β-1,3-glucanase activity was very high only in the pyloric caeca of *ayu* among the fish, and it cannot be detected in chickens. In the pig, it was very high in the cecum, rectum and colon.

S. Hibino et al.

Table 19   Distribution and localization of enzymes.

		Proteinase	Chitinase	Glucanase
Ayu	stomach	+	+	-
	pyloric caeca	++++	-	+++
	intestine	+++	-	++
Carp	intestine	+	+	t
Rainbow trout	stomach	+	+++	t
	pyloric caeca	++	-	t
	intestine	++	t	+
Eel	stomach	+++	++++	-
	intestine	+	t	-
Chicken	gland stomach	+++	+++	-
	gizzard	+	+	-
	pancreas	++++	t	-
	duodenum	+	+	-
	small intestine	++	+	-
	cecum	+	+	-
Pig	stomach	+++	++	t
	pancreas	++++	+++	-
	duodenum	t	t	t
	jejunum	+	+	t
	ileum	+	t	t
	cecum	t	t	++
	rectum	t	t	++
	colon	t	t	++

++++ very strong;   +++ strong;   ++ fairly strong;
  + detectable;   - not detectable;   t trace.

CONCLUSION

The observation of the change of yeast in guts by electron microscope showed that changes of cell were recognized in the organs, except the stomach. Especially, changes of cell in the cecum, rectum and colon of the pig were much more remarkable than in those of the chicken.

The results of the enzyme assay showed that: (i) pig, chicken, eel and rainbow trout had high activities of chitinase;

and (ii) pigs and *ayu* had high activities of β-1,3-glucanase.

There is much information which shows the excellent effectiveness of these two enzymes on the digestion of yeast (7,8,9).

It is noteworthy that chickens had no detectable activities of glucanase in the cecum, rectum and colon, but that pigs had high activities of glucanase in those organs. Microbiological examination of the cecum of pigs showed the existence of glucanase-producing bacteria which may belong to Bacteroidaceae. These facts may cause the different digestibility of yeast for chickens and pigs.

Young birds and young pigs had much more enzyme activities than baby ones, which fact may, perhaps, cause the better digestibility of yeast in young animals.

DISCUSSION

As reported previously by Jeuniaux, chitinase is present in the digestive tracts of vertebrates such as goldfish and bats (11). In our experiment, we recognized that chickens, pigs and fresh-water fish had chitinase, and that *ayu* and pigs had β-1,3-glucanase. It is natural that these animals have such enzymes, considering their natural foods, e.g. insects and earthworms for chickens, plankton and algae for fresh-water fish, etc.

It is interesting that animals fed with yeast from n-paraffin had much greater activity of a few enzymes, e.g. glucanase in the pig, chintinase in the eel and rainbow trout, than had the control animals.

In comparison with the good digestibility of yeast from n-paraffin, the low digestibility of other single cell proteins, e.g. chlorella, etc., is well known. It is fortunate that pigs, chickens and fish have such effective enzymes for yeast digestion as chitinase and glucanase. So, the yeast from n-paraffin may be practically available as a feed for livestock, poultry and fish.

S. Hibino et al.

ACKNOWLEDGEMENTS

We wish to thank S. Otsuka and T. Onihara of ZEN-NOH who have determined the digestibilities of yeast in chickens and pigs. We also wish to thank those research members of the Fish Laboratories at Nagano, Osaka, Shiga in Japan, who kindly provided fish.

REFERENCES

1. Shacklady, C.A. *et al.* *14th World Poultry Congress*, Madrid (1970).

2. van Weerden, E.J. *et al.* *8th International Nutrition Congress*, Prague (1969).

3. van der Wal, P. *et al.* *8th International Nutrition Congress*, Prague (1969).

4. Otsuka, S. *et al.* *14th World Poultry Congress*, Madrid (1970).

5. Onihara, T. *et al.* *58th Japanese Zootechnical Science Congress*, Chiba, Japan (1970).

6. Phaff, H.J. *Ann. Rev. Microbiol.* **17**, 15-30 (1963).

7. Bacon, J.S.D., Farmer, V.C., Jones, D. and Taylor, I.F. *Biochem. J.* **114**, 557-567 (1969).

8. Domanski, R.E. and Miller, R.E. *J. Bacteriol.* **96**, 270-271 (1968).

9. Monreal, J., de Uruburu, F. and Villanueva, J.R. *J. Bacteriol.* **94**, 241-244 (1967).

10. Okutani, K. *Bull. Misaki Marine Biol. Inst. (Kyoto Univ.)* **10**, 1-47 (1966).

11. Jeuniaux, C. *Nature* **192**, 135-136 (1961).

RESPONSE OF LIVESTOCK AND POULTRY TO SCP

C.A. Shacklady

BP Proteins Limited, London, England

INTRODUCTION

The object of this paper is to try and cover the use in animal feeds of bacteria and yeasts grown on hydrocarbons and simple derivatives of hydrocarbons. For this reason, no mention will be made of algal and fungal protein preparations which, in any event, seem intended by their producers for direct administration to humans. With regard to the yeasts grown on hydrocarbons, the bulk of the references will be to the work carried out on the products made by BP Proteins since this is not only the most extensive but also that of which I have direct knowledge. Furthermore, they are the only ones currently being used on a regular commercial basis as far as I am aware.

There are two ways in which this subject may be approached. One is to consider it in terms of a particular type of SCP and discuss the use of this for various classes of stock. The other is to classify the stock and consider the application of the various types of SCP to these classes. I think the former treatment is better adapted to a relatively short paper and so I have chosen to adopt it. The forms of SCP to be discussed, therefore, will be:-

i)   Bacteria grown on methane.

ii) Bacteria grown on methanol.

iii) Yeasts grown on alkanes either as pure n-alkanes or the n-alkanes in a middle distillate fraction.

BACTERIA GROWN ON METHANE

At the time of writing there is no commercial production of such material although one oil company has announced that it is working in this field.   Relatively little published work appears to exist regarding the use of methane oxidising bacteria for animals possibly due to the small scale on which the preparations have been made.   D'Mello (1) in 1972 published a study of the amino acid composition of 6 strains of methane utilising bacteria from which he suggests an assessment of their potential use in animal feeds might be made.   The most evident difference between these organisms and the yeasts grown on hydrocarbons is the generally higher level of nitrogen in the bacteria.   Methionine is higher and lysine lower as a percentage of the protein in bacteria compared with the yeasts.

In a later paper, D'Mello (2) describes the use of one of these strains, *Methylomonas albus*, as a source of protein for young chicks.   The experiment was on a small scale and of short duration, presumably due to limitation in the amount of material available, but D'Mello concluded that there were no significant differences in growth, feed conversion efficiency or nitrogen retention between the control group and that in which 10% of the bacterial protein replaced - mainly - its equivalent in soya bean meal.   He suggested that the strain of bacteria used in his study is potentially a useful source of protein for non-ruminant animals.

BACTERIA GROWN ON METHANOL

Rather more information is available on these materials since the publication of the paper by Maclennan and co-workers (3) and the communication of Stringer and Litchfield (4) to the Federation of European Biochemical Societies (FEBS) in April 1973, the latter being more detailed from the point of view of experimental results. The organism used is a strain of *Pseudomonas* and appears to have compositional characteristics not unlike the methane utilising bacteria described by D'Mello, that is to say a high nitrogen and methionine content but a relatively modest content of lysine.

Stringer and Litchfield quote the result of a short-term toxicity trial with rats and say that no pathological changes were noted at a dietary level of approximately 15% of their SCP. Results of experiments with broilers and pigs lead to their claim that it may form up to 10% of the total diet with no deleterious effect.

YEASTS GROWN ON ALKANES

This class of SCP has been investigated much more thoroughly than any other so far, not only by its producers but also by research institutes, university departments and feed manufacturers. The initial announcement by BP of their activity in this field stimulated others to follow their lead and most major oil companies in Europe and the USA have done some work in it at some stage or other. In addition it is known that the USSR and several Central European countries have worked on hydrocarbon fermentation though the practical results of their work is a little difficult to determine. However, apart from BP, those who seem to have made the most progress in approaching a commercial process have been the Japanese. It is of interest to note, in passing, that in Japan it is the petrochemical and fermentation industries rather than the oil industry which has taken up this new technology.

As stated previously, most of my examples of the use of these materials will refer to the BP products since, within this class, they represent the most extensively tested products. Indeed it is virtually certain that no other feed ingredient has ever been

C.A. Shacklady

Table 1   Characteristics of alkane-grown yeasts.

	Yeast G	Yeast L
Moisture % wt.	7.0	8
Crude Protein (N × 6.25) % wt. on dry matter	60	68-70
Lipids after acid hydrolysis % wt.	8-10	1.5-2.5
Ash % wt.	6.0	7.9
Ca % wt.	0.01	0.3
P % wt.	1.6	1.5
Pepsin digestibility %	80	80

tested so rigorously and with such good results as these before
now.   You may have noticed that I use the plural form since
there are two basic products.   One was developed at Lavera on
the alkanes contained in a middle distillate fraction and I shall
refer to this as Yeast L.   The other was developed at Grange-
mouth on a substrate of pure linear alkanes.   This is referred
to as Yeast G.   Both are now commercially available under the
brand name TOPRINA.

You will notice that the main difference in gross analysis
between G and L is in the higher protein content of L and the
higher lipid and hence energy content of G.

The amino acid patterns of the two yeasts are not identical
but, in my view, the differences are so small as not to be of
nutritional significance.

One point I wish to stress is that in the normal process
of feed formulation these differences in protein and energy are
automatically allowed for and, when this is done, we can find no
difference in nutritional performance between the two products.
In other words, both behave quite predictably and in accordance
with the nutritional characteristics determined on the individual
yeasts.

I shall not attempt to describe in detail the experiments
carried out over the last 8 years.   The fundamental work was

Table 2   Amino acid content of BP yeasts, fish meal and soya bean meal in grams per 16 grams nitrogen.

Amino acid	Yeast G	Yeast L	Fish meal	Extracted soya bean meal
Isoleucine	5.1	5.3	4.6	5.4
Leucine	7.4	7.8	7.3	7.7
Phenylalanine	4.3	4.8	4.0	5.1
Tryosine	3.6	4.0	2.9	2.7
Threonine	4.9	5.4	4.2	4.0
Tryptophan	1.4	1.3	1.2	1.5
Valine	5.9	5.8	5.2	5.0
Arginine	5.1	5.0	5.0	7.7
Histidine	2.1	2.1	2.3	2.4
Lysine	7.4	7.8	7.0	6.5
Cystine	1.1	0.9	1.0	1.4
Methionine	1.8	1.6	2.6	1.4
Total S-acids	2.9	2.5	3.6	2.8

conducted in collaboration with Dr. van der Wal and his colleagues in Wageningen and is continuing.   It has been extended now to other institutes and commercial organisations in France, Holland, Germany, Denmark, Norway, Italy, Belgium, Australia, the USA and the United Kingdom.   We are now permitted to use one or other of the BP yeasts for animal feed purposes in all of the EEC countries with the exception of Luxembourg and the Republic of Ireland to which application is only now being made.

Since the first communication of the animal feeding experiments was made in Addis Ababa in 1967, a number of publications has come from our collaborative work with ILOB (Instituut voor Landbouwkundig Onderzoek van Biochemische Producten) in Wageningen and, whilst not exhaustive, a representative list of these is given in the References (5-11).

The main areas of activity have been with poultry, pigs and calves, although work has been done with other species also.

A.   *Poultry*

Experiments with practical diets for broilers have shown that

TOPRINA G or L can form up to 20% by weight of the total diet, replacing all other major protein sources without reducing growth rate, feed conversion efficiency or carcase quality. In experimental, semi-synthetic diets, where the yeasts are the only sources of protein, up to 30% may be used satisfactorily.

The normal protein requirements of laying and breeding birds is met when yeast at 12-14% dietary levels forms the sole high protein source and performance on these diets is at least as good as that on control diets based on fish and soya bean meals. In our experiments we have used up to 20% of yeast in the diet of such birds over several generations simply to demonstrate the margin of safety that it enjoys. Performance was entirely normal in every respect but there is no nutritional advantage in using such a high level of yeast. Having demonstrated the safety of this level over 3 generations we have reverted to the more practical level of 12-14% for the remaining generations and have no plans for discontinuing this work which has now attained the 6th successive generation.

In Japan Yoshida *et al.* (12) have described the use of hydrocarbon grown yeasts from four manufacturers (unnamed) for the first generation of breeding hens in what is presumed to be a multiple generation study. According to the summary of their experiment, in which 15% dietary levels of yeast were used, they encounted no nutritional or toxicological problems.

In the United Kingdom and in France the yeasts have been used very successfully in rations for turkeys at various levels up to 10% of the total diet.

Apart from the work at ILOB, Shannon and McNab (13) have reported excellent results in a broiler finisher diet when 20% of TOPRINA replaced all the fish meal (3%) and soya bean meal (22%) in the control ration.

Lewis and Boorman (14) have also described their work on TOPRINA at Nottingham during the Versailles Congress on Animal

Production. Their results agree with those obtained at ILOB.

B. *Pigs*

Pigs have been fed at ILOB in a multiple generation study in which the breeding sows and boars received 10% of yeast in their diets and the weaners, 15%. After weaning they have been taken to slaughter on diets containing 7.5 or 15% of yeast. In all cases comparison was made with a yeast-free control diet. The results are summarised in Tables 3, 4 and 5.

As with the poultry, these experiments are continuing.

In the UK Barber *et al.* (15) have shown that alkane grown yeast can replace fish meal on a weight-for-weight basis in the standard NIRD diet. More recently Braude has shown that this is still true even when no supplementary methionine is added to the yeast.

Oslage (16) in Germany, Faustini (17) in Italy, Nielsen (18, 19) and Madsen (20) in Denmark have all reported favourably on the use of alkane grown yeast in pig rations. Nielsen's latest experiment is of particular interest since he showed that, for early (21 days) weaned pigs, a diet with 28.7% of TOPRINA and 58.3% tapioca meal gave at least as good results after 10 weeks as the traditional Danish diet based on fish meal, dried skim milk, whey and barley.

In France Gaye and Maol (21) have described their experiments with pigs and Hoshiai (22) includes the result of his work with pigs in a paper from Japan.

C. *Calves*

Experiments on calves fall into two categories, one is concerned with the veal calf, the other with the calf intended for beef or as a dairy herd replacement. The former invariably requires the feeding of a liquid diet, the latter may include both liquid and solid feeds.

Veal calf production is of considerable importance in Italy, France, Holland and Germany and the use of substitutes for dried

Table 3   Average number of pigs per litter and birth weight.

	Total no. of piglets	No. of litters	Average no. per litter	Average birth wt. (grams)
Control group	1545	154	10.03	1315
10% yeast group	1446	141	10.26	1232

Table 4   Weight gain in suckling period.

	Weight gain (grams per day)
Control group	345
15% yeast group	347

Table 5   Average daily weight gain and feed conversion efficiency.

	Average daily wt. gain (grams) weaning (25 kg) to slaughter (110 kg)	Average feed conversion efficiency (kg feed per kg liveweight gain)
Control group 1	664	3.11
7.5% yeast group	678	3.04
Control group 2	666	3.09
15% yeast group	689	2.99

milk is the subject of a great deal of research in view of the
price and supply position with milk products.   Our own work in
this field has been concentrated essentially in Holland and France
and the results are very encouraging.   In general terms we find
that 20% of dried skim milk can be replaced by an approximately

equipart mixture of yeast and dried whey.

Even higher levels of replacement are feasible from the nutritional point of view, the first limiting factor being a non-nutritional one, i.e. some reddening of the flesh of the calf. This is being overcome in two ways: one is by reducing the level of available iron in the yeast; the other is by the use of chelating agents in the milk replacer mixture.

As far as rearing calves is concerned, there is no such limitation on carcase colouration and our colleagues in France have succeeded in effecting the total replacement of skim milk in the rations of these animals. This has involved the use of about 28% of yeast in the mixture. A slightly lower level has also been used quite successfully in similar circumstances in the United Kingdom. In Italy, Mazzarracchio has just commenced a study with calves but no results are available at this stage.

In terms of actual growth rate, the diet containing 28% of yeast produced an average daily gain of 950 grams which is quite satisfactory in absolute terms and extremely good when it is remembered that the ration contained no dried skim milk at all.

D. *Other Young Stock*

In many areas lambs are much more important than calves and we have recently been interested in the use of TOPRINA in the liquid and solid feeding of young lambs. Some success has been achieved by our associates in France in the use of liquid milk replacers and this aspect is being developed.

Of direct interest to Italy is the work being done at Sassari by Mura, Rossi, Lucifero and their associates as part of a programme designed at the request of the Ministry of Health via its Veterinary Directorate in conjunction with the Ministry of Agriculture and co-ordinated by the Istituto Superiore di Sanita.

The Sassari experiments have indicated that 15% of TOPRINA can replace, quite effectively, its nutritional equivalent of fish and soya bean meals in the rations of early weaned lambs and,

indeed, may have certain advantages which could lead to even
earlier weaning being practical.   Preliminary observations on
the results have already been communicated by Mura and Rossi to
a Veterinary Conference in Lodi, Italy and the full report is in
the course of preparation.   The experiments are continuing.

At ILOB we have obtained excellent rates of growth with piglets weaned at 3 days of age on to liquid feeds containing 10%
TOPRINA.   In another experiment at the same institute the use
of the same diet in solid form was also successful but did not
give quite as high a rate of growth as the liquid diet.   It is,
however, probably more practical in its application to current
feeding systems.

E.   *Various Other Animals*

In addition to those already mentioned, alkane grown yeast
has been used, to a lesser extent, in a variety of animals.
Corrias (23) in Turin has used TOPRINA as the sole high protein
source in the rations of breeding bulls at the AI centre there.
Results have been indistinguishable from those on more conventional diets in terms of semen production and potency.

The same worker has also incorporated up to 30% of TOPRINA
in the feed of trout and reports very good results.   This con-
firms the report of Hoshiai (*loc. cit.*) on results obtained in
Japan with other varieties of fish.   It appears that there is
great potential for the use of SCP in this field.

In France, commercial manufacturers have shown that a level
of 10% of yeast in their formulations for rabbit feeding is quite
acceptable.

The use of up to 30% in the rations of Japanese quail over
many generations has been described by de Groot.   Twenty generations have now been produced.

Finally, the most recent use for TOPRINA is in dry feeds for
mink and here again the early indications are encouraging.

In summary, therefore, we are justified in saying that, as

far as we know, there is no species of livestock - whether mammalian, avian or fish -for which SCP in the form of TOPRINA is unsuitable.

I have chosen my words very carefully in the last sentence because I can speak only for the two products with which I have been associated. This does not mean that any and every SCP will behave in a similar manner and it is for that reason that each preparation must be evaluated separately both as regards its safety and its nutritional value. In absolute terms, it is the safety of a product which is more important. Its nutritional value represents its worth in the market place and the market is well able to take care of itself in that respect. But it must be assured that it is handling a material that has been shown - by procedures already discussed - to be "safe" - as this term is generally understood.

CONCLUSION

Although this paper has dealt mainly with alkane grown yeasts there appears no reason why other SCP should not be used equally successfully once they have been shown to be non-toxic, provided that their individual nutritional characteristics are accorded due regard.

The fact that these materials are, in some cases, new in themselves or are produced by novel methods is absolutely no reason for judging them by different - and more severe - standards than those applied to products already in use. A great deal of play has been made, for instance, about the relatively high nucleic acid content of some SCP and the fact that some of the organisms contained uneven numbered fatty acid chains. In the case of organisms grown on hydrocarbons, some rather ill-informed comments on potential carcinogenicity have been made from time to time.

As regards nucleic acids I cannot believe that there exists

any biochemist unaware of the difference in the way in which
these are metabolised by man on the one hand and domesticated
farm animals on the other.   What might be something of a metabolic embarrassment - not toxic - to man presents no problems
with lower species of animal.   In terms of animal nutrition,
the nucleic acid content of SCP is almost totally irrelevant.

Uneven numbered fatty acids are not only perfectly natural
products, and metabolised in the normal manner, but are quite
widely distributed in nature.   Anyone drinking milk is getting
a reasonable intake of them and those who have any doubts about
the normality of odd numbered fats might seek enlightenment from
the work of Schlenk (24) and others.

The absence of carcinogens and carcinogenic activity - certainly in the TOPRINA products - has been demonstrated by the
analyses of Grimmer (25) and by the long-term feeding studies
with rats conducted by de Groot, Til and Feron at the Central
Instituut voor Voedingsonderzoek (CIVO) at Zeist in Holland.

I confess that I am at a loss to understand the reasoning
of those who hesitate to give wholehearted approval to materials
which have been tested as exhaustively as certain of these Single
Cell Proteins and yet do not see anything incongruous in accepting, for instance, maize which has been deliberately genetically
altered - as in the case of opaque 2 - without bothering to
determine what other effects this genetic manipulation may have
had.

In assessing the evidence relating to the safety of any new
produce, reasonable caution is desirable, excessive demands are
not.   All it may do is delay the advent of a useful feed ingredient on to the market.   Toxicology and nutrition both have their
place in the scientific appraisal of a product but neither is, nor
ever has been a substitute for common sense.

ACKNOWLEDGEMENT

Permission to publish this paper has been given by The British Petroleum Company Limited.

REFERENCES

1.   D'Mello, J.P.F. *Jour. Appl. Bact.* 35 (1), 145-148 (1972).

2.   D'Mello, J.P.F. *Br. Poult. Sci.* 14, 291-301 (1973).

3.   MacLennan, D.G., Gow, J.S. and Stringer, D.A. *Process Bioch.*, 22-24 (June, 1973).

4.   Stringer, D.A. and Litchfield, M.H. FEBS Meeting, Dublin, 15-19 April 1973 (1973).

5.   van der Wal, P. and Shacklady, C.A. *2nd World Cong. Animal Prod.*, Maryland (1968).

6.   Shacklady, C.A. *Biotech. & Bioeng. Symp.* 1, 77-97, Interscience Pub. (1969).

7.   Shacklady, C.A. *Proc. 3rd Int. Cong. Fd. Sci. & Technol.* 743-747 (1970).

8.   van Weerden, E.J. and Shacklady, C.A. *Br. Poult. Sci.* II, 189-195 (1970).

9.   van der Wal, P., van Hellemond, K.K., Shacklady, C.A. and van Weerden, E.J. *Proc. Xth Int. Cong. Anim. Prod.*, Versailles (1971).

10. Shacklady, C.A. *World Rev. Nutr. & Dietetics* 14, 154-179 (1972).

11. Shacklady, C.A. and Gatumel, E. "Proteins from Hydrocarbons," Academic Press, pp. 27-52 (1972).

12. Yoshida, M., Tada, M., Bansho, H., Matsushima, M., Ogata, K., Iion, M. and Umeda, I. *Japan Poult. Sci.* 9, 173-181 (1972).

13. Shannon, D.W.F. and McNab, J.M. *Br. Poult. Sci.* 13, 267-272 (1972).

14. Lewis, D. and Boorman, K.R. *Proc. Xth Int. Cong. Anim. Prod.* (1971).

15. Barber, R.S., Braude, R., Mitchell, K.G. and Myers, A.W. *Br. J. Nutr.* 25, 285-294 (1971).

16. Oslage, H. Report to German Min. of Agriculture (1971).

17. Faustini, R. Personal communication (1973).

18. Nielsen, H.E. and Danielson, V. Danish Research Inst. Yearbook, pp. 35-38 (1971).

19. Nielsen, H.E., Sriwaramand, P., Danielsen, V. and Eggum, B. B.   Danish Research Inst. Yearbook (in preparation) (1973).

20. Madsen, A., Mortensen, N.P. and Larsen, A.E.   Danish Research Inst. Yearbook (1971).

21. Gaye, A. and Moal, J.   *Proc. Jour. Rech. Porc en France*, 169-173 (1972).

22. Hoshiai, K.   *Chem. Econ. & Eng. Rev.* $\underline{3}$, 7-15 (1972).

23. Corrias, A.   Personal communication (1973).

24. Schlenk, H.   *Fed. Proc.* $\underline{31}$, No.5, 1430 (1972).

25. Grimmer, G. and Wilhelm, G.   *Dtsch. Lebensmitt. Rdsch.* $\underline{8}$, 229-231 (1969).

THE PLACE OF SCP IN MAN'S DIET

Doris Howes Calloway

Department of Nutritional Sciences
University of California, Berkeley, USA

The increasing pressures of population and predicted food shortages have created a demand for new sources of human nutrition. This demand has focused ever-increasing attention on the possible use of single-cell organisms to supplant the normal human diet, rather than to supplement it in the traditional way.

Microorganisms are technologically attractice, in large part, because as Dr. Ganzin has noted they offer the promise of increased food production without reliance on traditional agricultural methods. Moreover, according to Prof. Gaden, some may serve a secondary role as biological processors of human and industrial wastes. Algae, for example, are able to provide edible, protein-rich cells as a by-product of sewage treatment, while some yeasts of the *Torulopsis* genera flourish in bagasse or sulphite-rich residues from paper production. Recent attention has concentrated on yeasts that may be grown on petroleum. Some bacteria flourish in methane and a wide variety of other substrates; bacteria could serve as sources of protein or as producers of specific supplementary amino acids to be added to vegetable proteins.

CONTRAINDICATIONS

But the use of single-cell proteins (SCP) directly as human food may be hampered by several serious shortcomings. Man has

learned to use bacteria, yeasts and molds in food processing but
many of these potential SCP sources contain pharmacoactive or
toxic substances.   While some of these endogenous toxins are
normally consumed at low concentrations without obvious detriment
to man, major dependence on one or several biomasses could elevate the dietary intake to toxic levels.   It is also possible
that SCP grown on waste products, such as sewage, or on petroleum
fractions, could sequester various toxins from the medium.   (It
is, of course, only fair to note that potential toxicity is not
an exclusive property of SCP.   Legumes contain a variety of undesirable and unsafe compounds that must be reduced in preparatory
procedures.)   Processing methods used to remove toxicants must
be thorough and complete reliable, as Dr. Hoogerheide has noted.
This inevitably adds to the cost and competitive position of the
final product, a point that Dr. Abbott has discussed.

Nor are most sources of SCP as digestible as we might wish.
(Another property shared to a variable extent with plant sources
of protein.)   In this regard, we must consider both the production of certain indigestible compounds such as intracellular
polymerized lipids and cellulose and other structural components
of cell walls.   We should perhaps also note that an edible substance is not always a palatable one.   Prepared *Aerobacter
aerogenes*, for example, tends to become unpleasantly slimy when
wet.

In human feeding studies consumption of certain SCP sources
has led to a wide range of gastrointestinal complaints, from relatively mild symptoms such as bulky stools and flatulence to more
serious nausea, vomiting and diarrhea.   Particularly distressing
to us as investigators is the fact that killed and purified bacterial cells caused these adverse reactions in man but not in any
of an array of animal species tested.   Other pathophysiologic
reactions have also been noted, such as peeling of the skin of the
palms of the hands and soles of the feet and itching, pain and

edema of the great toe. These latter symptoms may be due to the high nucleic acid content of the cells. It is this factor that perhaps constitutes a universal and major limitation to the use of SCP as food for man, unless safe processes for nucleic acid removal prove to be economically competitive.

Uric Acid

The final metabolic product formed in man from the purine moiety of the nucleic acids is uric acid (Fig. 1). Uric acid is only slightly soluble at physiologic pH's and if the blood uric acid content is elevated, crystals may form in the joints, causing gout or gouty arthritis. With excessive renal clearance loads, solubility of uric acid in urine may be exceeded and stones may be deposited in the urinary tract.

These problems have not been reported when SCP has been fed to experimental and farm animals. Most mammals degrade uric acid further, to the more soluble compound, allantoin, which is easily excreted. However, swine are unable to oxidize one of the purines, guanine, and are susceptible to development of guanine-gout on the same basis of poor solubility. Birds do form uric acid, as man does, but at the levels normally present, this compound serves a useful role in regulating water loss from the cloaca.

In man, the level of uric acid found in the plasma and urine is affected by two main factors: the purine and protein contents of the diet. (We are not considering here individuals with gouty tendency, genetic disorders and the like.) In our studies, 75 g protein per day is considered a control diet. We found the average urinary uric acid excretion of men fed a purine-free control diet to be about 350 to 400 mg per day; their plasma contained about 50 mcg uric acid per ml. Urinary excretion was less, 300 to 350 mg per day, and plasma uric acid was higher, 60 mcg/ml, when a protein-free diet was fed. Similar values were observed with feeding of 22 to 37 g protein per day. Steady

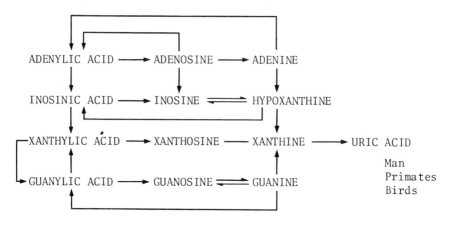

Fig. 1   Pathways of nucleic acid metabolism.

state, endogenous uric acid production of men with marginal
levels of protein intake thus appears to be the amount present
in the urine, 350 mg per day with 20% coefficient of variation,
plus about 100 to 300 mg per day degraded by intestinal bacteria.
The small increase in plasma level with low-protein feeds we believe to be due to diminished plasma volume rather than increased
body pool size, but have no direct evidence on this point.

Urinary uric acid output increases linearly with increased
intake of purine-free protein, but plasma uric acid level is unchanged or decreased.   Urinary uric acid excretion with 300 and
600 g protein in the diet differed from the control (75 g protein)
by factors of 2.3 and 3.1, respectively.   At the highest level
of intake, daily output was 1253 mg and great care had to be
taken to maintain urine pH on the alkaline side and the volume
high enough to prevent crystallization.

Addition of nucleoprotein or nucleic acids to the diet results

not only in increased urinary uric acid excretion but also in
marked elevation of plasma uric acid.   To quantify this effect,
we added 2, 4 and 8 g yeast ribonucleic acid (RNA) to the control
diet.   Urinary uric acid excretion increased by 147 mg for each
gram of RNA added.   With 2 g RNA in the diet, urinary uric acid
was 670 mg and similar to excretions reported with normal diets
that include moderate amounts of meat and vegetables.   At the
8 g level, urinary uric acid was 1393 mg, indicating that a four-
fold increase in dietary RNA (taking 2 g as a "normal" intake)
has a more marked effect on urinary uric acid than does an eight-
fold increase in dietary protein.   Plasma uric acid was increased
from 50 to 60 mcg/ml with 2 g RNA but all values fell within normal limits.   With 4 g RNA added, all men tested had values above
accepted upper limits and the average was 77 mcg/ml.   Values
rose to 94 mcg/ml at the highest level of RNA.

A third study using ^{15}N-labeled uric acid to measure uric
acid pool size and turnover rate has helped to explain the difference in response to protein and nucleic acid.   A control
diet was fed with and without 4 g yeast RNA and a purine-free
diet containing 390 g protein.   Urinary uric acid was 388 mg
with the control diet, 1095 mg with high protein and 1043 mg with
RNA.   Plasma values were 51, 53 and 92 mcg/ml, respectively.
During the control diet period, uric acid pool size was found to
be 1100 mg and turnover time was 1.7 days.   The high-protein
diet had no effect on pool size (1170 mg) but caused a sharp increase in turnover rate, reducing the time to 0.88 days.   In
contrast, RNA had no major effect on turnover time (1.3 days)
but caused nearly a doubling of pool size, to 1890 mg.   These
data indicate that dietary RNA exerts no feedback inhibition of
endogenous synthesis.   These findings suggest further that in
healthy men, dietary protein free of nucleic acid would not be
expected to increase risk of gout whereas dietary RNA would do
so.   Both substances would increase the risk of renal stone for-

mation.

Clifford *et al.* have reported that the various purines do
not have equivalent hyperuricemic effects.   Hypoxanthine (0.1
mM/kg body weight) was stated to increase plasma uric acid by
25 mcg/ml, adenine by 16 mcg, xanthine by 7 mcg and guanine by
only 2 mcg.   These findings suggest that the nucleoprotein portions of different SCP might not be equally hazardous.   However,
we found the nucleic acids present in algae *(Chlorella sorokiniana)*
and yeast *(Torulopsis utilis)* to elevate plasma uric acid in proportion to the amount fed irrespective of source.

These high levels of serum and urinary uric acid derived
from dietary precursor ribonucleic acid can be reduced by admin-
istering allopurinol, a hypoxanthine analog which inhibits xan-
thine oxidase, but the technique is by no means suitable for mass
feeding.   Thus, nucleic acid remains a serious obstacle, and
necessitates development of process to eliminate most of the
purine bases.   In our hands, admittedly inexpert, removal of
purines from bacterial cells was accompanied only with loss of
40% of the initial protein content.

One other point should be made before leaving the topic of
nucleic acids.   Only the amino groups of adenylic acid and
guanine would contribute to the body protein pool so 75% of the
nitrogen tied up in these compounds would be lost to human utilization.   As most SCP sources contain about 1 g nucleic acid per
10 g protein, this is a considerable loss.

These questions of toxicity, digestibility and nucleic acid
are the major difficulties recognized at the present time, but
there may be others as yet unreported.   Surprisingly enough,
considering the widely-held view that biomasses are good candidates for feeding expanding world populations, there is very little
reliable information available.   Until the recent work with petroleum-grown yeast, published data on long-term feeding of any
species was nil.   Biomasses recovered from prototype bioregener-

ative engineering models using human wastes have not been used as human food or are not reported.

Keeping in mind these general considerations, let us now examine the various sources of single-cell protein in more detail.

QUALITY OF SCP SOURCES

Bacteria

At the present time, bacteria seem to represent the least viable source of SCP, although data from many animal feeding studies are difficult to interpret because the test materials (rumenal contents and activated sludge) have often been mixtures of bacteria with other microorganisms such as protozoa and fungi. The protein of some preparations is of good biologic value (equal to casein in some cases), but protein quality and digestibility are quite variable and often low. Methionine is usually the limiting amino acid in terms of mammalian nutrition.

Bacterial cells are high in nitrogen content during rapid growth, but if the nutrient supply is inadequate, the cells will enter a resting state and accumulate storage products. Like algae and fungi, bacteria may store triglycerides of normal fatty acids, but more often storage lipid is composed of C17- and C19-cyclopropane acids or a polymer of hydroxybutyric acid.

Bacterial cell walls contain many compounds not present in other organisms. The primary structural component is often a complex polymer of the unusual carbohydrate, muramic acid, along with hexosamines and both D- and L-amino acids. Gram-negative bacteria have additional layers of lipid, lipoprotein, lipopoly-saccharide and proteins as part of the cell wall. Outside the cell wall, there may be a capsule or slime layer which is composed of hexose sugars and hexosamines. (It is suspected that this capsular material contains the endotoxin of Gram-negative bacteria.)

In rat studies, the protein of *H. eutropha* cells has the same biological value as casein, and is almost as well digested, despite

the relative indigestibility of its lipid content.   The high
lysine content of *H. eutropha* suggests that it might form an excellent supplement to cereal grains, which are low in this essential amino acid.   Nearly as high in the biological value of its
protein is *E. coli* although it is somewhat less digestible than
H. eutropha.   As protein, it has proved equal to fish meal in
the diet of chicks and rats.   It is probable that *A. aerogenes*,
as well as *Bacillus megaterium* and *Pseudomonas saccharaphilia*,
other candidates for SCP production, would have the same quality,
based on compositional data.

Unfortunately, bacteria cannot now be considered for human
nutrition.   Rodents appear to thrive on relatively high doses
of bacterial matter, but men fed 15 to 25 g of *H. eutropha* suf-
fered from vertigo, nausea, vomiting and diarrhea.   One subject
also complained of headache, weakness and pain in the extremities.
Symptoms appeared one to two hours after eating and subsided in
24 hours.   *A. aerogenes* produced similar reactions, and also
caused one subject to develop a rash.   Neither *H. eutropha* nor
A.aerogenes affected either blood pressure or body temperature.
One day later, concentrations of blood cells, glucose, serum uric
acid and key enzymes were the same as values prior to the test.

Since the bacterial cells had been washed free of medium
before feeding, the toxic material is apparently within or bound
to the cell; moreover, the time required for the onset of the
various symptoms indicates that digestion of the cell is needed
to release the toxicant.   Subsequent feedings of *H. eutropha*
from a different source produced lower levels of pathophysiologic
reaction, which may indicate the development of tolerance after
repeated exposure or simply reflect subject variation.   It is
also possible that differing growth conditions produce varying
amounts of the toxicant.

Nonetheless, the severity of these reactions, coupled with
their high proportion of nucleic acids (up to 20% of cellular dry

solids in *E. coli*, *A. aerogenes* and *B. megaterium*), make bacteria
a less than acceptable food source. As most other types of SCP
production rely on use of mixed cultures of yeast or algae and
bacteria, untoward responses to the bacterial contaminant must be
considered in safety evaluations.

Algae

Studies have shown that algae are a reasonably good source
of protein. In general, protein efficiency ratios and biological
values are lower than those recorded for good quality animal protein but higher than those for some vegetable proteins. However,
it should be pointed out that algal composition is affected by
the quality of its growth medium and environment.

Actively reproducing young cell masses, for example, contain
high proportions of protein and nucleic acid. As the cells
mature, they normally accumulate starch, but they may store lipid
if the medium is deficient in nutrients. Numerous other quantitative and qualitative differences exist between algal biomasses.

The amino acid content of various algal species often com-
pares favorably with that of casein. The quality of algal protein is limited by its low level of sulphur-containing amino
acids. This problem has been attacked, however, by the development of hybrid strains which contain much higher concentrations
of methionine and cystine.

The major limiting factor in the use of algal cells directly
as a source of SCP is poor digestibility. The cell wall, which
contains from 10% to 20% of the total nitrogen, has been found
entirely undigested in the feces of rats, pigs and humans consuming algal diets.

When measures are taken to decrease the rigidity of the cell
wall (techniques such as milling, boiling or lipid solvent extraction), *in vitro* and *in vivo* digestibility are usually increased. In some cases, the biologic value of the protein is
also increased, indicating that some of the bound amino acids are

F

thereby made available.

Attempts to feed humans large quantities of *Chlorella* have
met with mixed success. Some investigators have reported gastrointestinal problems with as little as 20 g of algae, and more
than 100 g is rarely tolerable. In many cases, the symptoms are
not severe enough to impair nutrient balance significantly, but
indications for caution are nonetheless present.

In one study, the protein, fat and carbohydrate digestibility
of a mixed food diet was not changed by the addition of 50 g of
lyophilized, boiled algae, but additions of 100 g or more resulted
in reduced assimilation of almost all nutrients. Pokrovskaia
et al. also have reported that calcium and magnesium assimilation
was depressed by the continued consumption of 120 g of dry cells
per day. We fed men 31 and 64 g dry algal cells per day as the
sole source of protein; true digestibility of protein was lower
with the larger amount present in the diet, 82 versus 89%. True
digestibility of casein was 97% in the same test.

There have been a number of pathophysiologic responses reported in connection with algal diets. Two men given 150 g per
day of dried green *Chlorella* developed edema of the face and hands,
petechial hemorrhages, cyanosis of the nail beds, and later peeling
of the fingers, itching, etc.. Some of these conditions could be
related to the high content of nucleic acids in the algae, as we
have noted above, but only minimal discomfort was reported by two
men fed algae decolorized by alcoholic extraction. Japanese
studies conducted with rats fed an alcohol-soluble fraction of
green algae revealed pathologic changes in the adrenal cortex and
renal glomerulus, suggesting that a toxin may be responsible for
the other adverse reactions.

To be fully utilized, algae would have to be processed to
fragment cell walls, as well as to remove nucleic acids, chlorophyll
and other compounds as yet unidentified. However, *Chlorella sorokiniana* supports nitrogen balance in man equally well as does casein

with the same proportion of RNA added.   About 6 to 7 g *Chlorella*
nitrogen a day will maintain equilibrium in men fed an otherwise
adequate diet.   There are no published data from man on usage
of *Spirulina* spp. although tests are now in progress.

Yeast

In general, fungal species vary in lipid content from less
than 1% to more than 50% of the dry solids.   As with algae, the
lipid content of most species can be altered quantitatively and
qualitatively by growing them in nitrogen- or mineral-deficient
media.   The lipid in young cultures grown in adequate media is
largely phospholipid, containing polyunsaturated fatty acids.
Triglyceride, which contains palmitic and oleic acids, accumulates
when growth is slowed.   Mineral content varies greatly with the
growth medium.

The biological value of *Saccharomyces* protein ranges from
60% to 90% in rat tests, but the *Torula* and *Candida* species are
lower in protein value.   In part, this difference is due to the
content of the sulphur-containing amino acids, which are the first
limitation in yeast protein of all types.   Naturally, tests of
methionine supplementation have demonstrated improved protein
quality.

Diets containing yeast as the only protein source resulted
in a slightly higher level of fecal nitrogen than a control diet
of casein, but the difference was not statistically significant.
Similarly, calcium, magnesium and phosphorus excretions exceeded
the dietary intake, largely due to increased fecal excretion of
these elements.   About 8 to 9 g of *Torula* nitrogen was adequate
to maintain balance in our healthy male subjects.

Torula yeast seems to produce few pathophysiologic reactions,
except for the dermatologic findings referred to above, which
occurred in 12 of 50 young men fed 45 to 135 g yeast per day for
3 to 4 weeks.   An antigen prepared from the yeast did not evoke
a dermal reaction in any subject, so the response was probably not

due to an allergy.   It is clear that yeasts will have to be
processed in order to remove the purine moiety of nucleic acids
before they can be considered as a viable source of SCP for man.
Petroleum-grown species have not been subjected to human testing
and this must be done once the process of purine-removal is
developed.

Other Fungi

The protein quality of other fungi is within the same range
as the yeasts.   As the sole source of protein, these support an
equal rate of growth in rats.   Young fungal cultures contain
less indigestible material and more of the free amino acid and
nucleic acids (from 8 to 14%) required for cell replication than
do older ones.   The few tests conducted with fungi indicate a
rather wide range of digestibility, running from a low of 44% to
a high of 90%.   Tests conducted with *Aspergillus sydowi*, for
example, revealed that only 48% of the protein and 51% of the fat
were digestible - although a surprising 81% of the fiber was
digested.

In human feeding studies, men were able to digest 72 to 83%
of fungal proteins, and only 43 to 62 g of protein was required
daily to promote nitrogen balance when *Agaricus compestris*,
Boletus edulis or *Cantharellus cibarus* were used as the sole
dietary source.

The habit of molds to form antibiotic and heptotoxic substances would have to be considered if these were proposed for
human use, as well as the usual problem of nucleic acids.

Leaf Protein

While they are not technically sources of SCP, higher plants
are perhaps the best unconventional, or underexploited, source of
protein.   Leaves are rich sources of protein (30 to 40% of dry
weight), but the 90% water content and excessive amount of fiber
(20 to 30% of dry weight) limits the amount of crude leaf that
can be consumed by nonruminant animals.   The amino acid content

of leaf protein indicates that methionine may be insufficient
for optimal growth in mammals.

The 80 to 90% digestibility of leaf protein concentrates,
produced by removal of most of the plant fiber, is better than
that of raw leaves, but can vary greatly with plant species, processing, age of the plant and the amount of stem included in the
test mixture.

Green leafy plants, of course, are a common part of the
human diet, but are seldom eaten in quantities greater than 10
to 30 g of dry weight per day.   In certain parts of Africa,
larger quantities are consumed, but no controlled studies have
been reported in which the nutritive value of the protein as
leaves was evaluated for man.   Leaf protein concentrates have
been found capable of replacing from 50 to 74% of milk protein in
children recovering from protein malnutrition, with only a slight
reduction in nitrogen retention and absorption.

Generally speaking, there are few pathophysiologic responses
to leaf protein, although some normally innocuous compounds might
prove troublesome if higher plants were to become the sole or
major source of dietary protein.   Carotenes are essentially harm-
less, but they could cause a yellowing of the skin and sclera.
Under some conditions of growth, plants may accumulate physio-
logically significant amounts of histamine.   It is thought that
when this occurs in nature, it contributes importantly to the development of grass tetany in cattle and sheep maintained on a
single biomass, in that case, a low magnesium forage.   Nitrate
concentration is another potential hazard that could vary in significance, depending on the nitrogen source in the substrate and
the activity of the man's intestinal bacteria in reducing the
nitrate to nitrite.

All things considered, leaf protein probably presents a
fruitful avenue for investigation into new methods of alleviating
world food shortages.

OTHER CONSIDERATIONS

As the morning speakers have emphasized, in considering the
use of SCP for human food, planners must look at total human
needs and economic capacities, not simply at safety and protein-
nutritional efficacy, the issues to which this presentation has
been addressed thus far.   According to Dr. Nicol, for most population groups where protein is now deficient or at risk, there
is an equal or greater need for food energy.   (Some cassava
areas are minor exceptions.)   Dietary protein will not be used
efficiently unless this need for energy is met simultaneously,
and at marginal intakes of both, small increments in energy have
more beneficial effect on protein nutrition (nitrogen balance)
than does an increase in protein intake.   In some areas, technologic effort and capital might be better spent for conversion
of sewage to fertilizer than for its conversion to SCP of human
food grade, if that resulted in higher yields of cereals, soy
beans, grain legumes or pasturage.   Conversion of sewage to
methane for power might prove to be more advantageous in other
areas if the total developmental strategy of the countries were
studied.

Conventional protein-rich foods are also carriers of a number of critical nutrients, not just protein.   Nutrients at particular risk in the various groups where protein is now deficient
are magnesium, potassium and calcium;   the entire group of B
vitamins;   and iron, zinc and probably other trace elements.   A
simple mixture of SCP and cassava or sugar will not replace the
nutrients of milk in the diet of children or meat, milk and legumes in the diets of adults.   With careful attention to fortifi-
cation, SCP and the more conventional protein isolates (such as
soy bean, cottonseed or leaf protein isolates) could be made to
mimic more closely the natural counterpart foods.   But at the
present state of knowledge, nutritionists cannot specify with

assurance how much and what balance of the trace elements must be added, or in exactly which form. An effective dose of some elements is uncomfortably close to the toxic level. Enrichment with some of the trace minerals poses formidable technologic problems. Research on these and related topics must proceed with the same emphasis and commitment by responsible commercial developers as they give to the quality and profitability of protein material if the products are to be offered for human use. Governments and the people they represent cannot fairly be expected to subsidize entirely the necessary basic research, because the problems are in large part generated by the technologic development. They are outcomes of turning to unconventional and highly processed protein isolates.

In my opinion, the use of SCP for animal feed is desirable and confers an urgently needed factor of safety for man on both toxicologic and nutritional grounds.

REFERENCES

1. Bengoa, J.M. "Nutritional Inquiry of the Working and Middle Class Families of Caracas." *Arch. Venezolanos Nutr.* 1, 347 (1950).

2. Bonner, P. *et al.* "The Influence of a Daily Supplement of Spinach or its Equivalent in Oxalic Acid upon the Mineral Utilization of Children." *J. Pediatrics* 12, 188 (1938).

3. Bowering, J., Calloway, D.H., Margen, S. and Kaufmann, N.A. "Dietary Protein Level and Uric Acid Metabolism in Normal Man." *J. Nutr.* 100, 249 (1970).

4. Bowering, J., Margen, S., Calloway, D.H. and Rhyne, A. "Suppression of Uric Acid Formation from Dietary Nucleic Acid with Allopurinol." *Am. J. Clin. Nutr.* 22, 1426 (1969).

5. Calloway, D.H. and Spector, H. "Nutrition Balance as Related to Claroic and Protein Intake in Active Young Men." *Am. J. Clin. Nutr.* 2, 405 (1954).

6. Calloway, D.H. and Waslien, C.I. "Bioregeneration of Food." *Env. Biol. Med.* 1, 229 (1971).

7. Calloway, D.H. and Chenoweth, W. "Utilization of Nutrients in Milk- and Wheat-based Diets by Men with Adequate and Re-

duced Abilities to Absorb Lactose. I. Energy and Nitrogen. " *Am. J. Clin. Nutr.* <u>26</u>, 939 (1973).

8. Clifford, A.J., West, D.L. and Clifford, C.K. "The Hyper-uricemic Effects of Adenine, Guanine, Hypoxanthine and Xan-thine and Their Concentrations in Foods." *Federation Proc.* <u>32</u>, 916 (abstr.) (1973).

9. Dam, R., Lee, S., Fry, P.C. and Fox, H. "Utilization of Algae as a Protein Source for Humans." *J. Nutr.* <u>86</u>, 376-382 (1965).

10. Denis, W. "The Effect of Ingested Purines on the Uric Acid Content of the Blood." *J. Biol. Chem.* <u>23</u>, 147 (1915).

11. Dirr, K. and Soden, O.V. "The Value of Yeast in Human Diet. 3. Digestibility of Bergin and Wood Sugar Yeast." *Biochem. Z.* <u>312</u>, 252-262 (1942).

12. Dirr, K. "Blood Uric Acid in Man when Wood Sugar Yeast is Used as Food." *Deutsch. Z. Verdau. Stoffwechselkr.* <u>11</u>, 120-122 (1951).

13. Fofanov, V.I., Kozar, M.I. and Dobronravova, N.N. "Some Indices of the Human Natural Resistance to the Dietary Re-placement of Animal Protein by *Chlorella* Proteins." *Kosmich. Biol. i. Med.* <u>1</u> (No.3), 121-127 (1967).

14. Fukui, T., Tokas, A., Miyoski, T., Machiguchi, M. and Sasahi, T. "Studies on the Digestion and Absorption of *Torula* Yeast *(Torula utilis, Mycotorula japonica)*. 2. Digestion and Absorption in the Human Body." *Shikoku Acta Med.* <u>16</u>, 706 (1960).

15. Funk, C., Lyle, W.G. and McCoskey, D. "The Nutritive Value of Yeast, Polished Rice and White Bread as Determined by Experiments on Man." *J. Biol. Chem.* <u>17</u>, 173 (1916).

16. Harper, A.E., Payne, P.R. and Waterlow, J.C. "Human Protein Needs." *Lancet* <u>1</u>, 1518 (1973).

17. Hayami, H., Shino, K., Morimoto, K., Okano, T. and Yamamoto, S. "Studies on the Utilization of *Chlorella* as a Source of Food (Part 9). Human Experiments on the Rate of Absorption of Protein of Blanched *Chlorella*." *Ann. Rep. Nat. Inst. Nutr.* (Japan), p. 60 (1960).

18. Hayami, H. and Shino, K. "Nutritional Studies on Decolorized *Chlorella* (Part 2). Studies on the Rate of Absorption of the Decolorized *Chlorella* on Adult Men." *Ann. Rep. Nat. Inst. Nutr.* (Japan), p. 59 (1958).

19. Hayami, H., Matsuno, Y. and Shino, K. "Studies on the Utili-zation of *Chlorella* as a Source of Food (Part 8)." *Ann. Rep. Nat. Inst. Nutr.* (Japan), p. 58 (1960).

20. Kawada, S., Matsuno, Y., Watanabe, K. and Ohta, T. "Nutritional Studies on *Chlorella* (Report 21). Effect of Administration of *Chlorella*-containing Diet to Human Subjects on Amino Acid Levels in Blood Serum and Urinary Amino Acid Excretion." *Ann. Rep. Nat. Inst. Nutr.* (Japan), pp. 54-55 (1960).

21. Kondrat'ev, Y.I. *et al.* "Use of 150 grams of Dried Biomass of Unicellular Algae in Food Rations of Man." *Vop. Pitan.* 25, 14-19 (1966).

22. Kondrat'ev, Y.I. *et al.* "Use of 50 and 100 grams of Dry Biomass of Unicellular Algae in Food Rations of Man." *Vop. Pitan.* 25, 9-14 (1966).

23. Kondrat'ev, Y.I., Bychkov, V.P., Ushakov, A.S. and Spehelev, Ye.Ya. "Use of a Biomass of Unicellular Algae for Human Feeding." *Probl. Kosmich. Biol.* 7, 364 (1967).

24. Lee, S.K., Fox, H.M., Kies, C. and Dam, R. "The Supplementary Value of Algal Protein in Human Diets." *J. Nutr.* 92, 281 (1967).

25. Lintzel, W. "Nutritive Value of the Proteins of Edible Mushrooms." *Biochem. Z.* 308, 413 (1941).

26. Miyoshi, T. "Studies on the Digestion and Absorption of Algae *(Chlorella, Scenedemus)*. I. Digestion Test on Algae." *Skikoku Acta Med.* 15, 1237 (1959).

27. Pirie, N.W. "Leaf Protein: Its Agronomy, Preparation, Quality and Use." IBP Handbook No.20, Blackwell, Oxford (1971).

28. Pokrovskaia, Ye.I., Tereschchenko, A.P. and Volynets, V.M. "Effect of Plant Diets, Including the Biomass of Unicellular Algae, on the Balance and Excretion of Mineral Elements." *Kosmich. Biol. i. Med.* 2 (No.3), 78 (1968).

29. Powell, R.C., Nevels, E.M. and McDowell, M.E. "Algae Feeding in Humans." *J. Nutr.* 75, 7 (1961).

30. Seegmiller, J.E., Laster, L. and Howell, R.R. "Biochemistry of Uric Acid and Its Relation to Gout." *New Eng. J. Med.* 268, 712, 764, 821 (1963).

31. Tamura, E. *et al.* "Nutritional Studies on *Chlorella* (Report 11). Human Excretion and Absorption of Decolorized *Scenedesmus*." *Ann. Rep. Nat. Inst. Nutr.* (Japan), pp. 31-33 (1958).

32. Udo, U., Young, V., Edozien, J. and Scrimshaw, N. "Evaluation of *Torula* Yeast for Human Consumption." *Federation Proc.* 18, 807 (Abstr.) (1969).

33. Waslien, C.I., Calloway, D.H. and Margen, S. "Uric Acid

Production of Men Fed Graded Amounts of Egg Protein and Yeast Nucleic Acid." *Am. J. Clin. Nutr.* 21, 892 (1968).

34. Waslien, C.I., Calloway, D.H. and Margen, S. "Human Tolerance to Bacteria as Food." *Nature* 221, 84 (1969).

35. Waslien, C.I., Calloway, D.H., Margen, S. and Costa, F. "Uric Acid Levels in Men Fed Algae and Yeast as Protein Sources." *J. Food Sci.* 35, 294 (1974).

36. Waterlow, J.C. "Absorption and Retention of Leaf Protein by Infants Recovering from Malnutrition." *Brit. J. Nutr.* 16, 531-540 (1962).

THE USE OF SCP IN FOOD

Herbert Stone and Joel Sidel

Food and Plant Sciences Department
Stanford Research Institute, Menlo Park, California, USA

INTRODUCTION

There is no doubt that single-cell protein (SCP) materials
can be processed in much the same manner as soy protein to yield
products having a wide range of physical and chemical properties.
Therefore, the use of SCP in food will be based on identifying
the most desirable end-use consistent with economic conditions
and will be limited only by our creativity.

There are numerous types of materials which fit the general
classification of single-cell protein (SCP); however, considerable disagreement exists amongst companies as to the name (or
names) which is given to them (other than trade names). In addition, there appears to be some consumer misunderstanding about
the connotation of SCP as being a petro-protein and "synthetic";
i.e., synthesized in a laboratory. Therefore, other appropriate
designations will be used; e.g., yeast-protein, bio-protein.
We refer to these materials as SCP throughout this report; however, it was not our intent to endorse the use of the term SCP.

In 1967, we initiated a series of studies on the development
of and uses of new proteins, including SCP and soy protein, in
fabricated foods for the United States market (3). We identified
a wide variety of food products that could utilize these proteins
including meat, poultry, seafoods, coffee whiteners, toppings,

Table 1   Estimated fabricated food consumption 1985 (millions of kilograms)

Country	Meat Analogs		Dairy Analogs	
	Total Weight	Protein Weight	Total Weight	Protein Weight
Belgium/Luxembourg	130	25	180	7
Denmark	60	12	110	4
France	570	120	300	10
Germany	550	110	520	18
Italy	475	95	700	25
Netherlands	170	35	310	10
Norway	10	2	40	1.4
Spain	250	50	210	7
Sweden	70	15	200	7
Switzerland	30	6	40	1.4
United Kingdom	500	100	850	30
Total*	2800	570	3500	120

* Totals do not add due to rounding.

dietetic foods, baked goods, and snacks.   These products were
not very different from those on the list developed by Hammonds
and Call (4,5) in their study of the protein ingredients market.
We estimated that by 1980 this market would have a dollar value
greater than $7000 million at the wholesale level.   In 1971
a second study was made in selected European countries (2), and
from the results, we estimated that by 1985 there would be a
market in Europe for as much as 700 million kg of protein for
meat and dairybased products (Table 1).   Since we prepared these
projections, there have been significant changes in the world
food supply, creating unanticipated problems in the availability
of raw materials and an increase in their cost.   Therefore, some
of our estimated projections for 1985 will be met sooner by SCP
and, possibly, to a greater extent than we had expected.
    If SCP is to be accepted with a minimum of delays (indepen-

dent of the safety question), we must consider the ways in which
it will be used and the economic benefits as well as identify
potential problems that might arise if it is used improperly.
To achieve this, we must first try to determine the reactions of
the food processor and the consumer to products containing SCP
or other new proteins.

ECONOMIC CONSIDERATIONS

The successful utilization of SCP in food can best be appreciated if we consider the economic benefits in addition to social
considerations.   Table 2 was prepared from available data on the
substitution of meat by various soy products;   however, the soy
products could just as well be SCP.   It is apparent that one can
effect considerable cost savings - as much as 40 to 50% - through
the partial replacement of meat in patties.   For purposes of this
discussion, we assumed that the soy proteins were satisfactory for
application as meat extenders, although this may not be true for
all the types of soy proteins available.   For example, it has
been observed that a granulated soy protein tends to lighten the
color of red meat and, if overcooked, results in the appearance
of light-colored particles dispersed throughout the meat.   For
the producer of SCP, knowledge of end-use will influence processing conditions and cost.

ATTITUDES ON SCP USE IN FOODS

A separate but closely related consideration in using SCP
in food is the assessment of the food processor's and the consumer's attitudes to these new proteins.   Although SCP initially
will be added to food in combination with other proteins, labeling
requirements and other procedures will serve to inform the consumer of the presence of SCP.

If SCP is to be accepted readily by the food manufacturer and
the consumer, there is need for a greater understanding of consumer

Table 2   Costs of beef-type patty mixes (estimated cents/kilogram).

	Price/kg (Cents)	All Natural Meat		Patty with Soy Concentrate		Patty with Extruded Soy		Patty with Spun Soy		Patty with Edi-Pro	
		Percentage used	Cost (Cents)	Percentage used	Cost (Cents)	Percentage used	Cost (Cents)	Percentage used	Cost (Cents)	Percentage used	Cost (Cents)
Boneless chuck	190.90	93.33	178.17	53.33	101.81	53.33	101.81	53.33	101.81	53.33	101.81
Fat trim*	4.88	6.67	.32	16.67	0.81	16.67	0.81	16.67	0.81	16.67	0.81
Soy concentrate	103.40			7.50	7.75						
Extruded soy	77.00					10.00	7.70				
Spun soy (wet)	72.60							10.00	7.26		
Textured Edi-Pro#	80.00									29.80	23.84
0.2% D,L-Methionine##	198.00			0.20	0.04	0.20	0.04	0.30	0.04	0.20	0.04
Water	0.00			22.30		19.80		19.80			
Total		100.00	178.49	100.00	110.41	100.00	110.36	100.00	109.92	100.00	126.50

*   Fat added to approximate the 30% allowed under current U.S. Department of Agriculture regulations.

Textured Edi-Pro 200 is a hydrated, textured protein with added vitamins and minerals, manufactured specifically for the U.S. Government school-lunch program.

D,L-Methionine added to the soy to achieve nutritional equivalency. The spun soy has a slightly lower biological value; therefore, the methionine is increased to 0.3%.

Source: USDA, SRI estimates.

attitudes and opinions as well as a concerted educational effort. Recently we initiated a series of surveys in the food industry and with selected consumers to learn of their reactions to SCP and other new proteins. Results from some of these surveys are reported here.

INDUSTRY OPINIONS

This first survey (Appendix A) was mailed to about 100 individuals representing companies currently producing, using, or planning to use protein in their products. For this evaluation, we did not attempt to identify specific companies other than by the general classifications of sales volume, major markets, and whether the respondent represented management, production, technology, or other fields. Of the 40 replies received to date, 32 were pooled for this evaluation.

These data showed that company sales or an indivudal's position in the company had little influence on the responses. Most respondents (83%) indicated their companies either had a policy that it would use SCP or had no policy on ingredient use. However, 17% of respondents stated there was a policy not to use these new proteins. Ninety percent of respondents also stated that the consumer would have to be educated to accept these new proteins.

Of particular importance were the responses of the use of SCP based on cost. Table 3 shows the pattern of SCP usage may be directly related to cost. In this particular instance, the comparison was with casein, and it was apparent that if SCP were priced 10% less than casein, the processor would be encouraged to use it. However, other factors may be equally important, as shown by the rankings in Table 4. These data identified product safety as the most important concern for SCP, followed by functional properties (water binding capacity, etc.), nutritive value, cost, flavor, and - least important - advertising. This pattern

H. Stone and J. Sidel

Table 3   Willingness to use SCP compared with casein in foods, as a function of cost.*

	10% less		equal		10% more	
	yes	no	yes	no	yes	no
Food Processor	14	2	9	8	5	11
Supplier	3	2	2	3	1	4
Processor and Supplier	3	1	4	0	1	2
Pooled	20**	5	15	11	7	17

* The assumption was made that SCP would be more readily available.
** Differences in total numbers due to incomplete responses.

Table 4   Rankings of the importance of various factors associated with use of SCP.*

	Processors**	Suppliers	Both	Pooled
Safety	1.7	1.8	1.2	1.6
Other functional properties	2.8	3.3	2.6	2.9
Nutritive value	3.4	2.8	3.6	3.3
Cost	3.4	2.8	3.6	3.3
Flavor	3.4	4.5	3.8	3.9
Advertising	5.5	4.7	5.6	5.2

* Lowest numerical value equivalent to most important factor.
** There were 17 companies listed as processors, 6 as suppliers, and 5 as both.

Table 5   Stated preference for a particular protein.*

	Preference for		
	SCP	Soy	None
Processor	0	14	3
Supplier	1	4	1
Both	0	5	0
Pooled	1	23	4

* The assumption was that if you had a preference, which would you use.

was basically the same for processors, suppliers, or both.

We also consider the type of protein preferred (Table 5). The fact that most respondents preferred soy was not unexpected. To date, no SCP is available in commercial quantities, and since the processor is familiar with soy products, he is more likely to respond positively to them. These results suggest that the SCP producer must educate the processor about the relative value of SCP as a food ingredient.

CONSUMER OPINIONS

A survey was also made of SRI employees. The questionnaire was similar to the one sent to food industry representatives but was modified, based on results from a pretest (Appendix B).

As in the previous survey, our primary concern was to identify consumers' views of important problems with SCP. These data were not analyzed statistically because of the limited sample size. The results reported herein were derived from about 200 respondents.

It was particularly interesting to note that, of those responding, about 88 to 90% indicated a willingness to use foods containing these new proteins - an attitude not very different from that of industry (83% acceptance) about the use of SCP or other new proteins.

Table 6 presents the ranking of items of importance for these new proteins, as determined by SRI respondents. The high degree of agreement between males and females is obvious. The fact that nutritive value and protein flavor were ranked as most important should be considered as indicative of what the consumer expects from foods containing these new proteins.

Attitudes about safety of SCP were considered separately, and these data are reported in Table 7. The respondents were almost evenly divided between those who believed that the government could establish adequate safety regulations and those who

H. Stone and J. Sidel

Table 6 Ranking of items important to these new proteins.*

	M	F	Pooled
Nutritive value	1.7	1.7	1.7
Flavor	1.7	1.8	1.7
Cost	2.5	2.7	2.6
Advertising	4.1	4.2	4.1

* Results from 189 respondents.

Table 7 Belief in government establishment of adequate safety regulations.

	M	F	Pooled
Yes	57	24	81
No	5	4	9
Maybe	55	37	92

Table 8 Stated preference for type of protein.

	M	F	Pooled
Plant protein	57	36	93
SCP	4	1	5
No preference	61	30	91

were not as convinced. This response was consistent with that reported by the participants in the industry survey and reflects a genuine concern by the consumer about product safety.

Results of the question of preference for type of protein (Table 8) - plant, SCP, or none stated - were consistent with previous results, although the fact that as many respondents had no preference implies a willingness to try alternative protein sources.

SUMMARY AND CONCLUSIONS

The primary objective of this presentation was to bring
into focus some of the important but not well-appreciated problems associated with the successful commercialization of these
new proteins.

There is no doubt that these new proteins can be incorporated
into foods to enable us to extend the available supply of food
without decreasing the quality or nutritive value of the finished
product.   However, the ease with which such products are accepted
by the food processor and the consumer can be greatly influenced
by how well we respond to their needs.   Whereas the processor
may feel that cost and functional properties are of considerable
importance (separate from the question of safety), the consumer
is most concerned with nutritive value and flavor.   It is also
apparent from this small sampling that the consumer is somewhat
skeptical about the government's ability to provide adequate
safety testing protocols.   For the past several years, consumer
confidence in food safety has changed dramatically from one of
complete acceptance to one of doubt.   If these new protein materials are to be commercially successful, a greater effort will
be required to demonstrate safety of the ingredients and/or products.

Finally, we should reemphasize the importance of communication
with the consumer.   As noted previously, in pre-tests, many of
our subjects were confused about what we mean when we say "single-
cell protein, SCP, petro-protein."   There is an obvious and urgent need to educate the consumer about this new food material
including its safety as well as its benefits.   It is incorrect
to assume that simple advertising or lowered price will be successful in the long term.

REFERENCES

1. Stone, H. "Food Products and Processes." Stanford Research Institute-International (1972).

2. Gentry, R.E. and Connolly, E. "Fabricated Foods in Western Europe." Stanford Research Institute Long Range Planning Service Report No. 449 (1971).

3. Gentry, R.E. and Connolly, E. "Fabricated Foods." Stanford Research Institute Long Range Planning Service Report No. 374.

4. Hammonds, T.M. and Call, D.L. "Utilization of Protein Ingredients in the U.S. Food Industry. Part I. The Current Market for Protein Ingredients." Dept. Agr. Econ., Cornell Univ., Agr. Exp. Sta. A.E. 320 (1970).

5. Hammonds, T.M. and Call, D.L. "Utilization of Protein Ingredients in the U.S. Food Industry. Part II. The Future Market for Protein Ingredients." Dept. Agr. Econ., Cornell Univ., Agr. Exp. Sta. A.E. 321 (1970).

APPENDIX A

Stanford Research Institute
Menlo Park, California 94025
(415) 326-6200

Undoubtedly you have read about the world food shortage and the current focus on finding sufficient protein to satisfy the nutritional needs of large segments of the world's population. One suggested solution is the production of protein by growing unicellular organisms (e.g., bacteria or yeast) on petroleum feedstocks. The organisms are then harvested, purified, and dried to produce a powder containing 60 to 90% protein. This powder can be added to foods, thereby improving the nutritive value of the food supply and extending existing supplies of conventional proteins (milk, eggs, protein). Such new proteins are often identified as single cell protein (SCP); they have been produced by many of the major petrochemical companies on an experimental basis. Their primary advantages are that they are less expensive to produce compared with milk, egg, or meat protein, they do not require extensive land, and they are not affected by environmental conditions. The disadvantages of SCP include a large capital investment and a biological limitation on the amount that man or livestock can tolerate.

With this introduction, we ask that you please complete the accompanying questionnaire and return it to me in the enclosed self-addressed, stamped envelope at your earliest convenience.

Thank you.

Herbert Stone, Ph.D.
Director
Department of Food and Plant Sciences

HS:ls
enclosure-

Would you please provide the following information about you and your company. If you are not in industry, please mark "other" in Question 1 and finish the test.

1. Your position in the company:

    Management   _____
    Production   _____
    Technical   _____
    Other   _____

2. Company sales:

    Less than $50 million   _____
    $50 million to $100 million   _____
    $100 million to $500 million   _____
    $500 million to $1,000 million   _____
    More than $1,000 million   _____

3. Company markets, primarily:

    Consumer   _____
    Institutional, catering, etc.   _____
    Remanufacture   _____
    Ingredients supplier   _____

We are interested in knowing your attitude and the attitude of your company toward the use of these new proteins. Specifically, we would appreciate your responses to the following questions about these proposed food ingredients:

1. Does your company have a policy that it will _____ or will not _____ use these proteins?

2. If an SCP of nutritive value equal to casein were available, would you consider its use, if .... ?

    a. if SCP's price was equal to the conventional protein, but SCP was more readily available? Yes _____ No _____

b.   if SCP's price was at least 10% less than the conventional protein, and SCP was readily available?
Yes ____ No ____

c.   if SCP's price was 10% greater, but SCP was more
readily available?   Yes ____ No ____

3.   Please rank the following items in order of importance
by placing a number next to each item relative to its
importance - e.g., 1 - most important, 2 - less important, etc., in relation to SCP:

Safety   ____
Nutritive value   ____
Functional properties   ____
(e.g. whipping solubility)
Cost   ____
Advertising impact   ____
Flavor   ____

4.   In your opinion, is current safety testing adequate
for these new proteins?   Yes ___ No ____

5.   Do you consider these new proteins primarily as:

Partial replacement for more costly proteins ____?
Total replacement in existing or new products ____?
Both   ____?

6.   If you had a choice, would you prefer any one of these
proteins?   Rank order the following list, with 1 as
most preferred, etc.:

Soya or other vegetable proteins   ____
SCP (bacteria, yeast)   ____
No preference   ____

7.   In your opinion, do you think that consumers will have
to be educated before they will accept these new proteins?

____ Yes   ____ No

Comments:

Thank you for your participation in this survey.

APPENDIX B

Dear Employee:

Undoubtedly you have read about the world food shortage and
the current focus on finding sufficient protein to satisfy the
nutritional needs of large segments of the world's population.

One suggested solution is the production of protein by growing unicellular organisms (e.g., bacterial or yeast) on petroleum feedstocks. The organisms are then harvested, purified, and dried to produce a powder containing 60 to 90% protein. This powder can be added to foods, thereby improving the nutritive value of the food supply and extending existing supplies of conventional proteins (milk, eggs, protein). Such new proteins are often identified as single cell protein (SCP); they have been produced by many of the major petrochemical companies on an experimental basis. Their primary advantages are that they are less expensive to produce compared with milk, egg, or meat protein, they do not require extensive land, and they are not affected by environmental conditions. The disadvantages of SCP include a large capital investment and a biological limitation on the amount that man or livestock can tolerate.

With this introduction, we ask that you please complete the accompanying questionnaire and return it to me at Bldg. 100 at your earliest convenience.

Thank you.

Herbert Stone, Ph.D.
Director
Department of Food and Plant Sciences

HS:ls
enclosure-

We are interested in knowing your attitude about the use of these proteins in food products such as meat patties. Your responses to the following questions will be very helpful in focusing the future research and development efforts of companies that use these proteins.

1. Because of increased food costs, many food companies are considering new types of proteins (such as from soya beans or yeast) as meat extenders.
   Would you reject foods containing these new proteins?

   Yes ☐   No ☐

2. Please rank the following items in order of importance by placing a number next to each item relative to its importance to you - (e.g., 1 - most important, 2 - less important, etc.) in relation to these proteins:

   Nutritive value ____
   Cost   ____
   Advertising   ____
   Flavor   ____
   Other (specify   ____

3. The new proteins can be manufactured from single cells
    and from plants.   If you had a choice would you prefer
    protein grown from:

    Single cells (e.g., yeast, bacteria) ☐
    Plants (e.g., soya bean)   ☐
    No preference   ☐

4. Do you believe the government can establish adequate
    safety controls for these proteins?

    Yes ☐   No ☐   Maybe ☐

To further assist us, would you please complete the following background information about yourself.

    Female ☐   Male ☐

    Total in family   ____
    Do you do most of
    the shopping?   Yes ☐   No ☐

SESSION 3

CURRENT POSITION ON SCP PRODUCTION, STANDARDIZATION
AND USE

THE PAG POSITION AND RÊCOMMENDATIONS ON SCP FOR
USE AS FOOD

Max Milner

Protein Advisory Group of the United Nations System
New York, USA

ABSTRACT

The Protein Advisory Group began in 1955 to assist three
agencies of the United Nations (WHO, FAO, and UNICEF) in problems
relating to the safety and nutritional evaluation of a number of
unconventional protein foods including single cell proteins produced from a variety of substrates.   In 1969 the PAG appointed
an *ad hoc* Working Group on SCP to study and evaluate these products more intensively.   The *ad hoc* Group and the PAG have now
produced a number of pertinent reports, statements and guidelines
which have proven helpful to research, institutional and industrial interests involved in these developments.   The *ad hoc*
Group has also assisted in the preparation and updating of two
additional important PAG guidelines dealing respectively with
pre-clinical methods of testing for nutritional value and toxicological safety and with recommended protocols for human testing
of unconventional protein products including SCP.   The nature of
these activities and documents and their implication to the development and testing of satisfactory SCP products will be reviewed.

Stimulation by a group of United Nations agencies of the
production and consumption of a variety of unconventional protein materials began more than two decades ago when WHO, FAO
and UNICEF in a joint program, identified protein-calorie malnutrition as one of the most serious threats to the health and
development of young children in developing countries, particularly in the tropics and subtropics.   In these regions prospects
for expanded production of animal protein foods were clearly
limited.   Concurrently with the initiation of this program in
the early 1950's, these agencies recognized the importance of
careful nutritional, and toxicological testing and food acceptance evaluation of these novel proteins which in most cases had
little if any history of use in human diets.

Among the resources which seemed to have potential and
adaptability to child nutrition were soy protein concentrates
manufactured by modern solvent extraction and heat-processing
methods, peanut, cottonseed, sesame and other oilseed flours,
synthetic amino acids, fish and leaf protein concentrates and
proteins from microbiological sources.   The concern for toxicological safety and nutritional adequacy of these materials, and
the need to coordinate the viewpoints of the agencies on these
problems and the related programs with Governments led to the
creation by WHO of the Protein Advisory Group in 1955.   The PAG
became a tripartite FAO/WHO/UNICEF entity in 1960 and since 1971
it has been the PAG of the United Nations System.   Recently IBRD
and the UN have joined the other agencies as sponsors.

Some of the earlier programming efforts carried out by WHO,
FAO and UNICEF included a fish protein concentrate plant in
Chile (beginning about 1955), an extracted, spray dried and formulated soy protein beverage operation in Indonesia (about 1956)
and two small plants in India to produce edible peanut flour
(about 1960).   It was at this time that Incaparina and other
protein-fortified cereal formulations were developed and intro-

duced into Latin American markets.

As for the role of PAG, this Group reviews developments in all areas pertinent to new protein resources and foods.   Its Statements, Guidelines and recommendations relate comprehensively to broad nutritional requirements in the real-life settings of the developing countries, and not just to the protein requirement.

A particularly useful mechanism in PAG activities is its so-called *ad hoc* Working Groups consisting of specialists in disciplines related to any unique problem area, usually technical in character.   There is, for example, a PAG *ad hoc* Working Group on Marketing of Protein Foods, another on Feeding the Preschool Child and a third on Nutritional Guidelines for Plant Breeders. One of the most effective of these, activated in 1969, deals with Single Cell Proteins.   It was first convened in Marseilles to deal with a comprehensive agenda, which led to the release in 1970 of PAG Statement No. 4 on SCP.   This broad review of the status of SCP at that time emphasized that developments had entered a critical phase and that these current efforts would determine whether successful industrial production and large-scale utilization would be launched and the scale, if any, of the impact SCP would eventually have on world protein needs.   The Statement included a definition of SCP in terms of a wide variety of single cell and multicellular organisms.   The group expressed the belief, in retrospect perhaps prematurely, that the value of several types of SCP for animal feeding was well established and for this reason PAG's primary concern in the future should be its suitability for human food.   The statement went on to deal with the broad range of substrates useful for SCP production and the special technological, toxicological and economic problems associated with each one.   In terms of human food use, special concern was manifested for nucleic acid concentration in terms of human sensitivity to this constituent.   A major section of this

report, which has become even greater in subsequent statements
by the Group, dealt with testing for toxicological safety and
nutritional quality.   It proposed a limit of nucleic acid consumption by humans of 2 g per day, equivalent to a range of
10-30 g of dry, fresh SCP material.   Ingestion of higher levels
of SCP would require special processing to reduce nucleic acid
levels.

As for food uses of SCP, the statement emphasizes the poten-
tials of SCP as a protein and B vitamin supplement in a variety
of foods, although it cautions that the food technology aspects
of such use will need extensive exploration.   Another section
of the report deals with production and cost components, size of
industrial plant for maximum production economy and the feasibility for SCP processing from petroleum substrates in developing
countries.

A primary recommendation of the group four years ago dealt
with the need to develop a practical guideline for the production
of SCP for human consumption which would take into account all
information useful in defining the technology, safety, production
control and necessary protocols for toxicological and nutritional
evaluation.

The second meeting of the SCP *ad hoc* Working Group was held
in Moscow, USSR, under the chairmanship of Prof. A.A. Pokrovsky.
On the subject of general safety of SCP, the meeting report reemphasized the absolute necessity of thorough studies prior to
human feeding trials as outlined in PAG Guideline No. 6, "Preclinical Testing of Novel Sources of Protein," of any new single
cell protein product.   It notes that this refers not only to
products derived from different species of single cell organisms
but also to those obtained by cultivating a standard organism on
different or modified substrates or by means of a different or
modified processing technique.   A number of examples were given
of the variability in nutritional quality and acceptability as

food when a common organism is grown on different substrates.
This variability may also be manifested unfortunately in preci-
pitation of poorly understood gastro-intestinal allergies not
related to nucleic acid levels.   The Group further stressed
that evaluation by means of test animals are unfortunately not
enough since adverse reactions in man such as certain allergies
may not be apparent from even very thorough animal trials.

As for the effects on serum and urinary uric acid levels in
humans due to ingestion of nucleic acids, the Group cautioned
that these maximum levels may not be related just to concentration in the diet, but also depended on the origin of the food
containing the nucleic acids, for example, liver in contrast to
yeast.

The report also included a variety of methods for reducing
nucleic acid levels of SCP materials.   It also reviewed what it
considered to be insufficient information on nutritional evaluation of *Spirulina,* emphasizing that its traditional use as food
by certain societies in Africa and Mexico does not *per se* constitute adequate evidence of its nutritional value or safety.   A
similar judgement was rendered in the case of *Scenedesmus* for
human feeding, notwithstanding certain recent large-scale acceptability tests with human subjects.   Further testing of certain
foods based on microfungi grown on carbohydrate substrates was
also recommended.

At this *ad hoc* Group's second meeting it considered and approved for the first time a draft guideline for the production
of SCP for human food use.   This document deals with its subject
under the following headings:

1.   *Introduction.*   SCP is considered as a food and as a protein
supplement, which must be manufactured by the best food production
processes.

2.   *Types of organisms.*

3.   *Processing.*   Described in terms of defined raw materials,

process variables and quality control.

4.   Safety evaluation.   The procedures proposed are those in
PAG Guideline No. 6 - Preclinical Testing of Novel Sources of
Protein, followed by clinical testing using the protocols out-
lined in PAG Guideline No. 7 - Human Testing of Supplementary
Food Mixtures.

5.   Nutritional evaluation.   Guidelines 6 and 7 also apply to
such testing.

6.   Composition.   In terms of protein content (taking into
account the considerable levels of organic nitrogen not in the
form of protein), nucleic acids, lipids (including the identification of unusual types), ash, in which various elements including heavy metals must be identified, solvent residues and sanitary analysis.

The third meeting of the *ad hoc* Group occurred in Cambridge,
Massachusetts, in June 1973, following an MIT International Conference on SCP.   The first part of this report reviews the suitability of SCP for human consumption in the light of the most
recent knowledge, pointing out that a wide variety of fermentation
processes and related microorganisms have been used for centuries
by man and that extensive favorable experience with food yeast
existed.   The need to evaluate thoroughly and systematically any
new SCP product developed for human feeding was again emphasized,
including the need to determine idiosyncratic reactions to such
foods by a minority of individuals.   The Group commented on new
information presented at the MIT Conference including the Tate
and Lyle carob utilization process, the ICI bacterial methanol
substrate process, the Finnish Pekilo-protein process utilizing
a mycelial fungus grown on sulfite liquor, the status of testing
of yeast protein produced by B.P. Proteins, the industrial production and testing of yeasts from n-alkanes in the USSR, the new
SCP project of Liquichimica, and developments in the utilization
of solid animal wastes for SCP production for animal feeding.

The Group also commented at some length on the feasibility of SCP production in the developing countries.   Special note was taken of the need to correct protein values in relation to nucleic acid content and non-protein nitrogen compounds. Also discussed was the collaboration of PAG with other international groups involved in these efforts including IUPAC, the EEC and Codex Alimentarius.   Extensive consideration was given to recent comprehensive nutritional and toxicological testing in France and Mexico of *Spirulina*.   The Group emphasized the need to standardize these production processes and products in order to achieve reliable analytical, biological and nutritional evaluation in humans.

The Group also commented on developments in Japan earlier this year which has slowed SCP efforts there.   This statement is worth quoting *in extenso*:

"The Working Group was informed of the recent development in Japan where the use of the name "petroprotein", combined with a wave of concern for the pollution attributed to the petroleum industry plus other factors, has temporarily forced cancellation of programs and plans for producing SCP for animal feeding. The Working Group reemphasized that a number of SCP products, including those grown on a substrate containing petrochemicals, can meet stringent criteria for safety and nutritional value and can be produced under conditions which protect the environment.

The use of a term such as "petroprotein" is highly misleading to the public because it does not convey either the fact that chemically-pure substrates can be employed or that the protein is synthesized by living cells rather than by artificial methods.

There are a number of ways of minimizing difficulties in obtaining public acceptance of SCP.   These include avoidance of names with potentially negative connotations;   detailed analytical, microbiological and biological evidence of safety and effectiveness before claims are made;   and presentation of information to

the public in a responsible and educational way. Where human
food use is intended it is essential that extensive clinical as
well as preclinical testing precede public announcements. If
SCP producers and governmental agencies in various countries
scrupulously follow the PAG Guidelines, they will be better able
to answer criticisms and doubts.

The PAG should not hesitate to give its endorsement to any
specific SCP material which can be demonstrated to meet all of
its requirements, but it cannot give generic approval to SCP for
either animal or human feedings. Each SCP product must be judged
on its own merits regardless of the variety of organism or type
of substrate involved. International organizations, governments,
ministries and private industry should be encouraged to discuss
SCP problems with the PAG Secretariat, particularly in regard to
the application of PAG Statements and Guidelines."

In view of the rapid pace of developments in this field, the
PAG in adopting this report of the *ad hoc* Group, decided that the
Group should meet again before the end of this year. It will
convene in its Fourth Meeting, in New York next month. The following agenda will be considered:

1.   Review of guidelines proposed for testing novel sources of
protein ɔ or animal feeding, and the role of PAG in this field.
The proposals of the ILOB group, which you will hear about
tomo row, as well as those by two IUPAC subcommittees will be
evaɪ ɪtɛd

2.   New nformation on feasible nucleic acid levels in SCP used
in human iets.

3.   Nom. clature for single cell proteins.

4.   Sta us of SCP chemical and biological evaluation, and regulatory tivities by governments, in relation to the relevant
PAG gui ines.

5.   Pr ʒss in modifications of the CEC standards for food and
feed yeast.

6.   A possible informal referee role for PAG in supervising uniform evaluation of quality and safety of candidate SCP products.

A detailed report of this meeting will, of course, be prepared and made available to all interests.

Frequent reference has been made in this presentation, and in that of others given at this meeting, to PAG Guideline 6 and 7.   It is sufficient for me to have indicated why they have been developed, and how they are usefully applied.   As for their philosophy, rationale and application to testing and evaluation of SCP products, I will leave this aspect to other speakers on this program.

The PAG, through its Secretariat and the *ad hoc* Group, welcomes contacts and information exchange with all governmental, institutional, research and industrial groups involved in these problems.   It is our hope that the activities I have outlined will continue to prove helpful in achieving the early and effective production and utilization of SCP products for animal and human diets, on a scale large enough to make an effective impact on the global protein crisis.

G

DRAFT CONCLUSIONS AND RECOMMENDATIONS OF THE
UNIDO'S EXPERT GROUP MEETING ON PROTEINS
FROM HYDROCARBONS HELD 8-12 OCTOBER 1973
IN VIENNA

M.C. Verghese

United Nations Industrial Development Organization
P.O. Box 837, Vienna, Austria

FOREWORD

As part of the UNIDO work programme for 1973 an expert
group meeting, having as its title "The Manufacture of Proteins
from Hydrocarbons," was convened in Vienna, Austria, from 8 to
12 October 1973.

The main purpose of the meeting was to identify problems
related to the production and utilization of SCP for feeding
livestock in developing countries and to provide guidance and
recommendations for future UNIDO activities in this field. The
meeting was also aimed at facilitating the transfer of SCP
technology to developing countries and promotion of new investments.

The meeting was attended by more than 70 experts from 20
developing and developed countries representing both governmental
agencies and industrial firms. Representatives of PAG, FAO and
WHO also participated.

The agenda of the meeting was divided into five sections as
follows, and all papers presented were considered in one of these
sections:

(i)   Selection of feedstock;

(ii)   Acceptability and nutritional properties of SCP;

(iii)   Production aspects;

(iv)   Country situations; and

(v)   Marketing of SCP.

CONCLUSIONS AND RECOMMENDATIONS

1.   The meeting concluded that

-   SCP can make a very positive and perhaps an irreplaceable contribution towards meeting the world's protein needs.

-   the manufacturing technology now exists for normal paraffins, gas oil and several other available candidate substrates, and the owners of the technology have indicated their willingness to license to developing nations under appropriate terms and conditions.   The major deterrents to full commercialization at this time are market acceptance of the product and cost of the raw materials and non-availability of process technology.

-   either n-paraffin or straight run gas oil feedbacks have been shown not to present any special or insoluble health problems, and can be considered.   This will probably also turn out to be true for other feeds such as methanol, ethanol and methane.

It is recommended therefore that UNIDO should encourage all countries, particularly the developing countries which ought to be among the principal beneficiaries of the SCP technology, to work in this field wherever they have or could create conditions such that the work can make a positive contribution.

2.   The meeting concluded that two principal kinds of suitable conditions can be envisaged:

a.   Countries without significant domestic markets for the fermentation protein product, but with large sources of low cost raw materials and facilities well located for making these available.

It is recommended therefore that these countries should, after satisfying themselves that an available market exists relative to their location, and after fully appreciating the quality, legal and feed and food industry requirements of their potential markets, consider establishing

- pilot plants so as to be able to participate fully in the operation of an industrial facility.

- a means of transforming feedstocks on the spot so as to be able to export both the fermentation proteins and the by-products at world prices, or else to export the raw materials in some form.

b. Countries with a sufficiently large internal market (which may or may not be within the economy).

It is recommended that such countries should consider establishing a genuine National Programme which may include

- demonstration plants as instruments of transfer of technology and training of personnel, so as to be able to participate in the operation of an industrial facility, and to have produced adequate quantities of SCP for feed trials.

- suppliers of raw materials.

- the organization which will produce the SCP.

- the food technologists who will ensure its incorporation into foodstuffs in an appropriate way.

- the marketing organization which will demonstrate its acceptability, and will distribute and sell it.

- the health authorities and their associated specialized centres which will supervise and approve testing, production, transport and use.

National Programmes described above are essential because

- approval is given for a product, produced in a certain way from a specified feedstock.

- it is important to cut down as much as possible on the long delay in getting a new product accepted.

- each country will need to obtain as much of a consensus from its own specialists as possible on: how to fit fermentation proteins into its economy, who or what to feed them to, what technology is most appropriate.

3.   The meeting stated that the developing countries may have difficulties in the realization of such programmes due to lack of qualified personnel, capital, especially foreign currency.

It is recommended therefore that UNIDO should

- attempt to identify training difficulties and assist developing countries in overcoming them, where such constructive activity is envisaged.

- assist developing countries, with particular emphasis on those having foreign currency difficulties, who need to establish demonstration plant facilties, with financial aid for obtaining the equipment they need.

- attempt to interest IBRD in participating in the financing of a SCP project applicable to a developing country with foreign exchange problems.

4.   It is concluded that there is a lack of basic information for the implementation of the programmes referred to above.

It is recommended that UNIDO, possibly together with UNCTAD and and World Food Programme, undertake a study for wide diffusion, designed to bring out:

- the real unsatisfied protein requirements that fermentation proteins may be able to satisfy that are likely to appear over the next 15 years.

- the possibilities and problems that are likely to be encountered if these requirements are satisfied by other sources of proteins, particularly of soya, or if they are not satisfied.

- the price levels expected to prevail in the above context considering that there may be one price prevailing on the world market and another one for domestic markets where foreign exchange savings may be a major consideration, as in petrochemicals.

- a matrix giving the approximate size of plant, as a function of cost of feedstocks, location factors, etc., necessary to satisfy the price levels referred to above for a representative number of cases.

5. It is concluded that a clearing house is needed for collecting industrial-type information useful to developing countries which could be constructively active in the field of fermentation proteins and which might

- promote an international conference.
- collect information on possible industrial projects for protein production by other means.
- draw up a code of practice for facilitating the storage and shipment of fermentation proteins across national boundaries.

It is recommended that UNIDO establish such a clearing house.

6. It was noted that certain co-ordinated steps need to be taken in connection with UNIDO's participation in these activities:

- the need for further strengthening the UN family's approach to the subject by a concentration in particular by UNIDO and FAO on the industrial production and marketing aspects which need emphasis now that health and safety aspects seem sufficiently well in hand to enable viable industrial and agricultural ventures to be considered with a certain confidence.

- the need to ensure that developing countries take the precaution of reviewing the latest technological developments for themselves - possibly with UNIDO help - in view of the rapid evolution and improvement in production technology, and that they do not forget that effluent problems can be encountered.

- the need to encourage actively any collaboration between developed and developing countries in the field of SCP, and between the developing countries themselves, wherever technology transfer comes about.

- the need to consider that while SCP from hydrocarbons
is presently one of the most promising fields, there are other
sources for SCP production (e.g. carbohydrates, plants, agricultural wastes, etc.).

Also it should be understood that SCP production is taking
place within the framework of a general and integrated policy
for the increasing protein supplies from any source, whether
"conventional" or "non-conventional".

It is recommended that UNIDO should be particularly careful
to ensure respect of these needs.

7.   Several participants brought to the attention of the meeting
that the present guidelines issued by PAG are mainly for a SCP
product intended for human consumption.   It was suggested that
guidelines for SCP for animal feed may be appropriate.

The meeting therefore recommends that PAG consider this
suggestion favourably.

8.   The meeting concluded that at the present stage of development of SCP technology the raw materials most suitable to be
considered are gas-oil, n-paraffins, methanol, ethanol and
methane.

It is recommended that UNIDO undertake a study to determine
production costs of these raw materials at suitable locations.
The study should include most economic size of production facilities, capital costs, production costs, transport costs, etc..
Such a study will enable a comparison to be made of production
costs of SCP using various feedstocks.

9.   It was brought to the attention of the meeting that one of
the main elements of the work programme of UNIDO is transfer of
technology and making available formulas for Industrial Development between developing countries.

Developing countries who have developed appropriate technology or who have the necessary R and D facilities are requested
to consider making available such facilities to other developing

countries who have scope to develop the SCP industry, particularly
in the field of training, use of SCP samples for making experiments with feed lots for animals, making available various strains
of yeast, bacteria, etc..

10. The meeting concluded that "it is desirable to establish
public and governmental confidence in the quality control procedures used in the emerging SCP industry."

It is recommended that UNIDO request IUPAC or ASTM/IP or an
equivalent agency to set up a programme of co-operative research
to standardize analytical procedures, establish the precision
limits of such procedures, and recommend further analytical research and development on a co-operative basis wherever the precision may prove inadequate.   Analyses to be covered are:

- total aromatics in raw materials at the ppm level.

- specific species of polynuclear aromatics in raw materials
and products at the fractional ppb level.

- all hydrocarbon types, by group, in SCP products at the
low ppm level.

- carbohydrates, lipids and nucleic acids as constituents
of SCP.

- amino acids and protein in SCP.

- heavy metals in SCP product at ppm level.

- other analyses, particularly with reference to "Codex
Alimentarius".

11. The marketing and acceptance of SCP products require standardization of products and the existence of specifications stating
the limits of acceptability of the analytical constituents.   Such
standards would evoke the SCP industry to make sales to the feed
mix industry as standard grades rather than on the basis of individually negotiated specifications.

It is recommended that UNIDO convene a meeting of potential
manufacturers and feed-mix manufacturers in order to draw up
agreed standards.   IUPAC and competent trade and distribution

associations should be invited to this.   Each country is free
to consider these and appropriate governmental agencies on nutrition and public health.

12.   It is recognised that the cost of manufacturing SCP can be
reduced by the use of large units for the production of feedstocks situated near a source of raw materials and low cost
energy.   In some cases such large plants may have to serve a
market larger than the territory in which they are installed.

It is therefore suggested that in these cases the siting of
SCP plants be considered based on regional integration rather
than on a purely national basis, and it is recommended that
UNIDO, and other United Nations agencies, use their good offices
to promote such regional integration, however without sacrificing
national interests.

EVALUATION OF SINGLE CELL PROTEINS FOR NONRUMINANTS

Jack C. Taylor, Ernest W. Lucas, Donald A. Gable
and George Graber

*Bureau of Veterinary Medicine, Food and Drug Administration
Rockville, Maryland, USA*

The Federal Food, Drug and Cosmetic Act (1) provides several
definitions that pertain to the use of single cell protein (SCP)
as feed ingredients for nonruminants. The term "food" as defined in the Act means articles used for food or drink for man
or other animals. Therefore, any ingredient used in the diet
of animals is subject to the provisions of the Act and this includes animal, human and industrial wastes, as well as SCP derived from such products. A food is deemed adulterated if it
contains any poisonous or deleterious substance which may render
it injurious to health, if it contains any food additive which
is unsafe, or if it consists in whole or in part of any filthy,
putrid or decomposed substance.

The term "food additive" means any substance which may become a component of food and is not generally recognized as safe
among experts qualified by scientific training and experience to
evaluate its safety. Section 409 of the Act provides for the
submission of a petition proposing issuance of a regulation pre-
scribing the conditions under which a food additive may be safely
used.

A food additive should not be confused with a food or feed
ingredient which is generally recognized as safe and requires no
regulation for its safe use. The Food and Drug Administration
has jurisdiction only when a feed ingredient becomes adulterated

and is involved in interstate commerce.   One example of a recent problem was the poly-chlorinated biphenyls (PCB) contamination of fish meal.   This case resulted in the establishment of a safe tolerance of 2.0 ppm PCB in fish meal, or 0.2 ppm in finished feeds, 2.5 ppm in milk, 5.0 ppm in poultry tissues and 0.5 ppm in eggs.   Another problem now beginning to surface in the U.S. is the presence of various molds on corn.

The evaluation of single cell proteins for nonruminants presents a complex problem.   Contributing to the complexity are the steps involved in the production of a finished product, such as:

1.   Source of substrate
2.   Fermentation process
3.   Preparation for feeding to animals
4.   Consumption by animals
5.   Consumption of animals by man

The three basic categories of concern are (1) establishing nutritive value, (2) determining safety to animals, and (3) determining that food derived from animals consuming such products are safe for man.   This last part can be further divided into two categories;   namely, (1) determining if tissue residues exist, and (2) if tissue residues do exist, determining if they are safe.   Tests performed to satisfy these concerns do not necessarily need to be conducted in the same order as presented.   They may be reordered based on the amount of knowledge regarding characteristics peculiar to a specific substrate or SCP product.

Before starting animal feeding studies certain basic information should be collected on the proposed substrate and the finished SCP product.   Most important is a detailed description of the source of raw material to be used as the substrate.   The description should include a list of all possible harmful substances the media may contain, such as:

polycyclic aromatic hydrocarbons
microbial and fungal toxins

chlorinated hydrocarbons

carbamates

antibiotics

sulfa drugs

hormones

organophosphates

heavy metals and/or trace elements

pathogenic organisms

parasites

Chemical and biological tests on the basic media may be directed at groups of substances or at individual products. As a positive control for these tests, the basic media should be "spiked" with expected use levels for the various substances, and a sample then subjected to the microbial fermentation process. A *recovery study* should be conducted on a sample of the raw material, and a determination of the amount of substance present in the microbial protein should be made. This procedure will provide a means of determining whether the substances in question migrate from the raw material to the microbial protein, to what degree this occurs, and whether or not such substances are concentrated by the organism.

Certain residues in the microbial protein should be below the level capable of being detected by the most sensitive method available in order for the product to be considered free of residue. If residues are found in the microbial protein, this may necessitate further testing in that area to determine if animals consuming the product are either free of residues, or in cases where tolerances are established, below the tolerance limit for the compound in question. This is of vital concern since SCP products may be proposed for use for all species of animals. Not all substances which cause residues have tissue tolerances established, and where tolerances are provided, they do not always extend across all species of animals. Positive residue findings

may require extensive basic toxicology studies to establish safe
levels for residues in those cases where no tolerances exist.

Generally, the basic toxicology studies to evaluate human
safety include two year studies in a rodent; one to two year
studies in the dog, and three generation reproductive studies.
Additional details concerning design and parameters which should
be evaluated may be obtained from the Agency.

In the case of trace elements and heavy metals in feed and
food, where such substances are not added but occur naturally,
the food is not considered adulterated within the meaning of
Section 402 of the Act provided that the quantity of such substances in the food is not ordinarily injurious to health. Section 121.101f, Title 21 of the Code of Federal Regulations governs
the use of trace minerals in animal feeds when they are added for
nutritional purposes. Residues of naturally occurring trace
elements and heavy metals in animal tissues used as human food
are not permitted at levels higher than those ordinarily found
under normal conditions without basic toxicology data to support
an increased level, or to establish a tolerance.

Tests for naturally occurring toxins and pathogens should
include:

1. Allergen tests with rabbits and guinea pigs.

2. Tests for pathogenic organisms, such as salmonella,
    clostridia and coliforms.

3. Tests for mycotoxins and parasite eggs.

In the event of positive findings in these tests, some modi-
fication of the manufacturing process may be needed in order to
eliminate the problem.

Tests for toxins naturally occurring as a result of fermentation should determine if the organism produces any toxins and
if such toxins remain in the product and pose a potential hazard
to animals or man. The animal safety studies should be designed
to answer this question. These tests should include determination

of nucleic acids in the product, as well as any other toxic substances known to be produced by the organism.

In order to demonstrate animal safety, acute, subacute and
chronic studies may be necessary and are described, as follows:
1.   Acute studies in the target species.   The need for acute
studies will depend on the nature of the product.   In general,
we feel that for most SCP products, acute studies would not provide meaningful data.
2.   Subacute studies in the target species.   These tests should
be conducted to determine whether any adverse effects on animal
health occur when microbial protein is fed at the maximum possible
use level of the product in the diet.   When possible, it is advisable to include levels less than and greater than the proposed
use level.   Practical considerations (animal acceptance of the
product, diarrhea, textures, etc.) may determine this maximum
level.   These tests may be combined with or be an expansion of
the commercial utility studies.   Animals should be fed for a
normal production period.   Practical control diets should have
protein levels similar to those of the test diets.   As a minimum,
these tests should include studies in horses, cattle, swine, and
broiler chickens.   Confirmatory studies in other species (turkey,
duck, etc.) could possibly be shorter, around 4 weeks.
3.   Chronic studies.   These tests should include reproduction
studies in the target species when the intended use of the product includes breeding animals.   Diets should be a practical control type and an experimental diet containing the microbial protein material to supply the supplemental protein needs of the test
species.   The amount of microbial protein in the test diets
should approximate that percentage proposed for the target species.
The material should be representative of the product that will be
marketed.   All treated animals (parents and offspring of each
generation) should be maintained on the test diets.

Parameters in the animal safety tests should include daily

observation of the test animals in all tests.   On the subacute
and chronic tests all normal production parameters (rate of gain,
feed efficiency, percent of lay, etc.) should be monitored. All
animals that die (controls included) on any test should be nec-
ropsied.   Gross pathology should be conducted on all studies at
any time of death, including termination of test or when
slaughtered.   In the event of any abnormalities, histopathology
of the affected areas will be required.   Histopathology of the
liver, kidney, mesenteric lymph nodes, spleen, testicles and
prostate (male), ovaries and uterus (female) and gastrointestinal
tract should be conducted on a representative sample of animals
(minimum 10) from each treatment on the subacute and chronic
studies.   Observations in the reproductive studies should be
made on the parents and offspring of each generation.   Normal
reproductive parameters (numbers born and weaned, birth and weaning weights, fertility, hatchability, etc.) should be monitored
in the reproductive studies.   Observations for teratogenicity,
mutagenicity, and carcinogenicity should be made in the reproductive (chronic) study.

Abnormalities attributable to treatment encountered in these
studies may require additional work in the affected area. This
additional work may take the form of studies to determine the
cause of the abnormalities and to determine whether use level in
the diet or other use limitations are necessary to prevent such
problems.   Here again, the use of microbial protein as a general
feed ingredient depends on it being safe for animals of any
species, class and reproduction status.

Utility of the product as primarily a protein source and
secondarily as an energy source may be demonstrated adequately for
some species by determination of the protein efficiency ratio
(PER) and metabolizable energy (ME) value.   PER studies may be
conducted by the official method in rats, and/or by a modified
method using chicks.   Metabolizable energy may be determined in

rats and chicks.   For other species, it may be necessary to show
that the product can alleviate a nitrogen deficiency in the target species and that the product can serve as a source of energy
in a normal feeding trial.   Much of this utility data may be obtained in conjunction with the animal safety data.   Feeding
trials and metabolism studies in the target species will also be
considered as supportive evidence of utility.   Other data which
may be generated for commercial utility concerns the character
of the product.   Determinations of vitamin content, trace mineral
content, amino acid composition, etc., as well as their availability to the animal, may also be considered as supportive evidence of utility.

We consider manufacturing, chemistry, and quality control
data to be essential in evaluating SCP products.   A complete
description of the raw material so far as is known, the manufacturing process, and the finished product should be provided.
Any quality control measures taken to ensure that the raw material
and/or final product are of uniform quality and composition should
be described.   Any chemicals or contaminants which may enter the
product as a result of manufacturing, processing, or handling
should be described.   The analytical data concerning composition
of the final product should be provided.   Where stability data
are necessary, appropriate studies to demonstrate that the product
is stable in storage should be conducted.   All of these types of
data are valuable in determining the characteristics of the final
product, and some of these data may also be used in evaluating
safety of the product.

In conclusion, we have outlined general testing procedures
whereby SCP products may be evaluated from the standpoint of animal
utility, animal safety and human safety.

REFERENCES

1.   Federal Food, Drug, and Cosmetic Act.   U.S. Government
      Printing Office, Washington, D.C.   (January 1971).

2. Code of Federal Regulations, Title 21. U.S. Government Printing Office, Washington, D.C. (1971).

A RAPID METHOD TO DETERMINE THE CARBON FROM "PETROLEUM-SCP" IN FOODSTUFFS AND IN ANIMAL TISSUES

P. Resmini

Istituto di Industrie Agrarie
Università di Milano, Italy

The carbon present in a compound may have a recent biological origin, or an ancient geological one (for instance from petroleum, fossil carbon, rocks and so on). It is possible to recognize the carbon origin by measuring the activity of its isotope (^{14}C): in the first case, indeed, this activity should have the same value we observe in the atmospheric CO_2 (during the last year it was 18.5 - 19.5 dpm/g of carbon); in the second case, since the lifetime of (^{14}C) is 5730 years, there is no evident activity due to this isotope.

Of course the carbon of SCP, obtained from any type of petroleum products, has no (^{14}C) activity; on the contrary, all the organic components of a normal food have the same (^{14}C) level as atmospheric CO_2 (except the very small quantity of synthetic integrators, as some amino acids, vitamins, etc.). (^{14}C) low levels (natural levels) can usually be determined by liquid scintillation, by converting the CO_2 (obtained from the sample combustion) to benzene, but for many reasons this method is not feasible for routine analysis.

We suggest a rapid method to measure natural (^{14}C) level in any organic substance (foodstuffs, animal tissues, etc.) by means of a common liquid scintillation spectrometer (1). The method includes the following steps:

COMBUSTION APPARATUS

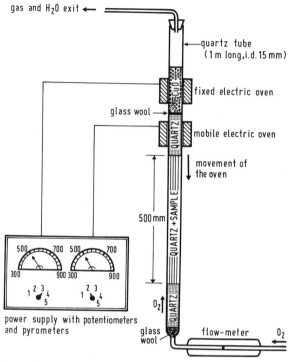

Fig. 1   Combustion apparatus.

1.   Combustion of 8 - 10 g of organic matter in an electric vertical oven (Fig. 1).

We burn the substance, in oxygen current, in a vertical quartz tube (1 mm long, inner diameter 15 mm) which is filled with: granular quartz, a mixture of quartz + sample, and copper oxide.

There are two electric ovens: one is fixed in a position corresponding to that of the copper oxide and kept at 700°C; the second oven is slowly moved downwards, during the combustion, its position corresponding to that of the sample, to prevent the formation of tarry products, and it is kept at 300 - 800°C according to the type of sample.   The oxygen flow is kept at 200 ml/min and the combustion is completed in half an hour.

RECYCLING ABSORPTION APPARATUS

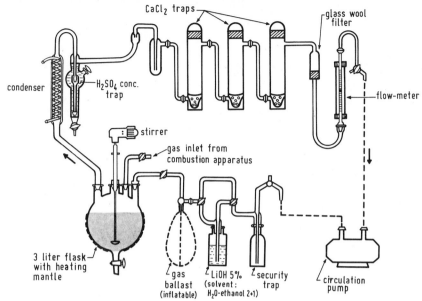

Fig. 2 Recycling absorption apparatus.

2.   The combustion gas and the excess oxygen are collected in a recycling apparatus where simultaneous absorption of CO_2 on LiOH solution is obtained (Fig. 2).

The gases are recycled by the pump in concentrated sulphuric acid for washing the CO_2, in granular and powdered $CaCl_2$ traps for drying the gas, and in a solution of 5% LiOH (H_2O-ethanol 2+1).   The excess gases are collected in the gas ballast;   in this way there is no loss of CO_2 and the pressure in the apparatus is constant. Li_2CO_3 precipitates from the alcohol solution and is then washed with methanol and dried at room temperature.   A salt of 96 - 98% purity is thus obtained in about 3 hours.

3.   12 g of Li_2CO_3 (corresponding to 1.9 g of carbon) are placed in a nylon vial with 17 ml of a special liquid scintillation cocktail: p-xilene 100 ml - PBD 500 mg - BBOT 300 mg.   The principle to measure (^{14}C) low levels by counting Li_2CO_3 has also recently been suggested by Moghissi (2).

Table 1   Levels of (^{14}C) (as dpm/g of carbon) in the body of chickens fed with petroleum proteins.*   Preset count of 40,000, with an average error, at 2σ confidence level, of 0.5 dpm.

Percentage of proteins in the food substituted by petroleum proteins.	Defatted meat	Fat	Feathers	(^{14}C) level in the food
0	19.2	19.5	19.0	19.3
50	12.1	16.1	10.7	15.0
75	9.2	14.9	7.6	11.2
100	7.0	7.2	7.1	6.9

* "TOPRINA" BP (58% protein, 11% fat, 6% ashes).

The filled vial is counted in a liquid scintillation spectrometer, LSA-01 Philips, with an efficiency of 47 - 55% and a background of 16 - 17 cpm.

By this method we can measure not only the quantity of petroleum SCP added to the foodstuffs, but also the distribution of the carbon from SCP in the body of animals fed with these substances.

The (^{14}C) levels obtained in a chicken-feeding experiment are reported here (Table 1).   We have tested three types of foods with different percentages of "TOPRINA" BP and, of course, with different (^{14}C) levels.

The greatest decrease of (^{14}C) activity has been found in the feathers, but we have lower values in the fat than the control.   If counting time is long enough (40,000 counts) we have for a biological product an average error in the measure, at 2σ confidence level, less than 0.5 dpm.

This means that, because the protein level in the chicken's food is normally of 22 - 24%, we can detect the presence of petroleum SCP in the food and in the chicken's body when less than 10% of this product has been used.

REFERENCES

1. Resmini, P. and Volonterio, G.   "A Rapid Method to Deter-
    mine the Carbon Origin in Any Organic Compound and its
    Application to the Food Control." FEBS Special Meeting
    15-19 April 1973, Dublin, Ireland.

2. Moghissi, A.A.   *In:*   "The Current Status of Liquid Scin-
    tillation Counting."   (Bransome, ed), Grune & Stratton,
    New York (1970).

SESSION 4
ROUNDTABLE DISCUSSIONS

The following section presents the summaries of the five
discussion topics. The discussion groups were organized so the
chairman of the group introduced the topic to the conferees.
Subsequently each of the chairmen examined briefly a specific
question that was related to the general topic of the group.
The conferees were then invited to offer viewpoints on the various subjects.   These summaries should not be considered to be
100% complete nor is it suggested that there was complete agreement among the conferees.   However, it is believed they represent a reasonably accurate review of the highlights of each discussion session.

TOPIC 1

CONTROL OF SCP PROCESSES

CHAIRMEN

Dr. F. Giacobbe
Compagnia Tecnica Industrie Petroli
Rome, Italy

Dr. G.I. Griesmer
Union Carbide
Geneve, Switzerland

Dr. J. Littlehailes
Imperial Chemical Industries
Teesside, England

Dr. P. Peri
Liquichimica
Milan, Italy

Dr. J. Senez, Chairman of the Group
Centre National de la Recherche Scientifique
Marseille, France

Dr. G. Solomons
Lord Rank Research Centre
High Wycombe,
England

The chairman initially presented a microbiologist's point of view of controlling the processes of SCP production of the group: (a) in other fermentation processes or industries, the purpose is to obtain by-products or metabolic intermediates, while in the case of SCP production, the object is that of obtaining a biomass, (b) that in SCP production based on hydro-

carbons and alcohols, the metabolism of hydrocarbons is an exclusively aerobic process, (c) in the production of SCP from
hydrocarbons there is some risk of a change in the metabolic activity of the organism when oxygen is exhausted or not adequate,
if oxygen is not provided to the organisms, the metabolism is
eventually completely halted, (d) current processes in industrial
SCP production are based on continuous cultures.   This presents
difficulties in the case of the other fermentation processes, and
especially those using mutants selected for maximal production
of a by-product or of a metabolic intermediate, because of the
risk of back-mutations or of secondary mutations resulting in un-
favourable metabolic changes.   In the case of SCP, however, the
risk of a mutational change of the culture in the course of a
continuous process is minimized, owing to the fact that the
selection and stabilization of strains is based on optimal substrate utilization and biomass production.

In regard to the choice of organism for SCP production, an
interest was noted in the use of mixed populations of culturally
related organsims as opposed to the current processes which are
based on a single organism.   In the light of experience gained
at large pilot plant and industrial scale, it has been shown
that in practice constancy of product over a long period of time
can be achieved.   It is obvious that both from safety and economic veiwpoints, such constancy of production is essential and
has to be routinely monitored.   Such testing must include
chemical, bacteriological, toxicological and nutritional examination, by conventional and established procedures.   With respect to contamination and continuous production of SCP in large
quantities, it must be borne in mind that even though usual food
sources are not bacteriologically pure, the purity and wholesome-
ness of SCP must be monitored constantly.   The transfer of technology from pilot plant to intermediate capacities, and ultimately
to full industrial scale production was discussed.   On the whole,

conditions prevailing in an industrial plant are similar to
those in a pilot plant; differences do arise from sheer, aeration and other physical factors. However, the scale-up in
size from laboratory production to pilot plant production is not
necessarily the same as from the pilot plant to the industrial
plant. If the results from standard tests in pilot plant production confirmed the results obtained from standard tests on
laboratory produced products, could it be concluded that these
same tests on the product produced on an industrial scale would
be similar? The group was not able to conclude that standard
tests on an industrial production scale would give similar results. Toxicological tests, at least, should be repeated on
the product from the industrial production. It was also
suggested that less time could be allotted to pre-tests and more
to end product tests. However, adequate tests must be performed
on the initial material so that continued development of the
product would be warranted.

The group drew attention to the fact that when a SCP process was scaled up manufacturers must be fully aware of the need
to monitor the various stages or steps of the process, including
fermentation, recovery, drying and processing of SCP, in order
to ensure the identity of the final product with the one on
which extensive testing was originally based. Specifically, if
complete nutritional, toxicological and complementary tests have
been performed on the product of the pilot plant, the product
deriving from scaling up to a full scale production plant should
be tested for constancy of product as stated above.

The group considered more specifically the production of
SCP from purified n-paraffins. In this regard it was stated
that present technology for the separation of n-paraffin using
molecular sieves provides a product of 99% purity. At this
point, the principal co-isolated materials are branched, fully
saturated paraffins. After release from these molecular sieves,

further purification processes eliminate polycyclic aromatics and other unsaturated products. The chain length of the n-paraffins has an influence on the growth rate and yield of the organisms, but no influence on the composition of the cells.

The group discussed the problem of nomenclature of SCP for marketing. In this regard it was considered if the specific name or collection number of the organism(s) should be included on the product label. Opinion on this point differed. All parties however, insisted that full disclosure of the process, including the identity of the organism, should be made available to the regulatory and legislative authorities. Alternative generic names for protein sources derived from microorganisms were also discussed. Even though a SCP product does contain other constituents besides proteins, no other name that was proposed to replace the name "single cell protein" was acceptable.

TOPIC 2

PROCESSING OF SCP FOR HUMAN FOOD

CHAIRMEN

Mr. S. Danielsen
Dansk Gaering Industries
Copenhagen, Denmark

Dr. R. Flannery
Amoco Food Company
Chicago, Illinois, U.S.A.

Dr. A. Spicer, Chairman of the Group
Lord Rank Research Centre
High Wycombe, England

Altogether 10 questions were placed before us and the conclusions we arrived at give a balanced expression of the panel's
view and the views of the participants who took a very active
part in the discussions.

SCP for human consumption is not a very far-off scientific
dream but a tangible development which will make its market debut
in the second half of the decade. PAG Guideline No.12 provides
a summary of the tests necessary to make SCP safe for human consumption. These tests, which we regard as minimum requirements,
span a time of above five years and should be supplemented by
feeding tests on primates and ultimately human beings to evaluate
possible allergy reactions in men for which neither rodents nor
farm animals would provide the answer. The material under test
must be provided by a representative pilot plant (not a laboratory-

scale production) on which the design for large-scale production would be based.   Only under these conditions need the tests on material from the ultimate factory plant not be repeated but such product would then be subjected to short-term confirmatory tests only.

Is SCP for human food dependent upon specific substrates? The answer is given in PAG Guideline No.12, which lists methane, methanol, ethanol, carbohydrates, carbon-dioxide and long chain normal alkanes as suitable carbon sources.   A representative of the E.E.C. Legal Commission, present at our Symposium, has asked us, however, to state that in forthcoming E.E.C. regulations all hydrocarbons will be excluded as substrates suitable for the production of SCP destined for the human food market.   Further proof, based on exhaustive testing, will have to be produced before hydrocarbons can be considered as suitable carbon sources. Our panel pleaded for the legalisation of the end-product rather than the process once testing has been successfully completed.

Can technological standards for SCP, such as purity, hetero-geneity, content of nucleic acid, etc., be formulated on the basis of present knowledge?   Yes, quite emphatically, Yes! We have enough scientific information based on years of research by competent teams to safeguard microbiological standards of purity.   The steady state reached in continuous fermentation will ensure uniformity and homogeneity of the biomass and nucleic acid content can be controlled to the quantity ultimately re-quired by food formulations.   A number of ways to reduce nucleic acid, which varies greatly in percentage in different organisms and different cell multiplication rates, have been published and much work to refine these processes has been undertaken by the companies engaged in SCP work.

To maintain or enhance the nutritional value of SCP, stan-dard fermentation or harvesting processes need to be adapted and modified.   In order to stabilize and render SCP edible, it has

to be subjected to a series of processes which do, in fact, reduce its nutritional values.   These processes then have to be
modified in order to maintain or improve the original nutritional
values.   Aseptic conditions for the fermentation stage are a
conditio sine qua non;   and sanitary downstream processing is
equally vital.   Heat input during drying must be controlled to
ensure the biological availability of heat labile amino-acids
on which the nutritive value of the protein depends.   The fermentation process lends itself to the addition of a variety of
micro-nutrients which will not only improve the yield but also
the quality of the end-product.

Can SCP products be fortified so that they are nutritionally
equivalent to the material being replaced?   Most SCP's have a
high lysine content and are rich in vitamins of the B complex.
When added to cereal mixtures, such as wheat or rice products,
they would upgrade their biological value by a considerable percentage and act in a similar manner to milk proteins.   SCP contains, after all, every micronutrient required for optimum cell
growth, such as iron, phosphates, calcium, magnesium and minor
trace elements.   Sulfur amino acids may be added during the
fermentation stage to enhance the biological value of the biomass, apart from a variety of adjustments which can be made to
eliminate any concern for the nutritional aspects of SCP.

Can the mixtures of amino acids or hydrolyzates from SCP be
used for human food and in what areas?   The market for such products appears, at the moment, rather limited but a variety of
savoury flavours could be based on such extracts or hydrolyzates
and such uses would materially assist in the solution of the
important B.O.D. problem, which without doubt will be resolved
by different manufacturers in a number of ways.

Which way is preferable for processing SCP for human food,
as structure-forming material or as additive?   SCP products will
answer both demands.   Some will be structure dependent and thus

H

be used ideally as an additive, and these may well be the applications in the near future.   Ultimately, structure forming
SCP's will answer the demand for meat or fish analogues or a
variety of new foods in which the texture will depend entirely
on the SCP product.

What functional properties do we expect from SCP?   Let us
remember that the cells harvested as biomass are whole cells,
incorporating cell wall material, cell-bound protein, carbohydrate
and lipids, apart from other chemical ingredients.   Once a cell
is opened, there are two options: (a) one can obtain protein
plus cell debris;   (b) separate protein (isolates).   Moreover,
there are two kinds of isolates, denatured and non-denatured
ones.   Each of the forms offers many alternatives in functional
characteristics and the ultimate choices depend on technology and
economics.   We must not compare SCP with protein isolates or
concentrates in our evaluation of functional properties and different SCP will display different functionalities, such as water
and fat absorption or adsorption, to a greater or lesser degree.
In the early stages of SCP marketing, food processors would be
more interested in its functional properties than in its nutritional ones.   Clearly in the developing nations, the nutritive
value would be given greater priority.   There will therefore be
continuous exchange of information between SCP manufacturers and
food processors in order to produce a wide range of SCP types
with many different functional qualities.

With proper technology, functionality can be built into SCP,
as has been done with soy.   SCP evolution may probably go through
these three phases: from nutritive additive to a balanced food
analogue, and hopefully to end up as a protein soluble in water.
However, in time to come, isolates or concentrates can and will
be produced from SCP with distinct functional properties, some
of them synergistic in action with other proteins.   Their flavour
will be bland enough to allow incorporation into other food mix-

tures.

What are the differences between SCP and vegetable proteins (e.g. soya) as regards spinning and other texturizing processes? We must accept that the biomass as harvested cannot form the dope for spinning.   Protein isolates of 80/90% purity are required for a spin edible filament.   An isolate from SCP could be used and properties would differ if a denatured or non-denatured protein is used, similar to isolates from soya or other oilseeds.   The biomass can be texturized in a number of ways - by thermal extrusion, puffing or deep oil frying - and interesting textures and flavours result from such processes.

Further discussions centred around the ingestion and digestibility of quantities of cell wall material present in SCP for human food.   Toxicological work will have confirmed the absence of noxious effects of cell wall constituents, whilst the presence of cellulose polysaccharides could have desirable metabolic effects, providing much desired roughage in man's present-day diet. Their water retention capacity would also enhance the satiety symptom, thus assisting calorie control for people in need of reduced food intake.

Foods containing SCP are likely to enter the market in the second half of this decade.   They will have benefited a great deal from the experience gained in marketing protein isolates and concentrates from legumes and oilseeds.   Advanced food technology will have given them highly acceptable textures and flavours, whilst their price competitiveness can hardly be doubted.

TOPIC 3
NUTRITIONAL VALUE AND SAFETY OF SCP AS HUMAN FOOD

CHAIRMEN

Prof. G.L. Gatti
Istituto Superiore di Sanità
Rome, Italy

Prof. A. Pocchiari
Istituto Superiore di Sanità
Rome, Italy

Dr. B.L. Oser, Chairman of the Group
Food and Drug Research Laboratories
Maspeth, New York, U.S.A.

Dr. K.W.G. Shillam
Huntingdon Research Centre
Huntingdon, England

Dr. V. Young
Massachusetts Institute of Technology
Cambridge, Massachusetts, U.S.A.

At the outset, it was pointed out by the chairman that the Protein Advisory Group undertook to draft Guidelines for the testing of SCP on the premise that a need existed to explore and develop novel sources of protein which, prior to clinical evaluation in human subjects, had to be carefully tested in the laboratory for purity, nutritive value and safety. Whereas safety for man can not be established with absolute certainty, present techniques based on exhaustive animal tests provide reasonable assurance that new foods can be administered without risk to human subjects under

205

carefully controlled conditions.   However, it was recognized
that advances in safety evaluation procedures, e.g. tests for
fetotoxicity, and experience gained from tests in man, might reveal effects not shown in preclinical studies such as impalat-
ability, nausea or other effects of a subjective nature.
Examples were also cited of foods long used by man or animals
before the presence of toxic components was recognized as in
soybean, cottonseed and rapeseed meals.   Many types of food consumed over long periods with apparent impunity, including varieties of yeasts and fungi, have not been subjected to the rigorous
scientific tests for nutrition and safety available today.

The PAG Guidelines, it was pointed out, describe in general
terms, methods for investigating the composition and purity (freedom from contaminants) of SCPs, from both the chemical and microbiological standpoints;   their nutritional value, particularly
in relation to digestibility and protein utilization;   and safety
evaluation in the rodent as measured by growth, food consumption
and efficiency, hematological and biochemical parameters, reproduction and lactation, and gross and microscopic pathological
changes.

It was emphasized that the objective of the preclinical
studies described in Guideline No.6 are regarded as achieved
"when it has been determined that the levels and conditions of
feeding of the novel dietary component are sufficiently safe to
warrant a cautious program of study in human subjects".

PAG Guideline No. 7 for human testing of supplementary food
mixtures presupposes the satisfactory execution of the preclinical
studies.   Procedures are described for determining the palatability and physiological tolerance of the novel dietary component
by experimental subjects, their responses in terms of growth,
nitrogen utilization, hematological, biochemical and physiological
functional tests, under various feeding conditions, depending upon
age and nutritional state.   Precautions necessary when using in-

fants, children, or malnourished subjects are emphasized.

PAG Guidelines are intended to serve as "general recommendations rather than as a series of mandatory procedures" and permit variations in the discretion of competent investigators as
determined by the nature, source, and intended use of the dietary
component under test.

The question concerning the choice of the organism or the
process for producing SCP as a human food versus an animal feed
was discussed in general terms.   In view of the apparent speci-
ficity of the allergic type of reaction to the ingestion of some
SCP sources by human subjects and the lack of comparable adverse
effects in experimental and farm animal species and even non-
human primates, it is clear that a SCP product found to be suitable for animal feed will not necessarily be safe or nutritionally
acceptable as a human food.   Processing modifications may serve
to render a SCP product suitable for human consumption but with
the limited clinical data available guidelines cannot be made
with respect to the nature of the processing modifications or
whether certain organisms or substrates are more or less acceptable as a basis of SCP production for human food.

The question of whether a higher level of RNA could be
tolerated if uric acid lowering drugs were used was also discussed.   It was pointed out that studies concerning acceptable
levels of RNA intake were confined to healthy adult subjects and
that there was a need for information for children and other age
groups.   It was felt there was little likelihood that the current PAG position of a maximum additional intake of 2 g nucleic
acid per day would be raised.

The use of uric acid lowering drugs (i.e., allopurinol or
the uricosuric type) was considered but it was concluded that
they cannot be recommended in conjunction with the utilization of
SCP in human food.   The only appropriate measure is to limit the
dietary intake of nucleic acids and swine derivatives.   In the

context of SCP contributing a significant proportion of the daily
protein need, an RNA-reduced product is to be recommended in the
development of SCP for human consumption.

Quoting from Guideline No. 6, "Products intended for incorporation into animal feeds may not require as extensive testing
as is suggested here for human foods, but foods derived from such
animal sources must be considered from the viewpoint of the possible presence of residues in meat, milk, or eggs, transmitted
from animal feeds."   The presence of such residues is generally
revealed by appropriately selected, highly sensitive chemical
analytical procedures.

In contrast with the testing of human foods which require
preliminary evaluation of experimental animals, SCP intended for
animal feeding is best tested in the target species.   It was
noted that the nutritional requirements of avian species are different from those for rodents, and those of ruminants are different from those for non-ruminants.   A by-product of tests in
domestic and farm animals such as chickens, pigs and dogs, is
the additional information contributed with respect to potential
risk for the human species.

It was proposed that Guidelines for the testing of SCP for
animal feeding should take into account (a) the degree of novelty
of the product with respect to species of microorganism, substrate,
and conditions of processing;   (b) whether products derived from
the animal are a source of food for man;   (c) whether the animals
are used for breeding stock;   and (d) the types of feed ingredients
presently used in animal rations.

Safety of SCP must be demonstrated at the pilot plant stage.
What range of tests should be applied to the commercially-produced
material to insure identity with the pilot plant material on which
utility and safety were demonstrated?   Moreover, if there are
subsequent slight changes in production technology in a commercial
plant, or further plants are constructed, what examinations should

be made to insure that the production is safe? It appears unreasonable to expect a commercial operator to put his plant "in
mothballs" while conventional long-term safety tests are made as
such tests can take 3 years from initiation to completion. On
the other hand, from both safety and commercial viewpoints, the
risk should be minimized. In the case of feeds for human consumption, the manufacturing process is not judged, but rather
the quality and safety of the final product is monitored. Therefore, legislation concerning a product containing SCP should
occur only on the final product after it has been extensively
tested.

This problem was rasied earlier at the conference when it
considered PAG Guidelines were advisory and that individual state
authorities should regulate this matter. But most, if not all,
state authorities do not have clear-cut opinions or regulations
on exactly what should be done. The situation is not improved
by the fact that full details of production technology, for good
commercial reasons, will not be released by the manufacturers.
How too can the manufacturers always be certain that they know
exactly what is going on inside the fermentation chamber?

Tentatively the following procedures are suggested.

1. *On the Pilot Plant Material*

(a) Constancy of the process as indicated by reproducibility
of composition of successive samples over a reasonable period of
time. Composition to include viable microorganisms, hydrocarbons, heavy metals, amino acids, nucleic acid (in the case of
human use), vitamins, etc., as recommended by IUPAC for example.

(b) Thorough pre-clinical examination for safety using the
stringent toxicological procedures that have been developed for
food chemicals. Any additional tests, specific to SCP, are a
subject for considerable discussion and will not be considered
here.

2. *On the Commercial Product*

(a)   Full range of compositional quality as for the pilot plant material.

(b)   Short-term feeding studies in rodents employing growth, biochemical, and hematological parameters.

Both composition and safety tests should be done at the outset and routinely at reasonable periods thereafter.

It is not too unreasonable to expect the manufacturers to adopt such procedures, if they must go into commercial production at this point in time, and lengthy delays in marketing should be avoided.   Constant surveillance and revision of these checks will be necessary in view of new scientific facts coming to light and fresh scientific thought.   There are many gaps in our current state of knowledge and there certainly appear to be no simple and instantaneous predictive tests which would permit declaration of safety to our complete satisfaction.

The panel considered the need for supplanting the general term SCP with more specific but non-pejorative terms applicable to this class of substances.   Questions were raised as to whether the naming of SCPs should reflect the genus or species of microorganisms or the basic substrate, and whether the regulatory agencies would interpose requirements for specific nomenclature in the interest of informing consumers.   Mention was also made of the need for interlingual uniformity of terminology and a request for recommendations was made on behalf of the PAG.

The role of PAG in recommending SCPs as a suitable source of protein, particularly for use in developing countries, was discussed.   It was pointed out that aside from published or submitted summary reports, the details of investigations for nutritional or safety evaluation of production lots of SCP have not been examined for the purpose of arriving at such judgements. Whether PAG should have the opportunity for independent appraisal of these products, as a prerequisite to making recommendations, will be considered at the forthcoming meeting of the SCP working group.

TOPIC 4

UTILIZATION AND SAFETY OF SCP AS ANIMAL FEED

CHAIRMEN

Dr. K. Aibara
National Institute of Health
Tokyo, Japan

Dr. R. Fahnenstich
Degussa
Frankfurt, West Germany

Dr. R. Ferrando
École Nationale Vétérinaire
Alfort, France

Prof. G. Giolitti
University of Milan
Milan, Italy

Dr. I.R.P. van der Wal, Chairman of the Group
ILOB
Wageningen, The Netherlands

I   GENERAL

The discussion of this topic was lively and well attended, probably reflecting the general feeling that the application of SCP as an animal feed ingredient is the most relevant for the time being.

In the discussions it was obvious that for some products, large amounts of experimental data obtained with farm animals are already published. For many other products under investigation, however, little information is made available.

This situation is setting limits to the possibilities for a discussion of the merits of many SCPs. Nutritional and safety aspects are specific for SCPs and experimental results obtained with one cannot be transferred to another.

Although helpful, a detailed chemical, bacteriological and physical analysis does not provide a complete and reliable base for a judgement of a product. The number of constituents found in a living organism, which may be of relevance with regard to safety, are far too numerous to be completely defined, leave apart to be completely analysed. A more satisfactory base for an evaluation of SCPs can be found in a biological testing with animals. This has not only to be taken into account during the final evaluation for obtaining clearance for use, but also during the selection of product modifications during the development stage and for quality control in full-scale production plants.

The experimental results obtained with a novel source of protein depend on:

a.   *Nature of the Substrate*

Substrates under study are: manure, wood, molasses, whey, cassava, carob bean sugar, olive wastes, starch offals and urban sewage. Derivatives of mineral oil and natural gas drew much attention in the past few years, partly because of the availability of huge amounts of well-standardised qualities of these products. All of these substrates have their specific risks with regard to toxic residues and contamination with pathogenic organisms. Apart from differences in the basic substrate, also differences in other ingredients added to the culture medium may affect the safety of the end product.

b.   *Nature of the Microorganisms Involved*

Yeasts, bacteria, fungi and algae have their own specific aspects with regard to safety and nutritional value. This is also the case with uncountable numbers of strains within each of these categories.

c. Nature of Processes

It became obvious that even with a given substrate and micro-organisms, nutritional value and safety of the end product can be strongly affected by process modifications. Temperature and solvents applied as well as microbial infections are to be considered among the relevant variations.

The effects of the factors mentioned make it clear, that discussing experimental evidence of SCPs can only be fruitful if the products are well-defined and specified.

II THE UTILIZATION

a. The utilization of SCP in animal feed is a realistic item. Farm animals form today by far the leading system to convert raw SCPS into an acceptable human food with a high organoleptical and nutritional quality.

b. The relative shortage of high protein sources like soya and fishmeal in the world markets will tend to increase in the forth-coming years. The need for alternative feed proteins is therefore urgent.

If the increase in demand for protein over the past ten years (approximately 8% per year) is going to continue at the same rate, the production of soya and fishmeal almost certainly cannot be increased sufficiently. To meet this rise in demand per annum, approximately an extra three million hectares of soya per year would be required. According to the forecasters, however, the acreage of soya in the main exporting country, the USA, will decrease in 1974.

c. The high biological quality of most of the SCP product makes them especially suitable for *inclusion in rations for monogastric animals* among which pigs and poultry form the largest potential consuming groups.

d. When included in practical rations for farm animals SCP alone can provide in principle all the amino acids essential for

the physiological functions of farm animals, if included at sufficiently high levels.   Such high levels will not be reached
in practice.   First of all, grains provide, as well as energy,
a substantial part of the amino acids required by the animal.
Secondly, the SCP will have to compete as a protein source with
other high-quality protein sources like soya, groundnuts and
fishmeal, and also with synthetic amino acids.

By linear programming the inclusion rate of SCP in rations
can be calculated by taking into account:

- the nutrient requirements of the animals
- the nutrient contents of SCP
- the price of the nutrients in SCP and in alternative
amino acid sources.

For German conditions a calculation was carried out at price
levels of soya of 80 DM/100 kg, fish of 150 DM/100 kg, lysine of
16 DM/kg and methionine of 5 DM/kg.

Under these conditions the shadow price for a hydrocarbon
grown yeast with 65% of crude protein would be 143 DM/100 kg for
broiler feed, 120 DM for laying hen feed and 139 DM for protein
concentrates for pigs.   At prices below these limits it would be
economically attractive to include the SCP in the rations at
levels up to 12% in broiler feed, 5% in laying hens' rations and
13% in protein concentrates for pigs.   It was concluded that,
although changes in price interrelationships will exert an influence on the percentages mentioned, it is unlikely that SCP would
reach even then a much higher inclusion rate.   Therefore in test
rations designed for evaluation experiments, an inclusion rate
of 20% of an SCP with the protein content mentioned, offers a
safety margin already.

III   THE SAFETY OF THE PRODUCT

The use of a *SCP product in animal feed should not lead to
negative effects on the animals.*

In animal husbandry, negative effects on performance in the order of size of 5% during early growth, production and reproduction are economically of decisive importance and therefore generally unacceptable. From an experimental point of view, differences of this size can be reasonly well measured for most parameters at a statistically significant level, if the experimental technique meets adequate standards. It seems, therefore, reasonable to require that negative effects of this magnitude can be excluded with certainty on the basis of scientific evidence before a new SCP is approved for inclusion in practical rations.

Possible negative effects have to be measured by the classical, physiological, histological and chemical characteristics of organs and tissues according to the standard criteria of toxicology.

Although it was felt in the discussion that no special reason for mutagenetic and teratogenetic effects is to be feared, attention should be paid to these aspects.

Apart from being safe for the animals, SCP has *to be safe with regard to the animal products destined for human consumption.* The chemical composition of these edible products with regard to toxic residues asks for special attention by means of sophisticated analytical and biological testing. The organoleptic characteristics of the edible tissues have to be studied.

IV   TEST ANIMALS

Because digestion, resorption, nutrient requirements and susceptibility for possible toxins are specific for each animal species, it is considered essential to carry out tests with SCP with the main categories of animals for which the product will be used, that is poultry and swine.

The rat, as a standard test animal, is considered as recommendable for the classical toxicological studies.

By carrying out the tests in this way on a small rodent (rat), a bird (poultry) and a larger mammalian species (pig), a satisfactory basis for the nutritional and toxicological evaluation is obtained.

V   TESTING SCHEME

The testing scheme has to be adapted to the characteristics of the product and the situation under which it will be used. However it seems advisable to have a standardized testing scheme as a generally accepted base, in order to promote the comparability of the experimental results and the international communication about their interpretation.

The Protein Advisory Group of the United Nations is proceeding towards the target of formulating standard guidelines for testing.   They include multiple generation tests with the animal species mentioned.

POLITICAL AND SOCIAL ASPECTS OF SCP UTILIZATION

CHAIRMEN

Dr. M.J. Forman, Chairman of the Group
Agency for International Development
Washington D.C., U.S.A.

Mrs. H. Henderson
Writer and social critic
Princeton, New Jersey, U.S.A.

Dr. G.D. Kapsiotis
Protein Food Development - Food Policy and Nutrition Division
FAO
Rome, Italy

Dr. K. Katoh
National Food Research Institute
Tokyo, Japan

Dr. E. Smit
Philips/Duphar
Amsterdam, The Netherlands

The World of the 1970's is characterized by a number of factors which will have an impact on the potential for utilization
of SCPs.   Among these factors are:

1.   Rapid advances in a number of SCP technologies and a favorable prognosis for even further refinements in the future.

2.   A growing world demand for protein.

3.   Improved mass communications technology which makes possible
rapid and extensive information exchange among peoples within

countries and between nations.

4.   A rise of "consumerism"* which can influence the implementation of policies by government and industry.

In considering the potential for the utilization of SCP, a
distinction must be made between its use as an ingredient in
mixed animal feed and as a food ingredient for direct consumption
by humans.   It would appear that there already exists a large
potential market for SCP in the animal feed industry.   Conversely,
the potential for SCP use in foods for direct human consumption
would appear to be quite a few years off.   Producers are currently concentrating on the feed rather than the food potential,
and consumer concerns are therefore not related to SCP as a human
food ingredient, but rather on its impact on the food products
derived from the fed animals.

It is important to note that there is a great range in de-
grees of development and other differences between countries, and
therefore individual circumstances in each country will dictate
the feasibility of utilization of SCPs in the mixed feeds industry.
For example, the recent divergent experiences in Japan and Finland
were influenced by combinations of factors which were very country-
specific and would be unlikedly to be duplicated exactly anywhere
else.

In Japan, there has been a long history of expressed public
concern for environmental problems caused by industry and there
have been much publicised cases of pesticide residues in milk,
methyl mercury in seafood and various other toxic substances in
human food products.   There are well organized consumer groups
and newspapers with a tradition of public service campaigning.
There is also a very active political opposition to the party in
power.   In this set of circumstances, the news of a plan to begin
producing SCP based on hydrocarbons and the hint that the product

---

* Organized consumer expression of concern with the products being
served it by industry.

contained carcinogenic substances set off a wave of protest, fueled and led by consumer groups, various scientists opposing the government and a powerful newspaper.   The pressures mounted to the point where the plans had to be shelved.

In Finland, recognition of the increasing need for protein for animal feed and a desire by the government to minimize imports from other countries led to the government encouraging and assisting industry to set up SCP production with no hesitation nor problems whatsoever.   Factors such as a country's protein needs, desire for self-sufficiency, potential for domestic production, consumer attitudes, and other economic and political considerations will influence the timetable of development and acceptance of SCPs.

Discussions of political and social aspects of SCP utilization cannot be considered without examining some economic aspects.   In the recent past, products generated from the petroleum-chemical industries have had a stabilizing effect on cost of natural fibers and timber.   The availability of SCP can be just as beneficial to prices of feedstuffs in the feed manufacturing industry.   Even though there is some concern about SCP taking such a share of the market that the growth of some other established protein industries would be slowed is unfounded. Taking into account the present consumption of protein-rich substances and their expanding rate of growth, it appears that there will always be a need for all of the SCP, soy products, fish meal, and other protein sources that can be produced.

Companies who are developing production facilities for SCP must consider that any policy that limits the development of sound basic agriculture should be rejected.   Also, these facilities should be placed in an area where other agricultural products are readily available so that manufactured feeds can be produced without the necessity of shipping individual feeds excessive distances.

Some concern was expressed that hydrocarbons were not the most desirable substrate for SCP production.   Carbohydrates seemed to be more appealing to the layman; however, they were more difficult to collect in one geographical point, and their ultimate yield was of the order of 10% in comparison to less than one-to-one for hydrocarbons.   Also, that the quantities of the petroleum fractions used were a negligible percentage of the amount of crude oil used, and that by using a petroleum substrate to produce protein, an environmental pollution problem was being solved.

The three most important considerations likely to influence the introduction of SCPs are:

1.   Safety or the *image* of safety.   Apprehension in governments or among people of possible toxicity and safety when used, will create serious obstacles to utilization.

2.   Government policies, concerning SCP utilization, will be influenced by the desire for such things as food and/or feed, self-sufficiency, favorable trade balance, reduced vulnerability caused by dependence on imports, stabilizing domestic food prices, as well as pressures from industrial, labor and consumer groups.

3.   Mass media communications.   Rapid and widespread information diffusion through mass communications concerning the acceptance and proven viability of SCP in one area will tend to enhance acceptance in other areas.

Additional considerations *should* influence the introduction of SCP, but these may tend to be ignored in favor of expediency. In innovation and the application of *new* technologies of any kind, prudence would dictate considering the overall impact on economies and societies.   Certainly mankind's experience would indicate that short-term and narrow economic benefits may become long-term liabilities to society as a whole.   For example, the choice of processes (ingredients, substrates, etc.) will affect such factors as: depletion or conservation of energy resources, conservation or waste of other resources, environmental pollution, employment, distribution of income and wealth, social disruption and the release for human use of food sources utilized in animal feeding.

Social and political factors have often provided barriers to economically viable technological advances.   They may however also serve to facilitate the introduction of new technologies. Whether social and political factors become positive or negative forces may well depend upon the degree to which those striving to introduce and gain acceptability of the new technologies are sensitive and considerate of societal needs and political realities.

ADDENDUM TO TOPIC 5 SUMMARY
STATEMENT ON CURRENT STATUS OF SCP PRODUCTION
IN JAPAN

Kiyoaki Katoh

National Food Research Institute
Tokyo, Japan

In discussing what is the nature of the Japanese consumer groups' opposition against SCP grown on hydrocarbons, I would like to begin with discussing the unique structure of Japanese society and the influence of the mass communication media.

I think, and many sociologists agree, that Japan is a unique country, because it is an extremely uniform, homogeneous society. For a long time the nation has been comprised of people of the same race, of the same color, of the same origin as far back as 2,000 years or more, who speak the same language mutually understandable from North to South, wearing the same kind of clothes, eating essentially the same type of foods based on rice and, moreover, today, 100,000,000 of the population are having almost the same living standards, with not too many of the rich or the poor. That means, they live, on an average, in the same standard apartment house, own a small compact car, and enjoy the same TV programs offered by a limited number of networks, and they read in the commuter trains one of the four major leading newspapers that are distributed nationwide. The daily subscription of those four papers totally reaches 20 million copies.

Needless to say, the literacy rate is 100%.   What is important is that this very homogeneous population of 100 million is becoming more and more concentrated in urban areas, the so-called "megalopolis", where industrial activities are more vital.

This background means that the reaction of the public is strongly influenced by powerful mass media.   Essentially, the nation of Japan is not accustomed to the multilateral point of view of one certain problem or to admitting different opinions of different groups of people among themselves.   They tend to react quite straightforwardly to every problem, and the problems easily become "all or nothing", or "yes or no" questions.

On the evening of August 25, 1969, readers of one of the leading nationwide newspapers were surprised to see a big headline attacking the so-called petro-protein in Japan, that is SCP grown on n-paraffin.   This article quoted an abrupt comment from the Chief of Food Safety Section of Health Authority (officially Ministry of Health and Welfare), who said that because of suspected contamination of carcinogenic materials in SCP, the government was warning the industries that their plans for manufacturing SCP from n-paraffin would be delayed until safety assessment could be made by Food Sanitation Investigation Council (FSIC), an Advisory Board of the Health Ministry.

Since BP's historic success in making protein from petroleum was reported worldwide in 1963, petroleum protein sounded one of the rosy dreams of scientific and technological achievements of mankind.   However, this report in the newspaper became the very first occasion when the people got the impression that there was something questionable about the safety of hydrocarbons.

In October 1959, the Ministry of Health and Welfare organized a special committee on SCP grown on hydrocarbons as a part of the Food Sanitation Investigation Council, and they spent a year determining 22 checkpoints for safety evaluation of SCP, particularly based on petroleum derived materials.

In order to meet the requirements of these standards set by the government, the industries compiled their safety investigation data as a report, and each company submitted its own to the Ministry of Health and Welfare.   It took another year and one-half for the Food Sanitation Investigation Council to investigate these reports of the industries and to assess their individual products.   When FSIC was apparently reaching its conclusions, one particular leading newspaper started a strong campaign led by a reporter who was fiercely against the approval of SCP by the government.   This campaign, by which other newspapers were apparently influenced, definitely pushed consumer groups to stand up, make a dispute and demand the immediate halt of SCP development plans.   Sharp headlines in the newspaper, saying the SCP grown on hydrocarbon may be carcinogenic, was strongly appealing to consumers.

But this carcinogenicity campaign was actually not realistic. The industries had already established strict control of the raw material, and minimized the content of aromatics to less than 1 ppb, not only in the n-paraffin substrate, but also in the final product.   Yeast from n-paraffin contains less than 1 ppb of aromatics, yet, from a resoures point of view, particularly in a country like Japan, where the nation is heavily dependent upon imported protein sources, the value of the product became enormous.

I believe it is a fair attitude for any mass communication media to provide news and critical reviews without fear or favor, taking all aspects of the issue into account and to communicate all relevant information to the public.   Unfortunately, the idea of suspected carcinogenicity of SCP grown on hydrocarbons as told by the mass media has become a widespread conviction of the public.   This is, of course, a misunderstanding.   Why is the Japanese public so concerned about safety and who are the Japanese consumers?

They are the consumers of a country which achieved incredibly rapid economic growth and industrial development by sacrificing her environment. They are the consumers who have already learned that the nation's environment, at least some part of it, is no longer safe to harvest a healthy rice crop because of accumulated cadmium ion in the rice paddies. They have come to realize that their environment is no longer safe to milk a cow and even to feed their babies with breast milk because of BHC and other pesticide residues. They now know that their environment is no longer safe to catch coastal fish or shellfish because of a biological concentration of methyl mercury. This is, of course, the famous Minimata Disease. They are the people watching birds and fowls dying from an unknown cause, which is most likely because of concentrated poly-chlorinated biphenyl and are afraid of what is going to happen next to themselves. They are the prople who can no longer trust some food companies because of a terrifying accident of arsenic contamination in baby milk, or of widespread poisoning from PCB leaking out in the manufacturing process into edible oil products. In addition, there are even more serious problems of food additives and deceptive food products. Under these constraints, when every day the newspapers repeated the reports and articles, it is a very natural reaction for the consumers to try to stop the production of a product they believe to contain carcinogenic substances.

SCP from hydrocarbons was essentially taken as another food toxicity issue; for even if it is used exclusively as feed, it comprises a part of the food chain for humans. The value of SCP as a potential protein resource was almost completely overlooked until the recent soybean embargo shock of Mr. Nixon. They took it as another ambition of the chemical industries to get involved in the feed business in order to secure more profit.

What I have been talking about is the consumer's reaction in general, in Japan. However, there are more organized groups

of local consumers in the large metropolitan areas who have fed-
erated themselves under the name of Consumer Groups Liaison Committee to Ban Petro-protein.   This group is made up of house-
wives who are more seriously concerned about the SCP issue and
who have been most often referred to by newspaper reports.
Their activity was brought to its height when it was reported
that the industries involved autonomously withdrew from the SCP
development plans.   Their demands are essentially represented
by the following documents.

APPENDIX I

In spite of the publicity received by this group, I do not
think that they really influenced the Ministry of Health and
Welfare to take action against SCP.   Here, I would like to
introduce to you a document submitted to the Governor of Tokyo,
Professor Dr. Minobe, a renowned economist in Japan.   The document was submitted by the Tokyo Metropolitan Consumers' Council,
an advisory group of intellectuals and consumer representatives,
to the Governor, and was written under the strong advisory opinions
of Tokyo University Medical School professors.

APPENDIX II

In this document, I find the oppositions against SCP grown
on hydrocarbons to be more realistic and logical.   First of all,
from a resources point of view, they are opposed to depending
upon petroleum for food resources because it is a limited and not
a renewable resource, and for Japan an imported resource costing
a great deal of valuable foreign currency.   But what is more
critical, is that they are against hydrocarbon yeast protein
because it is unconventional.

This is basically a matter of aesthetics or philosophy about
what our food really ought to be.   Rejection of an unconventional
material that is to be incorporated even as a feed ingredient is

significant, not only for hydrocarbon derived protein, but also
for any other type of SCP based on unconventional raw material.
This is the rejection that all those who are involved in SCP
development have to overcome by showing that what looks so new
to us, so unconventional to us, is, as a matter of fact, really
good and is not very unconventional.

Surprisingly, there has been a complete lack of public information and public relations in Japan about SCP grown on hydrocarbons.   It was only a small circle of industries involved and
scientists in that particular area who knew about it.   Accumulated results of animal feeding trials and toxicology tests
carried out by various neutral research establishments have never
been brought to the attention of the public concerned.

In the threat of escalating inflation and environmental deterioration in Japan, and increasing frustration of consumers or
public in general, what the ruling political party is now the
most afraid of is losing the votes and support of urban consumers.
It has been revealed that the mayorship of several major cities
in Japan is occupied by leftists of the opposition party.   Since
the opposition party took the SCP issue as a political weapon to
use against the present government, the issue has become purely
political rather than scientific or technological or economical.
The ruling party, from a political point of view, exclusively
decided to get rid of this dispute and gave the industries involved so-called "administrative guidance" to withdraw quietly
from the proposed SCP venture.

In the newspapers it was reported as an autonomous with-
drawal, but that is not true.   Those who look at the records of
the National Diet Session, Agricultural and Forestry Committee,
Finance Committee, Science and Technological Committee, International Trade and Industries Committee will be disappointed and
aggravated by the fact that discussions and arguments were made
about SCP without knowing, exactly or accurately, what SCP grown

on hydrocarbon really is and what has already been tested and
what is known about it. Accurate public information to both
government and opposition party leaders, to news agencies, consumers and the public was lacking.

One of the high officials of FAO has recently told us in
Tokyo that the reactions of consumers are interesting and sometimes even mysterious. He told us he saw an increasing demand
for natural products in European markets. This trend reflects
an increasing demand for silk, leather from raw hide, essential
oils, natural spices and flavors. Natural products, unlike
synthetic products from chemical and petrochemical industries,
do not cause pollution in the course of their manufacturing.
Natural products are generally biodegradable. In most cases
natural products are superior in quality to synthetic products.

The trend of consumers' demand is the same in Japan. What
was unfortunate was that the newspapers wrote that SCP from n-
paraffin is artificial and synthetic, hence not natural. Yeast
is a living organism and natural. It seems to be very difficult
to change this first impression of artificialness. It will
probably take a long time to remove this misunderstanding and to
have them realize that it is natural. But we must try to make
every effort to let them know that SCP is natural.

Getting back to more fundamental problems of what our foods
really are supposed to be, I must point out that since the ancient
era, drinking and dining together has been a symbol of mutual reliance and friendship. It was even a ritual. Any food should
have a quality which we can totally rely upon, just as a baby or
a child relying on foods their mothers give them. Unfortunately,
many food industries have betrayed our reliance.

I would like to conclude my remarks just by quoting a phrase
of the New Testament:

"What father among you, if his son asks for a fish, will
instead of a fish give him a serpent; or if he asks for an egg,

will give him a scorpion?"

(Luke 11: 11, 12)

APPENDIX I

PETITION REGARDING THE USE OF PETRO-PROTEINS AS FEEDSTUFF

We have learned that the Ministry of Health and Welfare and the Ministry of Agriculture and Forestry are moving toward authorizing the use as livestock feedstuff of petro-proteins made from petroleum with the use of yeasts.

It is also said that the industries including Kanegafuchi Chemical Co., producing PCB pollution, Dainippon Ink and Chemicals and Kyowa Fermentation have invested heavily in petro-protein production facilities.

At present, our living environment is being disrupted by pollution, and we are being threatened by food pollution through agricultural chemicals, heavy metals, industrial raw materials, food additives, and the like.   At such a time, we cannot help but feel extremely anxious not only about the safety checks applied to petro-proteins themselves, but also about the approval of the use as feedstuff of large quantities of petro-proteins, which animals have never before experienced, without well-founded data covering several generations on the influences of petro-proteins on living beings.

What is needed now is not the hasty promotion of an industry for making feedstuffs out of petroleum, but rather the urgent adoption of measures for protection of natural protein resources including seafoods and fishmeal.

The large-scale production of petro-proteins is a grave problem affecting the lives of all of us.

We strongly request a thorough study of this problem.

List of Questions:

1.   Is it possible to extract pure normal paraffin uncontaminated by carcinogens; 3,4 benzopyrene; heavy metals; mercury; arsenic; and other toxic substances?   Is a monitoring system of constant checks established within the production process?

2.   Can the presence of mycotoxins in the microbial strains themselves be thoroughly investigated?   Could the manufacturers refuse on-the-spot inspections in the name of industrial and trade secrecy?   Who will do the inspecting?

3. It is said to be difficult to differentiate by analysis between petro-proteins and normal proteins. Would this also be true for checks to make sure that petro-proteins have not been mixed directly in foodstuffs?

4. Could such petro-protein feedstuffs have any long-term chronic toxicity in animals, particularly in fish?

5. Will there be a capability for systematic safety checks of the entire volume of finished products?

6. Will the responsibility for accidents be clearly defined?

Five Major Consumer Organization
Local Consumer Organizations Liaison Office

APPENDIX II

OPINIONS ON THE USE OF PETRO-PROTEINS AS FEEDSTUFFS

(Tokyo Metropolitan Consumers Council, February 19, 1973)

We have become aware of the importance of influences on the lives of the Metropolitan citizenry of the possible use of the so-called "petro-proteins" and we find ourselves in doubt concerning the safety of such petro-proteins. Thus, we have prepared the following opinions as the result of our discussions.

I. The problems as we see them

1) We feel that there are many unknown and difficult-to-comprehend elements in connection with petro-proteins, a food source which is after all unrelated to the food sources and food surviving the long selection process during the thousands of years of human history. There is thus a necessity to carry out not only full chemical analysis but also sufficient long-term biological experimentation on several generations of a variety of species of animals. There can be no precipitous judgements of safety based only on experiments covering only a few years on a very narrow range of animals such as rats and mice.

2) There is also the problem that feedstuff manufacturers and the Government have not established a system to clearly define responsibility in the event that accidents should occur involving meat for human consumption from animals raised on petro-protein feeds.

Basically, it is difficult for us to agree with the idea of attempting to resolve the human food supply problem through the use of petroleum, a natural resource which itself is limited. Instead, there should be thoroughgoing efforts to obtain food resources from natural resources which can be regenerated.

This problem particularly relates to attitudes toward food and to the Government's policies regarding food.   In other words, a policy which gives economic efficiency top priority and advocates the supply of cheap foods in this way should be discouraged.

II. Measures which should be taken by the Metropolitan Government

1)   Not only are there doubts of the above sort regarding the Ministry of Health and Welfare's view that the safety of petro-proteins has been proved at the experimental level, but steps have not been taken to establish the system of responsibility mentioned above.   The Governor of Tokyo should thus, without delay, strongly petition the Ministry of Health and Welfare, the Ministry of Agriculture and Forestry, and other concerned governmental agencies not to allow the production of petro-proteins.

2)   Regarding the experiments to be carried out by the National Government on the safety of petro-proteins, the Tokyo Metropolitan Government, too, should immediately establish a research and survey system of its own in order to assess the problems.

3)   The Tokyo Metropolitan Government, in addition to collection and organization of important data from both domestic and foreign sources regarding this matter for the use of consumer organizations, should also draw the attention of related metropolitan agencies and the general public to the importance of this problem.

CLOSING REMARKS

Peyton Davis

*Stanford Research Institute, Menlo Park
California, USA*

The importance of developing another source of protein for feed and food use has been stressed. However, it must be understood by those responsible for shaping policies for the distribution and use of SCP products, as well as by those who are producing SCP, that the need for additional protein is and will be increasing each day. As we have heard, there are several reasons why we must proceed quickly toward the goal of having SCP available in the marketplace.

Historically, the problem of the world food situation has centered on the limited food supply for a growing population. There are now indications that increasing affluence will make this situation even more acute. The demand for animal protein has grown as a result of increased overall income. This means that higher prices can be paid for animal products. But the cost of animal protein varies significantly around the world depending on a country's productive capacity. For example, in June 1973, a pound of boneless sirloin selling for $1.99 in Washington, cost $3.94 in Bonn, $2.47 in Paris, $2.75 in London, and $12.92 in Tokyo.

These high costs, in part, reflect a tremendous increase in the demand for animal feed in the face of continuous adverse cir-

I

cumstances for productivity.   Even though record production of
wheat is expected this year in the world market, food and feed
still will be scarce throughout the world.   Thus, SCP will be
needed to help meet man's future feed and food needs.   In addition, attempts must continue to increase agricultural production
and the distribution and availability of feed stocks.   Furthermore, SCP production does not make a demand on agricultural resources.

    During this symposium, we have heard of the variety of
analytical, biochemical, microbiological, toxicological, nutritional, and clinical tests necessary to standarize SCP products
- all of which are essential to ensure reproducible quality.
Use of less desirable SCP products would result not only in
directly harmful consequences but also in serious repercussions
that could lead to consumer fear and apprehension by the licensing
agencies.   These problems must be avoided if this new industry
is to take its proper place.

    The use of SCP by man requires more extensive research.   To
include SCP in foods at levels that significantly would extend
the other protein source, the nucleic acid content would have to
be reduced.   For use in foods at levels that would cause improvement in the nutritional parameters, a very bland SCP product would
be needed.   If food manufacturers are to include SCP in food formulas, SCP must have equivalent or superior functional properties
to currently available protein sources and be competitively
priced.

    This symposium has afforded the individuals involved in all
areas of the SCP industry a unique opportunity to meet and discuss
in depth questions of common interest.   This approach is essential, because if we do not understand the importance of the public's requirements or fears, we will not be able to collect the
data that will answer their questions completely.   Furthermore,
if these questions are not answered completely, anxiety and sus-

picion can develop. To answer these questions, a multidisci-
plinary effort is required, involving engineers, chemists, microbiologists, toxicologists, food technologists, nutritionists,
clinicians, economists, marketing experts, educators, and consumers. A coordinated effort will place SCP where it is needed
to help reduce protein shortages and malnutrition. This symposium has been extremely helpful in providing us with an opportunity to discuss SCP.

APPENDIX I

PROTEIN ADVISORY GROUP OF THE UNITED NATIONS SYSTEM
GUIDELINE NO. 6
PRECLINICAL TESTING
13 March 1972 (Revised)

PAG GUIDELINE FOR PRECLINICAL TESTING OF NOVEL SOURCES OF
PROTEIN

SUMMARY

An an essential prerequisite to planning an experiment on
human subjects to evaluate a new protein-rich food, the procedures
described in detail should be followed.   The objective is to ensure the safety of the new product for humans.   In addition to
toxicity tests on animals, extensive microbiological examination
of the product is needed from its production through its many-
step evolution to the ultimate package for the consumer. Studies
of the new product's nutritional value should then be done using
animal feeding tests and chemical tests of amino acid content and
availability.   Also, any other tests should be carried out that
will help predict how nutritionally valuable the new protein-rich
food will be when eaten by humans.

Although prior history of safe use may be taken into account
in the evaluation of a protein source proposed for general consumption, this alone is insufficient to preclude adequate preclinical testing by currently available, more objective animal
feeding studies.   Careful attention must be given to the development of new varieties of conventional foods of improved protein
quality developed through application of technological processes.
Before they may be used as human food sources, new foods must be
evaluated with respect to the quality of their protein content
and their safety for use.   This requirement may apply to new
varieties of conventional foods where the composition has been
genetically changed, but it applies especially to new foods developed by isolation from conventional sources by unusual techniques and to yeasts, bacteria, molds or algae, i.e. the so-called
single cell proteins.   Processes involving the use of solvent
extraction or unusual heating conditions, or the utilization of
food additives in a variety of combinations may result in changes
in digestion, absorption, metabolism or safety of the food in
question.

App. I.1

The development of a protocol for a specific food material will depend upon its similarity to a conventional food, the kind of technological process applied in its preparation, and the conditions of its intended use as prepared for consumption.

The guideline for preclinical testing of novel sources of protein which follows has been prepared in general terms to describe the categories of information which must be developed in some cases but not necessarily in all. It is intended that this guideline serve as general recommendations rather than as a series of mandatory procedures. The extent of animal testing considered necessary prior to undertaking trials in human subjects will depend on the degree of novelty of the protein product. In the event that the observations and results of a preclinical appraisal of a novel protein are to be submitted to a regulatory or institutional agency as a basis for clinical trials, it is advisable to review the proposed protocol in advance with such an agency in the interest of saving time and effort.

Products intended for incorporation into animal feeds may not require as extensive testing as is suggested here for human foods, but foods derived from such animal sources must be considered from the viewpoint of the possible presence of residues in meat, milk or eggs, transmitted from animal feeds. Controlled tests in farm animals may contribute useful information concerning safety or nutritional value for man.

With respect to single cell proteins (SCP), particular attention must be directed to the composition of the media from the viewpoint of the possible presence of chemical components regarded as hazardous to health. The source materials which form the substrates for the growth of potentially nutritive microorganisms are a) food and agricultural products such as molasses, whey and starch; b) industrial by-products such as cellulosic by-products and sulfite liquor; c) hydrocarbons such as petroleum fractions and natural gas; and d) alcohols. The microorganisms grown on these media include various strains of yeast, bacteria, and fungi.

It is important, therefore, to recognize the possibilities of the presence of contaminants derived from the source materials (e.g., polycyclic aromatic hydrocarbons from petroleum, mercury from sulfite liquor), from the media in which microorganisms are growing and from extraction or refining, as well as reaction products resulting from heat processing. Substances used as lubricants or binders (e.g., in texturization) should also be considered in this connection.

The physical and chemical identity of the industrial product should be established to be essentially the same as that of the material tested experimentally. To be truly significant, the studies should be conducted on the SCP product as made on a production scale rather than on laboratory batches. Minor vari-

ations in processing conditions need not necessitate repetition
of the entire series of preclinical or clinical studies.

1.   INTRODUCTION

1.1   *Categories of Information Needed*

1.1.1   Safety, as predicted from information concerning methods
of production, chemical and physical properties, content of
microorganisms and their metabolites, toxicological effects on
laboratory animals, and the responses of normal human subjects
to limited feeding studies.

1.1.2   Nutritional value, as predicted first from chemical composition with particular emphasis on amino acid content and availability, then by means of short-term rat feeding studies designed
to estimate the efficiency of absorption and utilization of nitrogen content.

1.1.3   Sanitation, with respect to the source of the raw material
and the conditions under which it is processed.   Esthetic considerations as well as potential pathogenicity should be taken
into account.

1.1.4   Acceptability from the standpoint of taste and other
organoleptic properties, including its tendency to induce "taste-
fatigue".   Cultural and religious patterns of food acceptance
should also be considered in this connection.

1.1.5   Technological properties from the point of view of incorporation of the product into currently acceptable foods and fabri-
cation into new food items.

1.2   *Tests and Procedures to be Used*

1.2.1   Chemical analyses for proximate composition of the basic
product, for the amino acid composition of its protein component,
for its content of nonprotein nitrogenous components, for the
presence of contaminants, residues of pesticides or solvents
(depending upon the source of the raw material), for naturally
occurring or adventitious toxins, and for food additives subject
to tolerance limits.

1.2.2   Microbiological examinations for viable microorganisms,
both pathogenic and nonpathogenic, aerobic and nonaerobic, veg-
etative and spore forming.   In the case of proteins of microbial
origin, consideration should be given to the composition of the
medium or substrate in which the organism is grown.

1.2.3   Safety evaluations based on feeding studies in rodents
and other experimental mammals.   The initial short-term studies
should be followed by long-term (at least 2-year) tests in rats.

1.2.4   Protein quality studies in young rats and other laboratory
mammals to indicate the value of the protein product for promoting

growth and nitrogen retention when fed as the sole source of protein and as a supplement to other foods.

1.2.5   Studies of acceptability in preliminary feeding studies
of the protein in normal human adults and children.   The extent
to which these tests should be carried out will depend upon the
novelty of the protein product as well as on the results of the
preceding studies.

1.2.6   Extensiveness of the preclinical testing program should
be decided for each new protein proposed for human food use based
on a consideration of its source, composition, and nature of the
process employed in its production.   As examples, the species of
fish used for the production of fish protein concentrate, the
microorganisms used as single cell proteins, and the extraction
systems employed in processing, may determine how much preclinical
evaluation is required.

1.2.7   Choice of procedures should be exercised with judgment
based on experience.   A product intended for use by infants will
demand more exhaustive preclinical evaluation than products intended for use by children above the age of one year.   No advantage is to be gained in employing a multiplicity of preclinical
evaluations directed towards the same endpoint in terms of the
information furnished.

1.2.8   Limitation of the tests and procedures should be kept in
mind.   Whereas animal testing procedures are capable of establishing safety with reasonable certainty, no methods are available by which safety can be assured in an absolute sense.   Furthermore, chemical or other nonbiological methods for predicting nutritive value have certain limitations despite the high degree
of correlation between the results of such tests and those based
on animal feeding studies.

2.   EVALUATION PROCEDURES

2.1   Chemical

A novel source of protein for human food should be subjected
to the following analyses:

2.1.1   Proximate composition, i.e. moisture (and total solids),
total nitrogen, "fat" (ether extract), ash, crude fiber, and
"available carbohydrate" (by difference).

2.1.2   Protein.   a) The nitrogenous components should be hydro-
lyzed and the amino acid spectrum determined by chromatography.
The essential amino acid composition should be expressed on a
$N \times 6.26$ (N = 16 per cent) basis and the ratio of the total essential amino acids to $N \times 6.25$ should also be calculated. b) The
available lysine content should be determined by the method of
Carpenter *et al.* (1-3).   Since lysine is the principal (though

not the only) essential amino acid likely to become bound and
thus unavailable as a result of heat processing, the slightly
modified Carpenter method is especially useful as a quality control procedure. c) The presence and amount of nonprotein
nitrogenous components such as glucosamines, amides, and amines
should be determined, particularly in the case of products derived from animals sources. d) The content of nucleic acid
should be determined in single cell proteins.

2.1.3 Fat. The solvent extract should be analyzed for the
presence and content of triglycerides, steroids and phospholipids.
If the ether extract is greater than a fraction of a per cent,
the fatty acid profile should be determined by gas chromatography,
with special reference to fatty acids of unusual structure. If
fat is present in calorically significant amount, the ratio of
polyunsaturated to saturated fatty acids should also be calculated. Single cell proteins derived from petroleum hydrocarbons
should be analyzed for total and polycyclic aromatic hydrocarbons
by a suitable quantitative method.

2.1.4 Ash. Ash should be analyzed for its content of calcium,
phosphorus, iron, iodine, alkali and alkaline earth elements, and
heavy metals. Products of marine origin should also be analyzed
for mercury, arsenic, and fluorine. In the light of current
concern over mercurial contamination of fish from lakes, streams,
and marine waters, attention should be directed to the possible
presence of inorganic and particularly alkyl mercury in protein
concentrates derived from fish or algae.

2.1.5 Vitamins. Analyses should be conducted for all of the
major vitamins except those for which a low lipid content or in-
stability under processing conditions indicate little likelihood
of their presence in significant amounts.

2.1.6 Food additives. Analyses should be conducted for those
food additives permitted in the product under investigation for
which tolerance limitations have been established.

2.1.7 Processing damage. Useful information concerning the
effect of heat on the product may be obtained not only by determinations of available lysine, as mentioned above, but also by
spectrophotometric examination for products of the Maillard
(browning) reaction, or, in the case of leguminous proteins, for
the heat-labile antitryptic factor or the concomitant enzyme,
urease. Useful information concerning the effect of alkali
treatment of the product may be obtained by the determination of
lysinoalanine (4).

2.1.8 Physical properties. Though not relevant to the preclinical evaluation of the nutritional quality or safety of novel
proteins, it would be expected that studies of their physical
properties (e.g. solubility, wettability, viscosity, etc.) would

be conducted to establish their technological utility as foods or food supplements.

2.1.9 Miscellaneous. Depending upon the nature of the raw material and the conditions employed in its production, special analyses of the protein product should be conducted for:

a) Solvent residues, such as polycyclic or chlorinated hydro-carbons;
b) Pesticide residues;
c) Naturally occurring toxic substances, e.g. gossypol, hemagglutinins, and marine toxins (it should be noted that there are no satisfactory nonbiological tests for the latter category of substances).

2.2 *Biochemical*

As an indication of the digestibility of the protein product, *in vitro* enzyme studies may be conducted to determine the rate and degree of hydrolysis by pepsin and pepsin plus trypsin under conditions simulating those in the human gastrointestinal tract (5-7). As discussed below, calculations based on the essential amino acid content of enzymic hydrolyzates have been adapted for estimating the biological value (utilization) of proteins.

2.3 *Microbiological*

While this is discussed more fully elsewhere, mention may be made of the need for microbiological examination of new sources of protein to determine the number or types of microorganisms indicative of unsanitary conditions of production or processing and to establish their freedom from toxigenic organisms. In the case of single cell proteins, taxonomic and toxicologic studies should be conducted on the organisms from which they are derived, to define their identity as non-pathogenic species. The end products should also be examined to rule out the presence of viable organisms.

2.4 *Protein Quality*

2.4.1 Predictive tests. Though the aforementioned chemical examinations yield valuable information for predicting safety and nutritional value, they cannot be considered substitutes for biological appraisals of protein quality in the intact animal. For example, amino acid profiles as determined either microbiologically or chromatographically on protein hydrolyzates fail to differentiate between free, bound, and nonbound forms, or between differences in rate and degree of digestibility. Moreover, interpretations of amino acid profiles are based on comparison with some more or less arbitrarily chosen "ideal" protein, such as that of whole egg or human milk, or on comparison with the FAO reference pattern or the amino acid requirements as observed in young adult males.

The utility as well as limitations of estimating the biological value of proteins from their essential amino acid content
(8-11) is discussed in several monographs (12,13). Their main
use is for screening products prior to animal testing.

The "chemical score" of Mitchell and Block (8,9) is based
on the ratio of the essential amino acid in greatest deficit compared with its content in a reference protein, e.g. whole egg.
The "essential amino acid index" (EAA) is predicted on the hypoth-
esis that the biological value of a protein is a function of the
levels of all of these amino acids in relation to their content
in the reference protein (10,11). Experience has shown that the
chemical score, based as it is on a single limiting amino acid,
tends to underestimate the biological value, whereas the modified
EAA index gives values which correlate more closely with biological
values. However, since these chemical ratings are based on
analyses of complete hydrolyzates of proteins, they fail to take
into account differences in digestibility of the proteins or
availability of individual amino acids.

2.4.2 Bioassay procedures. Ideally, the nutritional evaluation
of protein foods should be made in relation to their potential
role in the diet of the population for whom they are intended.
Whereas this would preclude assigning a single numerical rating
to a given protein which is applicable under all conditions of
use, it would avoid the fallacy of assuming that such a rating,
based on a single level of feeding as the sole source of nitrogen
to the test animal, provides a true measure of its nutritional
value as a supplement to the diet or to specific foods for man.

Experience over the years has shown that the most useful
preliminary tests for the appraisal of the nutritional value of
proteins are based on the short-term growth responses of rats to
the ingestion of suboptimal levels of the test protein. Variations of this basic procedure have been described in which the
responses are expressed in terms of weight gain per unit weight
of protein (N × 6.25) or nitrogen ingested. These methods do
not distinguish between the utilization of protein for maintenance
and that for growth.

a) Protein efficiency ratios

The most commonly used of these procedures involves the
determination of the Protein Efficiency Ratio (PER) in which the
average net gain in body weight per unit weight of protein
(N × 6.25) is compared with that observed for the reference protein, casein. Because of differences in response to the same
standard casein, in the same or different laboratories, PER values
are customarily adjusted to an assumed value of 2.5 for casein.

This procedure has been refined (14,15) to balance the fat
(i.e. caloric density) and mineral content of the test and refer-

ence protein diets insofar as possible.   The diets are fed *ad libitum* to groups of ten weanling male rats (weighing 40-50g at 20-23 days) for a period of 28 days.   In the case of low-protein sources (e.g. rice, cassava, etc.), it is not possible to achieve the usual 9- or 10-per-cent level of dietary protein specified for the PER test.   Hence, the tests are run in comparison with standard casein at correspondingly lower levels.   Conventional PER determinations are deficient as bioassays in that they are performed at single protein levels, thus ignoring differences in slope of the dose-response curve at the suboptimal level.   Improved design of the PER test may be achieved by either a multi-level assay in which the growth responses at two (or three) levels of the test protein are compared with two (or three) sub-optimal levels of the reference protein (16), or by means of a slope-ratio assay employing multiple levels in which the slope of response to the test protein is compared with that of the reference protein (17).   In the conventional PER test, the ob-served value (grams gain in body weight per 100 grams protein consumed) is adjusted to an assumed value of 2.5 for casein to compensate for interlaboratory variations due to age, strain, and pretest dietary history of the rat and difference in the actual casein used.

Because of its relative simplicity and low cost, the PER method is the most widely favored method for the evaluation of protein quality.   However, it has certain limitations.   For example, like any procedure based solely on gain in body weight, it takes no account of composition of the weight increment.   A more significant criticism, however, resides in the fact that it is a measure of the combined effects of digestibility of the dietary components and their utilization for tissue synthesis. More informative procedures permit differentiation between the proportion of dietary nitrogen absorbed, which is a function of the susceptibility of the protein source to the action of the gastrointestinal proteolytic enzymes, and the proportion retained in the body, which is a function not only of the essential amino acid composition and content, but of the total protein content and the caloric density of the diet.

b)   *Net Protein Ratio and Net Protein Utilization*

Less frequently employed are the methods based on estimation of Net Protein Ratio (NPR) in which the weight loss of a com-parable group receiving a protein-free diet is added to the weight gain of the protein-fed group;   or the Net Protein Utilization (NPU) in which the total body nitrogen of both the protein-fed and protein-free groups are determined.   These tests are gen-erally performed in groups of four to six 28- or 30-day-old rats fed the test or control diets for a ten-day period.   The differ-ences in terms of weight gain (NPR) or nitrogen retention (NPU)

are expressed in relation to the weight of protein or nitrogen
consumed.

The NPU procedure is more laborious then those based simply
on growth response since it involves tedious and time-consuming
analyses of carcasses.   In theory at least, it is the product
of the coefficients of digestibility of the nitrogenous component
of the diet and its retention or biological value.   When conducted under standardized conditions with respect to the age,
initial weight, etc., of the test animals, the NPU method gives
values which correlate quite closely with biological values,
since within classes of foods digestibility will vary only within
small limits.   However, NPU is subject to the same criticisms
as mentioned previously for PER.   It must be recognized that
nutritional assays employing suboptimal levels of dietary proteins reflect not only the qualitative adequacy of the essential
amino acid content but the proportion of the total essential
amino acid content in the protein.   Thus a protein containing
even a "balanced" essential amino acid combination may yield a
poor response if the ratio of essentials to nonessentials is too
low.

c)   Nitrogen balance procedures

For a more definitive and detailed appraisal of the nutritive value of a protein source, nitrogen balance procedures must
be used.   These were applied originally to studies in man (18)
but, in the laboratory, dogs (19,20) and especially rats (21,22)
have been widely used.   By this technique, one can differentiate
between the degree of digestibility of the nitrogen source and
the proportion of nitrogen retained for storage or anabolism.
Digestibility is measured in terms of the ratio of the absorbed
N (i.e., the difference between the ingested and intestinally
excreted nitrogen, the latter corrected for "metabolic N") to
the total N intake.   Nitrogen retention is calculated from the
ratio of the retained N (i.e., the difference between absorbed
N and that eliminated in the urine, corrected for so-called
endogenous N) to the absorbed N.   These values are based on
analyses for food, fecal, and urinary N over the 3 to 5 day collection period, which follows a similar adjustment period.
Several proteins, including the reference protein, may be tested
in successive weeks, the metabolic and endogenous N corrections
being derived from a basal collection period during which a
"protein-free" diet is fed.   If the rats are in an actively
growing stage over a series of tests, it is a further refinement
to repeat the basal period at the beginning and end of the series
so as to interpolate correction values for metabolic and endogenous loss appropriate for each week.   (The errors involved in
these interpolations are discussed in a critical review by Njaa
(23).)

In testing a series of proteins sequentially, any residual effect of the previous week's test diet not fully offset by the adjustment period can be balanced by assigning the rats to test and reference proteins according to a latin square design.

In addition to yielding more detailed information than growth methods, the nitrogen balance procedure is not significantly affected by differences in maintenance requirement since the test collection periods are very short.

In comparative tests of biological value by this procedure, greater precision can be achieved by standardizing the food consumption at a constant level (e.g., 8-10g per day) because the degree of nitrogen retention is influenced more by food intake than by the protein level of the diet (23).   It is recommended that instead of a protein-free diet, one containing a low level of protein (e.g., 3 to 4 per cent lactalbumin or whole egg protein) be fed during the basal period to avoid confounding catabolic with maintenance losses.   The diets are fed *ad libitum* which introduces a source of error inasmuch as the ratio of weight gain to food consumption may be influenced by the latter, which in turn is influenced by factors of palatability and toxicity of the protein source.

d)   *Limitations of bioassay results*

It should be pointed out that none of the animal assays for protein quality can be assumed to provide an absolute measure of nutritive value for man.   Aside from possible species differences, these procedures have certain limitations with respect to i) differentiation between maintenance and growth requirements, ii) the assumptions *in estimating* metabolic and endogenous losses, iii) the effects of *ad libitum* vs. controlled food intake, and iv) dietary levels of proteins, calories, and other nutrients not completely balanced between test and control diets.   Furthermore, any test of protein efficiency based on feeding a single source must be interpreted with reservation since, except for milk or milk substitutes, proteins are consumed as components of, or as supplements to, mixed diets.   Nevertheless, reasonably good correlation is observed between the growth and nitrogen retention procedures and the relative ranking of individual protein sources is quite similar to each of the methods described.   Especially in chemically-treated proteins the determination of the limiting amino acid by rat assay may give valuable information in relation to the chemically-determined composition of the protein. Special reference is made to the review entitled "Evaluation of Protein Quality" of the Committee on Protein Malnutrition of the Food and Nutrition Board (12) and those of Njaa (23) and Irwin and Hegsted (24) have discussed the limitations not only of the widely used short tests for rating proteins (e.g. PER and NPU), but of the more informative nitrogen balance procedures.   The errors involved in estimating corrections for endogenous and metabolic nitrogen excretion are relatively small compared to the basic error implicit in the evaluation of an individual protein as the sole source of this nutrient in the diet.

2.5 Safety (25)

2.5.1 Related factors

a) Nutritional adequacy of test diet

Growth depression or any other adverse effect observed in the course of short-term nutritional assays should be viewed in the light of possible toxicity of the protein source.   It is necessary to differentiate between growth failure due to nutritional inadequacy, and toxicity of either the protein *per se* or any adventitious contaminants. In order to avoid confusing nutritional insufficiency with toxicity in safety evaluation studies, the basal diet to which the test protein is added as a supplement should itself be nutritionally adequate for normal growth and development of the animal species employed.   The protein content of the basal diet rather than that of the test material should be relied upon to satisfy the amino acid requirements.

b) Identity of test animals

In applying the results of safety evaluation studies to products made, or to be made, commercially, the identity and reproducibility of the test material with that produced in practice must be established by chemical and other relevant procedures.

c) Natural toxicants

Naturally-occurring toxic substances found in plants include carcinogens (e.g., cycad nuts, oil of sassafras), goitrogens (*Brassica* species), hemagglutinins (e.g., ricin, phaseolotoxin in legumes), lathyrogens (e.g., vetch, sweet peas), cyanogenetic glycosides (certain beans and nuts), and estrogens (in seeds and leafy vegetables) (26).   Marine sources of protein, such as fish or shellfish found in tropical waters, and the algae or plankton on which they feed, may contain highly toxic substances. Naturally-occurring toxic agents can be avoided either by care in the selection of the raw materials or by appropriate methods of storage, heat processing, or extraction.

d) Microbiological toxins

Raw materials subject to microbial contamination and spoilage must be examined for the presence of pathogenic organisms (e.g., *Salmonellae, Shigella, Staphylococci,* and *Clostridia*) and for the endotoxic and exotoxic substances they produce.   Raw materials exposed to warm, humid conditions which induce fungal growth must be examined for the possible presence of mycotoxins, such as the aflatoxins.

e)   Extraction residues

Protein concentrates which have been isolated or refined by
means of solvent extraction should be analyzed for the possible
presence of solvent residues and any products which may be formed,
particularly by the use of reactive chlorinated hydrocarbons.
In the event that any such residues are present, toxicological
data should be available to establish safe limits.

Single cell proteins produced by growing microorganisms on
sulfite liquor, carbohydrates (e.g., molasses), or hydrocarbon
media must be evaluated to establish the non-pathogenicity of the
microorganisms and to rule out their metabolites or possible mutagenicity into toxigenic forms.   Depending upon the nature of the
raw materials, the media and the conditions of processing, analyses
for the possible presence of impurities or contaminants such as
solvent residues, heavy metals, fluoride, etc., should precede
any toxicological feeding studies.

f)   Multilevel feeding of test protein

When graded levels of the test protein are fed as supplements
to a natural type diet, it is not possible to maintain isonitro-
genicity.   From the toxicological standpoint, however, it is preferable to insure a sufficient level of complete protein in the
basal diet rather than to adjust for differences in nitrogen content.   This complicating factor can be avoided by using a semi-
synthetic type of diet in which casein constitutes the single basal
protein, provided it is present in all diets at nutritionally adequate levels.

g)   Comparability of test and basal diets

To the extent that the test protein source contributes high
levels of lipid, ash, or indigestible cellulosic material, adjustments may be required to balance out these factors in the test and
control diets.

h)   Highest feasible feeding level of test protein

In contrast with safety evaluation studies of food additives
generally, it is not feasible to include large multiples of potential use levels of proteinaceous foods in experimental diets employed in toxicological evaluations.   Nevertheless, as high a
level as possible should be included, keeping in mind the fact
that excessive amounts of even high-quality proteins, such as
casein, may depress growth and food efficiency.

2.5.2   Testing protocols.   The need for and experimental design
of a safety evaluation study in animals depend upon the novelty
of the protein as a food for man, in respect to both its source
and method of production.   The following discussion assumes that
the test material is sufficiently different from conventional
forms of dietary protein as to require rather thorough toxicologi-

cal appraisal before conducting feeding studies on human subjects.
Furthermore, it is assumed that any nutritional evaluations which
may have been conducted suggest that the test material is sufficiently safe to warrant more extended studies.

The protocol for a safety evaluation program requires de-
cisions with respect to:

a)   Choice of animal species

Rats are by far the best single species.   Mice are also used
but less is known of their nutritional requirements and their
size precludes obtaining sufficient blood or urine for examination.
Among the nonrodent species, beagle dogs, rhesus monkeys, and
miniature pigs have been used for short-term but not for chronic
(life-cycle) studies.

b)   Composition of basal diet

As a basal diet for short-term (e.g., 3-month) tests either
a "synthetic"-type (casein-starch) or a commercial natural-type
ration is suitable.   For long-term (e.g., 2-year) studies the
latter is preferred.   In either case the basal ration must
satisfy all nutritional requirements for the species in question.

c)   Dietary level of test protein

The test protein should be fed at two or three graded levels,
the highest being determined by its nutritional adequacy as a
sole source;   for example, 50 per cent of the total protein of
a test diet, provided it does not lower the overall biological
value.   If the test protein has been established to be nutritionally complete, it may be fed as a replacement for casein in
a "synthetic"-type diet, at least in a short-term toxicity test.

d)   Equilibration of test and control diets

If the test protein product contains a high ash content (e.g.,
certain fish protein concentrates), or is otherwise "unbalanced"
with respect to any specific nutrient(s), it may be advantageous
to equalize the level of this component in the test and control
diets to facilitate proper interpretation of the responses.

*e)   Age, weight, sex, and method of assigning animals to
groups*

Rodents are usually started on tests at or shortly after
weaning and are assigned to groups of equal size, balanced with
respect to litter distribution, sex, and average weight.   For
short-term tests, groups consist of 10 to 15 animals of each sex,
but for long-term tests at least twice this number is recommended.
In the case of the larger mammalian species the groups should include 3 and 6 of each sex for short- and long-term studies, respectively.

K

The use of neonatal animals as toxicological test subjects has been suggested for the evaluation of protein which might be included in the diet of infants. It has been demonstrated that newborn animals have not achieved the capability of the adult for enzyme induction and hence lack the ability to metabolize or detoxify foreign substances.

f) Individual or group housing

Animals should be housed individually during the initial period of rapid growth so as to permit reliable measurement of food consumption. Caging in pairs or larger groups may be resorted to at later stages. Metabolism cages should be used during periods when urine or faeces are collected.

g) Maintenance and sanitary controls

The animal quarters should be maintained in a sanitary condition and controlled with respect to temperature and humidity. The environment should be kept insect-free without the use of pesticidal aerosols. Cages should be washed preferably at weekly intervals.

h) Nature and frequency of observations

The gross inspections, clinical laboratory tests and pathological observations, and their frequency in both short- and long-term toxicological studies, are illustrated in the following tabulation:

TYPICAL CRITERIA USED IN TOXICOLOGICAL EVALUATIONS

Observations	*Frequency*	
	Short-term	*Long-term*
Physical appearance	daily	daily
Behavior	daily	daily
Body weight	weekly	weekly
Food consumption	weekly	weekly
Hematology		
Hemoglobin		
Hematocrit		
Leukocytes,	0,4,8,12	1,3,6,9,12,
total and differential	weeks	18,24 months
Platelets		
Reticulocytes		
Blood chemistry		
Glucose		
Urea N		
Protein, total		
Albumin/globulin ratio	as above	as above
Triglycerides		
Cholesterol		

continued

Observations   *Frequency*

                          Short-term   *Long-term*

Blood chemistry *cont.*
  SGOT, SGPT
  Alkaline phosphatase
  Uric acid
  Allantoin
Urine
  Volume, pH, sp. gr.
  Glucose
  Protein   as above   as above
  Ketone bodies
  Bile
  Occult blood
  Sediment
Autopsy (dead or sacrificed
        animals)   terminal   terminal
Gross pathological
  examination
Organ weights
  Liver, kidney, heart, brain,
  spleen, gonads, pituitary,
  adrenals, thyroid
Histopathology
  20 organs and tissues
  Electron microscopy of
    liver and kidneys

i)   Functional or metabolic studies

In special cases, tests for hepatic, gastrointestinal, or
renal function, metabolic balance studies, or neurological or
behavioral tests may be suggested.   Periodic ophthamologic
examinations should also be conducted.

Single cell proteins are known to contain a high level of
nucleoprotein, in some cases as much as 12 to 15 per cent.   The
effect of high levels of intake on uricogenesis in man therefore
must be considered.   Since the available evidence indicates that
all animal species except man and anthropoid apes metabolize
purines past the uric acid stage to allantoin, this phenomenon
can best be studied only in man (Dalmatian dogs excrete uric acid
not because of the lack of the uricolytic enzyme but because of
a low renal threshold).   Allantoin levels in blood and urine
should be included in toxicological studies of single cell protein.

j)   Reproduction and lactation, multigeneration studies

The degree of novelty of a potentially important food item (both as to source and method of production) should determine the need for reproduction and lactation studies in animals. While they may not be indicated in the case of a fish or cereal protein concentrate, such tests should be included in a protocol for safety evaluation of a single cell protein.   Though questions have been raised concerning the application of rat reproduction data to the human species, this problem is not peculiar to reproduction phenomena.   Chronic toxicological assessments may be designed to include multigeneration studies according to the following schedule:

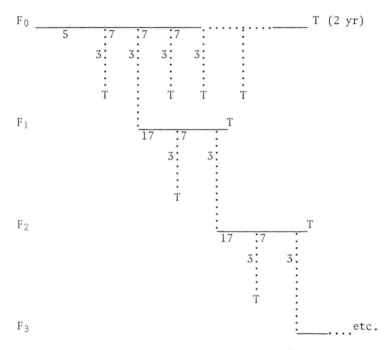

Chronological scheme of reproduction and lactation

The horizontal lines represent the generations of rats through their successive matings and the dotted vertical lines indicate litters;   termination of a litter or a generation is shown by the letter T;   the figures indicate the number of weeks elapsed at each stage, beginning with the first mating in F_0.

The observations recorded in reproduction studies include the proportion of successful matings, the number and weight of young born, and their ability to survive and grow during the nor-

mal lactation period.　Certain of these parameters are expressed
in terms of indexes for fertility (the proportion of matings resulting in pregnancies), gestation (the proportion of pregnancies
resulting in live litters), viability (the proportion of pups
born which are alive at 4 days of age), and lactation (the proportion of pups alive at 4 days which survive to weaning) (27).

k) *Duration of test period*

Short-term toxicological tests generally run from 3 to 6
months;　long-term tests from 1 to 2 years.　If potential carcinogenicity is suspected, studies should be designed to include
larger than usual groups of rats or mice and the test period
should run at least 2 or 1.5 years, respectively.

l) *Teratogenic or mutagenic studies*

Recent emphasis on teratogenetic and mutagenetic investigations is in part, at least, a response to public and political
pressure.　However, without belittling the significance of genetic aberrations as an aspect of toxicity, further research is
needed to establish the validity of present procedures for teratologic and mutagenetic tests for assessing safety under use conditions in man.　Current methods are being applied largely for
the purpose of accumulating data to establish their relevance to
human safety evaluation.

If the source or nature of the protein product is so unusual
as to demand more extensive study, or if abnormal responses are
seen in reproduction studies (2.5.2 (j)), the possibility of
teratogenic or mutagenic effects may be considered.

Teratologic studies are conducted in rats and rabbits with
particular attention to the time and duration of test dosage
before or during gestation.　Litters are delivered by cesarian
section and responses are observed in terms of implantation sites,
resorption, survival of the pups, and examination of the soft
tissues and of skeletal structure after clarification and staining.

Cytologic tests in tissue culture for evidence of chromo-
somal aberrations in animals have recently been emphasized for
the investigation of potentially mutagenic drugs and pesticides.
However, the significance of such tests as applied to the intact
mammalian species has yet to be established.　So far as is known,
no proteins included in the human diet have been investigated for
possible mutagenicity.

m) *Statistical analyses and interpretation of findings*

In the interpretation of the responses to toxicological
tests, the statistical significance or differences of responses
between test and control groups plays an important role.　Hence

the size of experimental groups as well as the quantitative rating of both objective and subjective observations are particularly relevant.   However, whatever statistical probability is adopted as the basis for defining significance, the chance that a single group may deviate from the norm without actually indicating a biological aberration cannot be ignored.   Judgement founded on experience of the investigator and past performance of the particular strain and colony of animals must be given due weight. Interpretation of experimental findings should take into account the quantitative relationship of the test vs. use conditions of the product under investigation, interspecies variations, the limited number and variety of observations incorporated into the safety evaluation program, and the relative size of the test and human populations.

For a discussion of the basic procedures involved in safety evaluation of food components, reference is made to the reviews of the United States Food and Drug Administration (28), the Food Protection Committee of the National Academy of Sciences - National Research Council (29), and the Joint Expert Committee on Food Additives of FAO/WHO (30).

Reports of investigations submitted for review and evaluation by PAG must include full details and data for control as well as test groups and appropriate statistical analysis of the findings. Brief descriptions of the observations and conclusions will not be acceptable.

3.   CONCLUSIONS

In any event, the object of the preclinical study is achieved when it has been determined that the levels and conditions of feeding of the novel dietary component are sufficiently safe to warrant a cautious program of study in human subjects.

4.   REFERENCES

1.   Carpenter, K.J.   Estimation of available lysine in animal-protein foods. *Biochem. J.* 77, 604-610, 1960.

2.   Boyne, A.W., Carpenter, K.J. and Woodham, A.A.   Assessment of laboratory procedures suggested as indicators of protein quality in feeds. *J. Sci. Food Agr.* 12, 832-848, 1961.

3.   Carpenter, K.J. and March, B.E.   The availability of lysine in peanut biscuits used in the treatment of kwashiorkor. *Brit. J. Nutr.* 15, 403-409, 1961.

4.   DeGroot, A.P. and Slump, P.   Effects of severe alkali treatment of proteins on amino acid composition and nutritive value. *J. Nutr.* 98, 45-56, 1969.

5.   Sheffner, G.A., Eckfeldt, G.A. and Spector, H.   The pepsin-digest-residue (P.D.R.) amino acid index of net protein utilization.   *J. Nutr.* 60, 105-120, 1956.

6. Sheffner, G.A. *In vitro* protein evaluation. *In:* Newer methods of nutritional biochemistry (Albanese, A.A., ed), Vol. III, Academic Press, New York, N.Y., U.S.A., 1967.

7. Mauron, J. Nutritional evaluation of proteins by enzymatic methods. *In:* Evaluation of novel protein products (Bender, A.E. *et al.*, eds). Proceedings of a symposium held in Stockholm, Sweden, 1968. Pergamon Press, New York, N.Y., U.S.A., 1970.

8. Mitchell, H.H. and Block, R.J. Some relationships between amino acid contents of protein and their nutritive value for the rat. *J. Biol. Chem.* 163, 599-620, 1946.

9. Block, R.J. and Mitchell, H.H. Correlation of the amino acid composition of proteins with their nutritive value. *Nutr. Abstr. Rev.* 16, 249-278, 1946.

10. Oser, B.L. Method for integrating essential amino acid content in the nutritional evaluation of protein. *J. Am. Dietet. Assoc.* 27, 396-402, 1951.

11. Oser, B.L. An integrated essential amino acid index for predicting the biological value of proteins. *In:* Newer methods of nutritional biochemistry (Albanese, A.A, ed), Vol. I, Academic Press, New York, N.Y., U.S.A., 1959.

12. Food and Nutrition Board. Evaluation of protein quality. United States Academy of Sciences/National Research Council, Washington, D.C., U.S.A. Publication 1100, 1963.

13. Food and Agriculture Organization/World Health Organization Expert Group. Protein requirements. FAO Nutrition Meetings Report Series No. 37; WHO Technical Report Series No. 301, 1965.

14. Campbell, J.A. Methodology of protein evaluation. FAO/WHO/ UNICEF Protein Advisory Group, United Nations, N.Y., U.S.A. PAG Document R. 10/Add. 37, 1961.

15. Association of Official Agricultural Chemists. Official methods of analysis. Tenth ed. AOAC, Washington, D.C., U.S.A., 1965.

16. Bliss, C.I. The statistics of bioassay. *In:* Vitamin methods, Vol. II, Academic Press, New York, N.Y., U.S.A., 1952.

17. Hegsted, D.M. and Chang, Y. Protein utilization in growing rats. I. Relative growth index as a bioassay procedure. *J. Nutr.* 85, 159-168, 1965.

18. Thomas, K. Biological value of nitrogenous substances in different foods. *Arch. Anat. Physiol.*, pp. 219-302, 1909.

19. Allison, J.B., Anderson, J.A. and Seeley, R.D.   Determination of the nitrogen balance index in normal and hypoproteinemic dogs. *Ann. N.Y. Acad. Sci.* 47, 245-271, 1946.

20. Allison, J.B.   The efficiency of utilization of dietary proteins.   *In:* Protein and amino acid nutrition (Albanese, A.A., ed), Academic Press, New York, N.Y., U.S.A., 1959.

21. Mitchell, H.H.   A method of determining the biological value of protein. *J. Biol. Chem.* 58, 873-903, 1924.

22. Mitchell, H.H., Hamilton, T.S., Beadles, J.R. and Simpson, F.   The importance of commercial processing for the protein value of food products.   I.   Soybean, coconut, and sunflower seed. *J. Nutr.* 29, 13-25, 1945.

23. Njaa, L.R.   A study on the Mitchell method for determination of the biological value of protein.   John Griegs Boktrykkeri, Bergen, Norway, 1963.

24. Irwin, M.I. and Hegsted, D.M.   A conspectus of research on amino acid requirements of man.   *J. Nutr.* 101, 539-566, 1971.

25. Oser, B.L.   The safety evaluation of new sources of protein for man.   *In:* Evaluation of novel protein products (Bender, A.E. *et al.*, eds), Pergamon Press, New York, N.Y., U.S.A., 1970.

26. United States National Academy of Sciences/National Research Council.   Toxicants occurring naturally in foods.   NAS/NRC, Washington, D.C., U.S.A.   Publication 1354, 1966.

27. Oser, B.L. and Oser, M.   Nutrition studies on rats on diets containing high levels of partial ester emulsifiers.   II.   Reproduction and lactation. *J. Nutr.* 60, 489-505, 1956.

28. Division of Pharmacology, U.S. Food and Drug Administration.   Appraisal of the safety of chemicals in foods, drugs and cosmetics.   Association of Food and Drug Officials of the United States, Austin, Texas, U.S.A., 1959.

29. National Academy of Sciences, Food Protection Committee.   Evaluating the safety of food chemicals.   Washington, D.C., U.S.A., 1970.

30. FAO/WHO/UNICEF Protein Advisory Group.   Preclinical testing of novel sources of protein.   United Nations, New York, N.Y., U.S.A.   PAG Guideline No. 6, 1970.

APPENDIX II

PROTEIN ADVISORY GROUP OF THE UNITED NATIONS SYSTEM
GUIDELINE NO. 7
HUMAN TESTING PROCEDURE
10 June 1970 Replaces Guideline dated 22 January 1970

PAG GUIDELINE FOR HUMAN TESTING OF SUPPLEMENTARY
FOOD MIXTURES

SUMMARY

Prior to tests using human subjects to evaluate new protein foods, every step in the PAG Guideline for pre-clinical testing of novel sources of protein should be executed.

The experimental plan is extensive but flexible. The aim is to use with maximum safety the fewest subjects possible to obtain significant data.

Included in this outline of tests are:

Determination of product acceptability and physiological tolerance;

Measurement of body weight and height;

Determination of nitrogen balance (NPU);

Measurement of changes in amounts of albumin, amino acids, and enzyme activity in blood plasma or serum.

The FAO/WHO/UNICEF Protein Advisory Group at its 17th meeting in New York, USA, 25-28 May 1970, adopted the following revised Guideline for human testing of supplementary food mixtures. That guideline was based on a previous PAG document (1) and on recommendations made at the 13th meeting of PAG, Geneva, Switzerland, August 1966, and on revisions suggested by Drs. N.S. Scrimshaw and M.A. Guzman for the 16th meeting of the PAG. The revisions now adopted were proposed during a WHO consultation on human testing of protein-rich foods, Geneva, Switzerland, 9-11 March 1970.

1. APPLICABILITY OF THE GUIDELINE

Tests for safety and suitability for human consumption, especially for feeding of infants and children, are essential in the development of protein-rich foods. When commonly used foods

App. II.1

are newly processed to supply protein in a food mixture or when
materials, not so far used as human food, are to be used as protein sources in a new food product, it is essential that certain
preliminary steps be taken before human testing of the product.
Some of these steps are outlined in PAG Guideline No. 6 (2) for
pre-clinical testing of novel sources of protein.

Some preliminary steps are:

a.   Identification of the source of edible protein, the
quantity available, and economic study of its development.

b.   Chemical evaluation of the quantity and quality of protein, if not already known, in each of the component foodstuffs
from which protein-rich food mixtures are to be made.

c.   Determination of various components in the proposed mixture based on considerations of nutritional or other relevant factors.   An evaluation of the probable price of the final product
would be desirable at this stage, taking into account the costs
of raw materials, processing, necessary packaging, storage conditions, shelf-life, commercialization, normal profits and all
other elements which enter into the operation.

d.   Measurement, chemically and biologically, of the nutritive value of the mixture and evaluation of damage to protein or
loss of nutrients available as a result of processing which may
be necessary for industrial production, or consumption.

e.   Assurance that it is free of harmful microorganisms.

f.   Tests indicating freedom from toxicity of the product
and its components.   Such toxicity may be due to the presence of
intentional additives, of toxic substances naturally occurring or
arising from mild infestation, or through the use of pesticides
and fungicides.   Qualitative and quantitative tests for determination of these compounds may be necessary, as well as animal
tests for determination of acute and sub-acute toxicity.   The
rules specified by the Food and Drug Administration, Washington,
D.C., USA, for acceptance of additives to common foods provide
useful guidelines (3).   These include among others, full acute
and chronic toxicity trials.

It is only when these steps have been satisfactorily accom-
plished that human tests should be considered.   It is imperative,
therefore, that all the requirements mentioned above be fully
satisfied before planning an undertaking which will involve human
subjects.

While there is no question as to the need for the clinical
testing of really new sources of protein or of the consequences
of new ways of processing protein concentrates, there is real danger that excessive and unnecessary testing of minor variations in

the formulae using previously tested ingredients or processes could needlessly hamper progress in this field.   It is therefore suggested that:

   i.   Proteins and processed protein concentrates previously not considered in the WHO/FAO/UNICEF programmes, or products previously considered but manufactured by new processes or by major changes in established processes, especially if these changes in processing raise any suspicions as to nutritional or toxicological properties of the product, must pass testing procedures of the type recommended in the proceedings of the Princeton Conference on Human Protein Requirements and their Fulfillment in Practice (4).

   ii.   Mixtures of well-known staples and protein sources which have already received favourable consideration should be accepted without insistence on clinical testing beyond acceptability and tolerance trials if there is no further processing which could cast a doubt on their safety.   It would be advisable, however, to ascertain by animal experimentation, the nutritional value of the final product (PER or NPU).

   iii. In case of severe or unconventional processing of mixtures even of well-known staples and protein sources the products should be accepted for tests in man only after they have satisfied the necessary laboratory analysis and animal testing for protein quality.   Clinical testing, although not mandatory in this case, may be helpful in ascertaining the value of some of these food mixtures in children's supplementary feeding.

   Understanding of the technological steps involved in the processing will help to decide in which of these categories a food mixture should be classified.

2.   CATEGORIES OF TESTS

   Human testing, as these observations will be termed, will fall into four main categories as follows:

   1.   Acceptability and tolerance tests;

   2.   Growth tests;

   3.   Nitrogen balance measurements;

   4.   Other criteria.

   The actual type of tests to be carried out will be determined by the considerations mentioned below.   Careful clinical observations will, of course, be concurrent in all studies.   One prerequisite is common to all, and that is full satisfactory information on items a. to e. above.

2.1 *Preliminary Acceptability and Tolerance Tests*

It is possible that the foodstuffs from which a protein-rich food mixture is made have been individually in use as human food in one or more parts of the world. Processing of mixtures on an industrial scale, however, may affect not only their suitability for the groups for which they are intended, but also their palatability and acceptability. Therefore, it may be necessary to determine the tolerance to the dosage level recommended for contributing significantly to protein needs. Under such conditions, "acceptability and tolerance" tests are indicated. These tests should be carried out in an institution or in a closely observed sample of the population. If it is decided to have several such tests for a given product, at least one of them should take place in the country in which it is intended to introduce the protein-rich food mixture.

A danger to be avoided is that persons evaluating the food supplement may be swayed by their own "acceptability" criteria to influence the reaction of the recipient to the detriment of useful supplements. Even young infants sense the emotional reaction of the mother or of other persons feeding them and may respond psychically by rejecting the food.

Mild disease processes, particularly infections, tend to reduce appetite and produce mild to moderate gastrointestinal upsets, which could be interpreted as poor tolerance and acceptability. Because of these factors, it is suggested that a simultaneous negative control be run in these trials. Sequential periods with and without the test food may also be useful. The total volume fed, the timing of the meals and the total intake should be kept consistent. If possible, test and control groups should be of similar age as well as have similar weights for their heights.

2.1.1 *Number*. Depending on the consistency of the results the number will vary. In any case, it is suggested that no less than twenty, and preferably closer to thirty, individuals be tested.

2.1.2 *Age*. The sample tested should consist of individuals of the age or ages for which the product is intended.

2.1.3 *Duration of feeding and observation*. Occasionally upon the introduction of a new type of food a short period of apparent intolerance may occur, which is overcome in two or three days. If the diet is going to be unacceptable because of a tiring or boring taste, this is generally noted within the first weeks of the feeding trials. It is therefore suggested that a period of at least four weeks be used before the clinical evaluation of protein quality or more extended tolerance tests are planned.

2.1.4 Method of preparation. This should be either in the form of a suitably flavoured gruel or incorporated into a local recipe.

2.1.5 Level of protein feeding. That needed to supplement the diet to the levels recommended by the FAO/WHO report on protein requirements (5), or preferably to cover more than 50% of the requirement of 97% of the population tested. An additional group fed the material *ad libitum* will provide information on maximum quantities acceptable per meal in the form supplied.

2.1.6 Level of calorie intake. Should be sufficient to maintain constant weight in adults or adequate weight gain in children (6).

2.1.7 Observations to be made. Children should be left to feed themselves or should be helped by an attendant, but in this case care should be taken not to force the food on the child. Refusal to eat the preparation is considered an indicator of poor palatability, provided that the trials take into careful consideration all of the potential interfering factors in this type of study. Even if acceptability is unsatisfactory as first tested, it may be possible to find an acceptable form of preparation by trial and error. This should be such as is practicable in homes and under conditions for which the food mixture is recommended.

Tolerance is judged by noting persistent gastrointestinal upsets, such as loss of appetite, flatulence, vomiting, particularly delayed vomiting, undigested stool contents, diarrhoea or intestinal hurry. Where legumes are involved, it is important to note the extent of bloating and flatus production.

Other clinical manifestations such as allergic reactions should also be recorded if manifested.

Large-scale, 3-6 months acceptability and marketing trials in selected future consumer groups should be started as soon as possible after this step. Careful consideration should be given to the statistical design and evaluation of these trials.

When protein-rich foods are introduced to the family, observations should include the reaction of mothers to the products. It should be explained to them that although the food will contribute to the nutrition of all the members of the family, it has been prepared in a form which is of special value for the health and development of infants and young children.

2.2 Growth Tests

The principal methods used for the evaluation of protein quality in man are measurement of growth and of nitrogen balance. These represent alternate approaches; which will be selected depends upon many factors, such as the type of subject to be

studied, the local conditions, the facilities and personnel available.   It is desirable but not essential that they be done in
the country of intended use.   Complementary information may also
be obtained by various types of measurements of blood chemistry
and liver function.   Both growth tests and nitrogen balance techniques should be carried out only in centres specialized in nutrition or allied disciplines.   The use of tolerance and acceptability experiments to evaluate the effect on growth should be
discouraged.

2.2.1   *Growth.*   Trials in which growth is measured may be planned
in many ways, depending upon the nature and age of the subjects
to be studied, and the circumstances in each case.   Therefore,
only very broad guidelines can be laid down.   Every trial should
be planned on a sound statistical basis, so that the results can
be accurately evaluated.   Ideally, a closely matched control
group should be studied.

2.2.2   *Observations which may be made.*   The most commonly used
index of growth is the rate of gain in body weight.   Evaluation
of protein value from the change in weight over a specified
period on a given protein intake is analogous to the measurement
of PER in animals, and is subject to the same criticisms: that
weight gain may not reflect accurately the change in lean body
mass.   This difficulty may be circumvented in part by measurement of the urinary creatinine output over a timed period, since
it is accepted that this provides an index of muscle mass.
Measurement of height or body length is of even greater significance, particularly in older children, because height is usually
less variable than weight.   However, since height increases more
slowly, the measurements have to be made over a fairly long
period.   Supplementary information can be obtained by serial X-
ray films of bone maturation and cortical thickness.   The investigator should not neglect general observations such as the character
of stools, amount of flatus, occurrence of allergic and other undesirable responses and general acceptability to mother and child.

2.2.3   *Age and type of subjects.*   Since growth is faster and
protein requirements are higher, the earlier the age, the greater
are the advantages in using infants and young children, rather
than older children, for measurements of protein quality.   The
children should be as normal as possible.   Each investigator
should determine the populations suitable for growth studies, but
it is recommended that children who are frankly retarded in growth
should not be studied because of great variabilities in responses.
It is suggested that all children should be above the 3rd percen-
tile in height and should have weight for height above 95% of
ideal, based on standards for well-nourished children such as
those which have been published, *inter alia*, in Western Europe
and the USA.

In testing a new protein, it is important to find out which is the lower age at which the protein supports adequate growth. Consequently the age will vary, depending on the results obtained from the initial tests. Weaning foods should be tried first in children 6 months to 1 year. Special infant foods should be tested in younger infants.

2.2.4 Duration. The duration of the trial must depend upon the extent to which constant conditions can be achieved. With infants aged about one year, under close supervision in a hospital ward, a reasonably accurate measurement of growth rate can be obtained by daily weighing over a period of 2 to 4 weeks. With somewhat older children, again under well-controlled conditions, e.g. in an orphanage, 3 to 6 months are necessary. Day care centres, orphanages and convalescent hospitals for children are likely to be convenient for such studies. It has been observed that children do not gain appreciable weight during the hottest months of the year, when temperatures reach 38°-40°C, so that short-term trials in such an environment should be avoided during these months. Similarly, epidemics of any infectious diseases are likely to invalidate trials.

2.2.5 Number of subjects. This will depend on the age and cooperativeness of the subjects, the duration of the trial, the extent to which infectious and other interfering factors can be eliminated, and the adequacy of the controls. Valuable information may be obtained from as few as five infants per group in a well-controlled study in an institution.

2.2.6 Frequency of observations. In general, the greater the number of serial observations, the fewer the subjects required, and the shorter the necessary duration of the trial. In studies on infants under hospital conditions, weights should be measured every day. In older children, weights should be measured at least every one to two weeks. In infants length should be measured bi-weekly, but in older children height measurements at intervals of 1 to 3 months will be enough (7).

2.2.7 Level of feeding. The trial will not be a true test of protein value if other elements in the diet are limiting. The diet must therefore supply adequate intake of calories (from fat and carbohydrates), and of vitamins and minerals.

The total protein intake should at least conform to the recommended allowances of FAO/WHO (5). The extent to which it may be higher than this depends upon the purposes of the trial - whether it is to determine the effect upon growth of a given protein supplement, or whether it is to find the minimum amount of a protein mixture which will support normal growth.

In general, the test protein should be the sole source of protein in the diet; for some special purposes it may be provided

as a supplement to a natural diet.   The control group should receive milk or egg as the source of protein with levels of protein
and calories adjusted to be comparable.

2.3 *Nitrogen Balance Measurements*

The measurements of nitrogen balance in man is comparable to
that of NPU in experimental animals.

2.3.1 *Conditions.*   Staff and facilities must be adequate for
the precise control of food intake, minimizing of cross-infections,
complete collection of urine and faeces, and the necessary biochemical analyses.   Experienced full-time personnel dedicated
to the work are required for preparing and weighing the diets and
giving close continuous supervision to the subjects.   Because
of the constant and monotonous diets, special skill is needed to
ensure that the intake is maintained through the period of observation.

2.3.2. *Subjects.*   Measurements of N balance may be made on
adults, children or infants.   There are advantages in using as
test subjects infants who are fully recovered from malnutrition,
mainly because of their being accustomed to metabolic techniques.
Acutely and severely depleted subjects, as well as children recovering from malnutrition, are not suitable for such studies
because another variable is introduced which complicates the interpretation of the results.   It is also extremely important
that the subjects have no infection.   Even mild infections induce a stress response which increases urinary nitrogen loss.

Most malnourished infants are not likely to reach a stage at
which the tests can usefully be done until they have received optimum treatment for one to two months.   Complete nutritional recovery must be estimated not only by normal weight for height and
serum and blood biochemistries but also by adequate lean body mass
for height (refer to 2.4.3).   It is difficult to specify an exact
age range for such tests.   Children six to thirty-six months are
convenient subjects, but this does not exclude children outside
this age range.   In any case it is essential that the groups be
carefully matched.   This is necessary because with recovery from
depletion nitrogen retention tends to fall.   The best plan is to
use each subject as his own control, with consecutive tests on
control and experimental diets.   Because the subjects may vary
in degree of depletion as the tests go on, the order of feeding
should be varied.

2.3.3. *Food*

2.3.3.1 *Calories, water, vitamins and minerals.*   The calories
supplied must be equal in all balance periods (test and control)
which are being compared, and should meet the level recommended
by FAO/WHO (6).   The proportion of fat to carbohydrate and the
nature of the fat must be similar in groups which are being com-

pared.   Water, vitamins and minerals, including potassium and phosphorus, should also be fed in adequate and constant amounts.

2.3.3.2 *Protein level.*   For tests of protein value the protein must be fed at a level or levels on the linear part of the curve of the nitrogen balance index (5,8).   This curve remains linear for some way into the region of positive nitrogen balance. In tests on human infants, it is undesirable to feed at maintenance level only.   It is necessary to choose a level above maintenance that is enough to allow reasonable nitrogen retention and growth, but not so high that the efficiency of nitrogen utilization falls off so much that differences in biological value disappear.   It has been shown (9) that in infants of about one year the average requirement for maintenance is 100 mg N/kg/day (in terms of cow's milk protein), and that almost all balances are positive at an intake of 130 mg N/kg/day.   From the evidence available it seems that the total obligatory loss of urine and faeces per kg of body weight is only slightly higher in infants than in adults.   It is recommended that for measurements of protein value the intake should not exceed an upper level of 300 mg N (i.e. slightly less than 2 g protein) per kg per day.   If the clinical condition of the child justifies feeding at lower levels, e.g. 1 to 1.5 g protein/kg/day, difference in protein value will be shown still more clearly.

A test at one level within the limits just specified is adequate if the sole concern is the measurement of protein quality. However, a further practical question may arise: can a food which has a poor protein value produce adequate retention and growth if fed at a higher level, e.g. 3 g protein/kg? To answer this question, tests must obviously be made at whatever level is indicated by the measurement of biological value, but it should be clearly recognized that tests at such high levels are not reliable measures of protein quality.

2.3.4 *Adaptation period.*   The number of days required for initial adaptation depends upon the age of the child and the magnitude of the change in quantity and quality of protein from that of the preceding diet.   In infants a three-day adaptation period is generally sufficient, but in older children and adults five days or more may be needed.   The individual investigator should provide evidence that the adaptation period used under his conditions is adequate.   Subjects recovering from an infection may need one to two weeks before the nitrogen excretion is stabilized.

2.3.5 *Length of balance period.*   Collections should be obtained for a minimum of six days.   Two three-day periods or, if defaecations are sufficiently frequent, three two-day periods represent a minimum study.   Where circumstances permit, balances can be conducted over a period of two to three months in such a way that 6 to 9 balance periods of six days each may be obtained in a single child.

2.3.6 Digestibility. In boys, separate collection of urine and faeces will make possible measurement of apparent digestibility as well as of apparent biological value. With many vegetable proteins digestibility is low, and the measurement of it is therefore important. In girls, even if faeces and urine cannot be adequately separated, it is still possible to measure the net protein utilization (NPU).

It is not generally necessary to measure the basal or "endogenous" urinary and faecal nitrogen loss, in order to estimate the true digestibility and biological value. For practical purposes it is probably accurate enough to use the figures published (10). It is important, however, that the calculated N intake be verified by actual analyses of aliquots, since values from food composition tables do not give a sufficiently reliable estimate for the purpose.

2.3.7 Necessary precautions. In summary, nitrogen balance measurements will be useful, reliable and reproducible if the following precautions are observed:

1. Calorie intake per kg is adequate and constant;
2. Protein intake per kg is kept constant within a single trial;
3. There are no complicating vitamin or mineral deficiencies;
4. Water intake is controlled and excessive sweat loss avoided;
5. No infections, even of seemingly mild degree, are present;
6. Subjects are reasonably content and not psychologically disturbed;
7. The subjects are in an adequate state of nutrition and receiving protein levels which allow discrimination of protein quality;
8. Adequate adjustment periods are used;
9. Meal times are standardized both between and within treatments;
10. Period(s) on the same diet are long enough to determine trends as well as the initial response to dietary change;
11. Food intake and collections of urine and faeces are obtained and measured accurately.

2.4 Other Criteria

2.4.1 Serum albumin. In children recovering from malnutrition changes in albumin concentration may give a rough indication of protein quality. Measurements should be made periodically and the blood sample should be taken at the same time in relation to meals.

Standardization of laboratory methods is desirable. Divergence of results for serum albumin and for growth and nitrogen re-

tention have been reported.   In some cases this appears to be
due to a rapid increase in lean body mass and blood volume con-
cealing active albumin synthesis (11) unless total circulating
albumin is measured.   Serum albumin also apparently behaves
differently from other parameters in response to vegetable as compared to animal protein and is slow to decrease on some experimental diets with low PER.   The significance of this difference
requires further study.

2.4.2   Plasma amino acid and enzyme levels.   Measurements of
plasma amino acid levels and ratios, and of the concentrations
of various enzymes in the plasma have been proposed as useful
criteria.   These methods still require further evaluation.

2.4.3   Creatinine height index.   It has recently been demonstrated that 24-hour creatinine excretion of a malnourished child
compared with that of a well-nourished child of the same height is
a good measure of the reduction of lean body mass due to malnutrition and its recovery with refeeding (12).   It can be used
to evaluate the degree of recovery of lean body mass.

3.   REFERENCES

1.   PAG.   Note on human testing of supplementary food mixtures.
      FAO/WHO/UNICEF Protein Advisory Group, United Nations, N.Y.
      10017, U.S.A.   Nutrition document R.10/Add. 91/Rev. 1,
      1966.

2.   PAG.   Guideline for pre-clinical testing of novel sources
      of protein.   FAO/WHO/UNICEF Protein Advisory Group, United
      Nations, N.Y. 10017, U.S.A.   PAG Guideline No. 6, 1969.

3.   U.S. Food and Drug Administration.   Appraisal of the safety
      of chemicals in foods, drugs, and cosmetics.   Assoc. of Food
      and Drug Officials of the United States, Austin, Texas,
      U.S.A., 1959.

4.   Waterlow, J.C. and Stephen, J.   Human protein requirements
      and their fulfillment in practice.   *Proc. of Princeton
      Conference, Joshia Macy Jr. Foundation, New York, U.S.A.,*
      1957.

5.   Food and Agriculture Organization/World Health Organization
      Expert Group.   Protein requirements.   WHO, Geneva,
      Switzerland.   WHO Technical Report Series 301, 1965.

6.   Food and Agriculture Organization.   Assessment of report of
      second committee, FAO 1957, on calorie requirements.   FAO,
      Rome, Italy, 1964.

7.   World Health Organization.   Medical assessment of nutritional
      status;   report of expert committee.   WHO, Geneva, Switzer-
      land.   WHO Technical Report Series 258, 1963.

8. Allison, J.B. Interpretation of nitrogen balance data. *Fed. Proc.* <u>10</u>, 676, 1951.

9. Chan, H. and Waterlow, J.C. The protein requirement of infants at the age of about one year. *Brit. J. Nutrition* <u>20</u>, 775, 1966.

10. Fomon, S.J., DeMaeyer, E.M. and Owen, G.M. Urinary and faecal excretion of endogenous nitrogen by infants and young children. *J. Nutrition* <u>85</u>, 235, 1965.

11. Viteri, F.E., Alvarado, J., Luthringer, D.G. and Wood, R.P. Hematological changes in protein caloric malnutrition. *In:* Vitamins and Hormones, Advances in Research and Applications (Harris, R.S., Wool, I.G., Levine, J.G. and Thimann, K.V., eds), Vol. 26, Academic Press, New York, U.S.A., 1968.

12. Viteri, F.E., Arroyave, G. and Béhar, M. Estimation of protein depletion in malnourished children by a creatinine height index. *VIIth International Congress of Nutrition.* Abstracts of papers 46-47. Pergomos-Druck, Hamburg, Germany, 1966.

PROTEIN ADVISORY GROUP OF THE UNITED NATIONS SYSTEM
GUIDELINE NO. 15
EVALUATING NOVEL PROTEINS FOR ANIMAL FEEDING
7 June 1974

PAG GUIDELINE ON NUTRITIONAL AND SAFETY ASPECTS OF NOVEL
PROTEIN SOURCES FOR ANIMAL FEEDING

SUMMARY

Urgent worldwide demand for animal protein foods has stimulated major commercial development and production of protein concentrates for animal feeding. These include some novel products
such as single cell proteins grown on unconventional substrates
like hydrocarbons. This document proposes nutritional and safety
criteria which may be helpful to the manufacturers of such novel
proteins and to government regulatory agencies when evaluating
their suitability for feeding farm animals.

1. PROBLEMS AND ISSUES

The need for urgent action to expand the world supply of protein for human food and animals feed has been well documented.
Present and projected critical shortages of protein, in affluent
as well as less affluent nations, have stimulated agricultural
and industrial research and development in many countries aimed
at meeting this need. Novel technologies for massive and economic production of single cell protein (SCP) from fermentation
processes employing various substrates have led to construction
of large production plants built by companies in several countries;
more are certain to be built in the near future. These developments have several implications. For one, they imply that a
revolution in animal and human feeding will take place over a relatively short period; millions of people will consume meat, milk
and eggs from animals receiving new forms of protein in their
feeding rations. Before very long, humans will receive such protein foods as direct components of their diet. They also imply
that private industry will be encouraged by governments, as well
as international and bilateral agencies seeking to stimulate development, to make huge investments in plants to produce such
forms of protein. Yet another implication is that in antici-
pation of the introduction of novel proteins into the diets of

their populations, the governmental agencies of many nations will
seek guidance in the establishment of regulations consistent
with those governing more conventional feedstuffs.   These will
reflect the need to insure that the new proteins will have a
beneficial effect on the nutrition and health of their peoples.

We are thus challenged today with an unprecedented conver-
gence of circumstances:

a)   immediate and increasing worldwide demand for protein;

b)   immediate demand for industry as well as agriculture
     to produce new forms of proteins, including single cell
     proteins, utilizing available technologies;

c)   immediate demands for many governments to evolve ob-
     jective regulations controlling the quality and safety
     of novel protein sources, such regulations to be capable
     of harmonization at the international level to the
     greatest possible extent;   and

d)   an almost equally immediate demand to allow unrestricted
     and unimpeded international export and import of such
     products, which will require international similarity
     of national regulations.

A logical answer to these challenges is for an internationally-
respected, impartial and professionally-capable group of experts
who represent the most competent scientific, regulatory and industrial expertise available in the world to a) critically evaluate
and constructively disseminate information on the various research,
development, testing and marketing efforts on novel types of protein in terms of safety and nutritional quality for their intended
use and b) encourage the international harmonization of pertinent
regulations and criteria as necessary to stimulate widespread production, marketing and consumption of acceptable new protein resources.   This effort should take into account the positions of
companies seeking through large investments to produce and market
such products and of governments which find it necessary to regulate product identity, quality and safety.   It was the consensus
of this *ad hoc* working group, representing broad international expertise in universities, governments and industry that such an
evaluation and guideline are urgently needed and that it should be
undertaken under the auspices of the Protein Advisory Group of the
United Nations System.

It may be emphasized that the PAG has no mandate or authority
as a regulatory body at any level in national or international
affairs.   The PAG acts with the prior approval of its sponsors
(FAO, WHO, UNICEF, IBRD and the United Nations) to study specific
substantive issues such as the one under consideration here.   It
then develops statements or guidelines providing the kind of up-

to-date information and informed, knowledgeable impartial judgments on the matter that a panel of reputable internationally-
recognized specialists, acting under its auspices, can provide.
Thus the PAG statement or guideline serves as a source of un-
biased information and advice which hopefully will be useful to
all interests concerned with a common problem.   As indicated,
the interests it serves include those of an industrial firm seeking to produce and market products which may be subject to governmental regulations and the government itself along with its regulatory agencies.

In the interests of public health it becomes essential to
establish acceptable criteria for determining the nutritive value
and safety of these protein materials in relation to their use
in the rations of the particular animal species concerned.   The
PAG has already developed guidelines for the preclinical testing
of novel proteins in laboratory animals (Guideline 6, Appendix I)
and for their clinical evaluation in human subjects (Guideline
7, Appendix II).   These guidelines were stimulated by the growing interest in the production for possible human use of microbial
biomass grown in some cases on unconventional substrates such as
hydrocarbons and simple alcohols.   At present, industrial research and development in various countries is mainly directed
toward the use of SCP as components of animal feeds.   Thus there
arise questions of safety and nutritive value not only concerning
these products for feeding various target animal species but also
concerning the human foods derived from these food-producing
animals.

In contrast with the need to use experimental animals as
models for testing new food components for direct consumption by
man, animal feeding materials can be tested under controlled conditions directly in the "target species";   that is, the domestic
and farm animals for which they are intended.   This does not
imply that laboratory animals, which are the conventional biological tools of the toxicologist and nutritionist, cannot provide additional valuable information.   However, the nutrient
requirements of animals vary among different species, e.g. those
of poultry and other avian species differ from those of mammals
and those of ruminants differ from those of nonruminants.   Hence,
the critical tests for utility and safety ultimately must rely on
the use of the appropriate target species fed on such novel
materials.

2.   THE NEED FOR GUIDELINES

The question then arises as to the necessity or usefulness
of establishing guidelines for testing novel proteins proposed
for animal feeds in addition to those already established for preclinical evaluation of novel sources of protein for human foods.
In the first instance such new guidelines will be useful to the

industrial producers of novel protein materials, e.g. selected yeasts or other microorganisms grown on hydrocarbon substrates or any other feed protein concentrate of animal or plant origin requiring extensive processing, use of solvents, etc. These companies will require some standards endorsed mutually by industry and governments by which to gauge the quality, uniformity, nutritive value and safety of products.

From the practical standpoint it is quite obvious that the material to be evaluated initially cannot be derived from full-scale plant production. To do otherwise would require plants to be built on a speculative basis, a requirement which would discourage commercial development of novel products. Initial production, testing and product acceptance must therefore involve products from pilot plants, under the reasonable expectation that the product will be matched in the ensuing commercial-scale production. Many complex factors must be considered for prior approval of novel proteins, including the quality of the raw materials, the acceptability of the critical processing parameters affecting nutritive value and safety and the purity and uniformity of the ultimate commercial output compared with the pilot-plant product previously evaluated and approved. In the case of SCP products, the stability of the microorganism to mutation must also be considered. This requires careful development of physical, chemical and microbiological specifications as well as nutritional and toxicological parameters appropriate for the target species. After commercial marketing of novel protein feed ingredients is approved, long-term studies of food-producing animals maintained on rations containing the novel protein should be continued under practical feeding conditions to confirm the earlier conclusions regarding safety and efficacy.

Other beneficiaries of guidelines would be government regulatory agencies responsible for the control of foods and feeds moving in the channels of trade which require their own assurance of suitability. Whether an individual country's rules require approval prior to marketing or simply prohibit the marketing of unsafe and nonefficacious products, it is clear that the industrial sponsor must develop the information necessary to formulate such judgments and share it constructively with regulatory agencies when required.

It is essential that regulations of various governments be harmonized so as to encourage rather than inhibit commercial production and international trade in these products. PAG guidelines could be highly useful in this regard.

National and international agencies concerned with the health and welfare of deprived populations in countries which lack the means for evaluation of new foods must of course rely on the advice and recommendations of professionally-competent, independent experts or groups such as the PAG.

3. THE PURPOSE OF GUIDELINES

It should not be construed that a published guideline constitutes a compendium of mandatory tests which, unless completely
and successfully satisfied, would preclude acceptance of any new
food component. Indeed, with the accumulation of experience in
routine testing of these products and their feeding to livestock
under practical conditions, it seems likely that more informative
and possibly more routine test procedures will emerge which will
permit improved testing efficiency and economy. It is recognized
that toxicologists and nutritionists experienced in these matters
should have the prerogative of deciding on the extent and design
of experimental protocols. However, there is a need for independent and internationally-coordinated evaluation of the statistical and biological validity of the conclusions reached.

For the guidance of those less experienced in these highly-
specialized disciplines it is considered useful to suggest procedures to support acceptable conclusions as to both functional
utility and safety of novel proteins. Many aspects of the criteria described in PAG Guideline 6 are applicable to proteins intended for animal feeding; particularly relevant are the sections
dealing with chemical, physical and biological evaluations. However, the criteria for the prediction of protein quality of foods
for human use, e.g. bioassays for Protein Efficiency Ratio, Net
Protein Utilization, Biological Value, while of interest are not
applicable for example to poultry. This explains in part the
importance of establishing the quality and safety of feed ingredients intended for nourishment and productivity directly in the
target species. As stated in Guideline 6, "Products intended
for incorporation into animal feeds may not require as extensive
testing as is suggested for human foods, but foods derived from
animal sources must be considered from the viewpoint of the possible presence of residues in meat, milk or eggs transmitted from
animal feeds."

4. TERMS OF THE GUIDELINE

When reviewing the elements of this guideline, reference
should first be made to the introductory pages of PAG Guideline
6 (Appendix I), particularly those dealing with the categories of
information needed (1.1-1.2.8) and evaluation procedures (2.1-2.3).
It should be pointed out, however, that certain of these criteria
such as those for protein quality and acceptability relate specifically to the testing of novel sources of protein intended for
human food. With respect to ingredients intended for animal feed
purposes, the guideline should cover aspects specifically applicable to the feed requirements of the species concerned as well as
aspects applicable to foods derived from these animals and intended
for human use. With respect to the species involved, the guideline should provide for the evaluation of the quality and efficiency

of the protein for maintenance, growth and reproduction, its
safety for the target species and its effect on productivity
from the economic standpoint.   With respect to the foods derived
from these animals, consideration of acceptability in terms of
flavor, color, texture, etc., would have been taken into account
prior to marketing any such product.   Safety for humans would
involve the possibility of contaminants or residues arising from
the source materials, e.g. substrate or media employed in the
case of SCP, and the processing conditions.   The protein mole-
cules themselves would be unlikely to present a hazard, inasmuch
as the normal processes of digestion and breakdown to individual
amino acids and anabolic conversion to tissue proteins are generally controlled by homeostatic mechanisms.   The quality and
safety of food from animals fed unconventional protein should be
predictable from the nutritional and toxicological studies of the
protein in the animals' feed.   Because of the impracticability
of identifying, by means of animal feeding studies, the minute
traces of residues or contaminants that might be transmitted from
the feed into meat, milk or eggs, detection of any such substances
which might be suspected to be present must depend on highly-
sensitive chemical analytical procedures.

   In view of the fact that some types of novel proteins may be
produced in the form of microbial biomass grown on agricultural
and urban waste, including feed-lot animal excreta, particular
attention must be directed toward insuring the absence of pathogenic organisms and metabolites (Table I), as well as of toxic
residues of pesticides or drugs.   The microorganisms selected
as the inocula for SCP production, whether the substrate is derived from industrial hydrocarbons, alcohols or other chemicals,
or biological waste materials, should be nonpathogenic notwithstanding the fact that the fermentation process need not involve

Table I   Suggested limits for viable and contaminating micro-
            organisms

Microorganism	Number per gram*
Viable bacteria	<100,000
Viable yeasts and molds	<100
Enterobacteriaceae	<10
Salmonella	<1 per 50g
Staphylococcus aureus	<1
Clostridia, total	<1,000
Cl. perfringens	<100
Lancefield Group D Streptococci	<10,000

* Levels indicated may be more relevant to industrially-produced
SCP biomass than to traditional animal feeding concentrates (fish
meal, soybean meal, etc.).

the use of pure cultures grown aseptically. However, once the microorganisms have been selected, it is necessary to control their stability from the standpoint of the quality of the end product.

After the processing conditions have been established to insure uniform quality, safety and nutritive value of the final product, chemical criteria should be determined as suggested in Table II.

Table II   Quantitative chemical criteria for defining novel proteins

---

A. *For all novel proteins (dry wt basis)*

Total solids	%
Total nitrogen	%
Total lysine	g/16g N
Available lysine	% of total lysine
Sulfur amino acids (methionine and cystine)	g/100g protein
Crude lipids	%
Ash	%
Lead	<5 ppm
Arsenic	<2 ppm
Mercury	<0.1 ppm

B. *Additional criteria for SCP from hydrocarbons (dry wt basis)*

Total residual hydrocarbons	<0.5%
Total residual aromatic hydrocarbons	<0.5%
Benzo(a)pyrene	<5 ppb

As indicated above, long-term studies of the safety of novel proteins should be performed on pilot-plant lots prior to large-scale production. It is necessary therefore to establish the identity and reproducibility of the commercial product with that previously tested by resorting to microbiological, physical and chemical tests. The criteria for comparison should serve as the basis for setting specifications for each manufacturer's product.

Quantitative analytical procedures of appropriate sensitivity must be used to determine the levels of any undesirable residues which could arise from the source or media from which the proteins are derived or from solvents and other agents employed in any stage of processing. Inasmuch as feeding experiments may not be sufficiently sensitive to detect all such residues as might transfer to edible products derived from animals receiving novel proteins in their rations, sensitive analytical methods must be used. For in-plant control, the methods of examination and analysis should either be identical with, or give results in conformity with, the methods recommended by the Fermentation and Food Sections of the International Union of Pure and Applied Chemistry.

5.   NUTRITIONAL AND SAFETY EVALUATION

The nutritional value of novel proteins for animal feeding should be determined in the species for which its use is intended and under the conditions for which they are intended.   In experimental diets conventionally employed for evaluations in rats, the test proteins are incorporated as the sole source of nitrogen.   Since novel proteins would be used in animal feed as a supplement or partial replacement of the soybean, fishmeal or other protein component of the total ration, test diets should be prepared in simulation or practical rations with the test material providing three or more levels ranging from 10 to 50 per cent of the total protein content of the ration.

To achieve optimum protein adequacy of proteins used in animal feeds, consideration may be given to supplementation with synthetic amino acids essential for the species in question, e.g. glycine for poultry.

In the design of experimental rations for toxicological evaluation, care must be exercised to insure that normal dietary requirements for the species in question are satisfied in order not to confuse nutritional effects, such as deficiency symptoms or impaired growth response due to nondigestibility or amino acid imbalance, with toxicity *per se*.   For this reason, the positive control diet should include high-quality animal protein such as meatmeal or fish protein concentrate.

6.   TEST SPECIES

For the toxicological assessment of a novel protein, a rodent species (preferably the rat), a nonrodent mammal (the dog) and an avian species are generally employed.   However, where the emphasis is on the biological quality as well as toxicological safety for animal feeding, studies should be conducted with chickens and pigs as prototypes of nonruminant farm animals; veal calves (which are also nonruminant) may also be used. Studies with sheep and older calves are conducted to represent the requirements of ruminants.   Many studies will be conducted on the rat in addition to the target animals since so much nutritional and toxicological information concerning mammalian nutrition has been accumulated through the use of this laboratory species.

7.   PROTOCOLS

The ultimate test of the nutritional value of animal feeds are the practical trials in which growth, feed efficiency, reproduction, health, survival and economic productivity are the bases

for evaluation.   Short-term feeding studies are only minimal
prerequisites for the introduction of novel feed constituents.
Because of the short duration of such tests relative to the total
life span, it is not possible in these tests to observe evidence
of long-term (chronic) or cumulative effects.   Thus, studies for
reproductive performance and for carcinogenicity (where substrates
or processing adjuncts suggest the need) are required, particularly if the proposed feed ingredient is to be incorporated in
the ration of breeders.

Reference should be made to PAG Guideline 6, Section 2.5.2,
for an outline of the basic method for safety evaluation of novel
proteins in rats.   Suggested schedules for short- and long-term
studies in the recommended species for testing animal feeds are
shown in Table III.   It should be noted that these are minimal
conditions with respect to numbers of animals and dosage groups.
Following these studies, controlled observations under practical
feeding conditions should be carried out with the target species
of animals.   Physical inspection of the animals, including observations of weight changes, feed conversion, hemocytology and
blood and urine chemistry should be conducted at intervals as
shown in Appendix I, Section 2.5.2h.   (Since allantoin is the end
product of purine metabolism in mammalian species other than
primates, blood uric acid determinations are usually omitted in
studies with rats or pigs.)

Table III   Recommended schedule of feeding studies in test
animals

	Rats	Pigs	Chicks
Duration			
Short-term	3 mo	3 mo	3 mo
Long-term	2 yr	1 yr	1 yr
No. dosage groups			
Test	3	3	3
Control	1	1	1
No. animals/sex/group			
Short-term	15	3	30
Long-term	30	6	30 male/100 female
Observations			
General	see Appendix I, Section 2.5.2h		
Special	teratogenicity (rats or mice)		
	mutagenicity (rats)		
	carcinogenicity (rats)		
	egg production and hatchability (chicks)		

Following the short-term tests, reproduction experiments should be set up, preferably with short-lived species.   In the case of rats, animals may be selected from the first litters and bred for several successive generations.   The one-year test period will generally permit only a second generation to be produced.

The observations to be made in mammalian species are described in Appendix I, Section 2.5.2.   Those chicks not sacrificed following the short-term test are mated (one cockerel per three hens) for studies of fertility, egg production and hatchability.

8.   REGULATORY ASPECTS

Regulatory requirements for novel protein products may vary from country to country.   Information concerning certain proprietary process details may be required (on a confidential basis) to provide assurance of safety and to insure adequate quality control as well as uniformity of the final product.

Examples of process details which should be reported in the case of SCP production are the nature and properties of the microorganism, the qualitative composition of the substrate raw materials employed, including major nutrient supplements, and the agents used for special purposes such as defoamers, emulsion breakers, etc..   General processing conditions, such as propagation method, extraction processes, concentration procedures, drying methods, etc., should be described to the extent needed to insure sanitary quality.   Similar criteria for other unconventional proteins for animal feeding will need to be described for each product.

Approval of a new protein feeding adjunct would require submission of a statement on the safety and quality of the product, with supporting data as outlined earlier in this statement.   From time to time, as reasonably necessary, the results of limited comparative toxicological data obtained with randomly-selected production samples may be submitted to regulatory authorities.

Changes in processing which might significantly affect the nutritional quality or safety should be reported before such changes are adopted.

Based on appropriate sampling of products in the manufacturing plant or in commercial channels, samples should be subjected to examination by procedures designed to establish safety as a feed, to confirm or measure basic quality requirements and to establish identity with the registered product.   The chemical and biological testing procedures, therefore, will include general methods applicable to all sources of unconventional protein and to feeds in general and methods selected especially to relate to the registered product.   Certain significant data should be included in label information.

Appropriate methods for the chemical, nutritional and micro-biological quality characteristics referred to in this document may be found in PAG Guideline 6.   Requirements for additional or improved analytical methods for evaluating novel proteins will be referred to appropriate committees of the International Union of Pure and Applied Chemistry (IUPAC).